Economic Regulation and the Federal System

This is Volume 42 in the series of studies commissioned as part of the research program of the Royal Commission on the Economic Union and Development Prospects for Canada.

This volume reflects the views of its authors and does not imply endorsement by the Chairman or Commissioners.

Economic Regulation and the Federal System

RICHARD SCHULTZ
AND
ALAN ALEXANDROFF

Published by the University of Toronto Press in cooperation with the Royal Commission on the Economic Union and Development Prospects for Canada and the Canadian Government Publishing Centre, Supply and Services Canada

University of Toronto Press
Toronto Buffalo London

Grateful acknowledgment is made to the following for permission to reprint previously published and unpublished material: *Bank of Canada Review*; Carl E.Beigie, Esq.; Canadian Radio-television and Telecommunications Commission; Chief Statistician of Canada; Cornell University Press; Economic Council of Canada; Steven Globerman, Esq.; Institute for Research on Public Policy; James Lorimer and Company Limited, Publishers; Methuen Publications; Prentice-Hall Canada Inc.; University of Toronto Press.

Printed in Canada
ISBN 0-8020-7287-9
ISSN 0829-2396
Cat. No. Z1-1983/1-41-42E

CANADIAN CATALOGUING IN PUBLICATION DATA

Schultz, Richard J. (Richard John), 1945–
Economic regulation and the federal system

(*The Collected research studies / Royal Commission on the Economic Union and Development Prospects for Canada*,
ISSN 0829-2396 ; 42)
Includes bibliographical references.
ISBN 0-8020-7287-9

1. Industry and state — Canada. 2. Federal government — Canada. 3. Canada — Economic policy. 4. Industrial laws and legislation — Canada. I. Alexandroff, Alan S. II. Royal Commission on the Economic Union and Development Prospects for Canada. III. Title. IV. Series: The Collected research studies (Royal Commission on the Economic Union and Development Prospects for Canada) ; 42.

HD3616.C33S38 1985 338.971 C85-099276-1

PUBLISHING COORDINATION: Ampersand Communications Services Inc.
COVER DESIGN: Will Rueter
INTERIOR DESIGN: Brant Cowie/Artplus Limited

CONTENTS

FOREWORD

When the members of the Rowell-Sirois Commission began their collective task in 1937, very little was known about the evolution of the Canadian economy. What was known, moreover, had not been extensively analyzed by the slender cadre of social scientists of the day.

When we set out upon our task nearly 50 years later, we enjoyed a substantial advantage over our predecessors; we had a wealth of information. We inherited the work of scholars at universities across Canada and we had the benefit of the work of experts from private research institutes and publicly sponsored organizations such as the Ontario Economic Council and the Economic Council of Canada. Although there were still important gaps, our problem was not a shortage of information; it was to interrelate and integrate — to synthesize — the results of much of the information we already had.

The mandate of this Commission is unusually broad. It encompasses many of the fundamental policy issues expected to confront the people of Canada and their governments for the next several decades. The nature of the mandate also identified, in advance, the subject matter for much of the research and suggested the scope of enquiry and the need for vigorous efforts to interrelate and integrate the research disciplines. The resulting research program, therefore, is particularly noteworthy in three respects: along with original research studies, it includes survey papers which synthesize work already done in specialized fields; it avoids duplication of work which, in the judgment of the Canadian research community, has already been well done; and, considered as a whole, it is the most thorough examination of the Canadian economic, political and legal systems ever undertaken by an independent agency.

The Commission's research program was carried out under the joint direction of three prominent and highly respected Canadian scholars: Dr. Ivan Bernier (*Law and Constitutional Issues*), Dr. Alan Cairns (*Politics and Institutions of Government*) and Dr. David C. Smith (*Economics*).

Dr. Ivan Bernier is Dean of the Faculty of Law at Laval University. Dr. Alan Cairns is former Head of the Department of Political Science at the University of British Columbia and, prior to joining the Commission, was William Lyon Mackenzie King Visiting Professor of Canadian Studies at Harvard University. Dr. David C. Smith, former Head of the Department of Economics at Queen's University in Kingston, is now Principal of that University. When Dr. Smith assumed his new responsibilities at Queen's in September 1984, he was succeeded by Dr. Kenneth Norrie of the University of Alberta and John Sargent of the federal Department of Finance, who together acted as Co-directors of Research for the concluding phase of the Economics research program.

I am confident that the efforts of the Research Directors, research coordinators and authors whose work appears in this and other volumes, have provided the community of Canadian scholars and policy makers with a series of publications that will continue to be of value for many years to come. And I hope that the value of the research program to Canadian scholarship will be enhanced by the fact that Commission research is being made available to interested readers in both English and French.

I extend my personal thanks, and that of my fellow Commissioners, to the Research Directors and those immediately associated with them in the Commission's research program. I also want to thank the members of the many research advisory groups whose counsel contributed so substantially to this undertaking.

DONALD S. MACDONALD

INTRODUCTION

At its most general level, the Royal Commission's research program has examined how the Canadian political economy can better adapt to change. As a basis of enquiry, this question reflects our belief that the future will always take us partly by surprise. Our political, legal and economic institutions should therefore be flexible enough to accommodate surprises and yet solid enough to ensure that they help us meet our future goals. This theme of an adaptive political economy led us to explore the interdependencies between political, legal and economic systems and drew our research efforts in an interdisciplinary direction.

The sheer magnitude of the research output (more than 280 separate studies in 72 volumes) as well as its disciplinary and ideological diversity have, however, made complete integration impossible and, we have concluded, undesirable. The research output as a whole brings varying perspectives and methodologies to the study of common problems and we therefore urge readers to look beyond their particular field of interest and to explore topics across disciplines.

The three research areas — *Law and Constitutional Issues*, under Ivan Bernier; *Politics and Institutions of Government*, under Alan Cairns; and *Economics*, under David C. Smith (co-directed with Kenneth Norrie and John Sargent for the concluding phase of the research program) — were further divided into 19 sections headed by research coordinators.

The area *Law and Constitutional Issues* has been organized into five major sections headed by the research coordinators identified below.

- Law, Society and the Economy — *Ivan Bernier and Andrée Lajoie*
- The International Legal Environment — *John J. Quinn*
- The Canadian Economic Union — *Mark Krasnick*

- Harmonization of Laws in Canada — *Ronald C.C. Cuming*
- Institutional and Constitutional Arrangements — *Clare F. Beckton and A. Wayne MacKay*

Since law in its numerous manifestations is the most fundamental means of implementing state policy, it was necessary to investigate how and when law could be mobilized most effectively to address the problems raised by the Commission's mandate. Adopting a broad perspective, researchers examined Canada's legal system from the standpoint of how law evolves as a result of social, economic and political changes and how, in turn, law brings about changes in our social, economic and political conduct.

Within *Politics and Institutions of Government*, research has been organized into seven major sections.

- Canada and the International Political Economy — *Denis Stairs and Gilbert Winham*
- State and Society in the Modern Era — *Keith Banting*
- Constitutionalism, Citizenship and Society — *Alan Cairns and Cynthia Williams*
- The Politics of Canadian Federalism — *Richard Simeon*
- Representative Institutions — *Peter Aucoin*
- The Politics of Economic Policy — *G. Bruce Doern*
- Industrial Policy — *André Blais*

This area examines a number of developments which have led Canadians to question their ability to govern themselves wisely and effectively. Many of these developments are not unique to Canada and a number of comparative studies canvass and assess how others have coped with similar problems. Within the context of the Canadian heritage of parliamentary government, federalism, a mixed economy, and a bilingual and multicultural society, the research also explores ways of rearranging the relationships of power and influence among institutions to restore and enhance the fundamental democratic principles of representativeness, responsiveness and accountability.

Economics research was organized into seven major sections.

- Macroeconomics — *John Sargent*
- Federalism and the Economic Union — *Kenneth Norrie*
- Industrial Structure — *Donald G. McFetridge*
- International Trade — *John Whalley*
- Income Distribution and Economic Security — *François Vaillancourt*
- Labour Markets and Labour Relations — *Craig Riddell*
- Economic Ideas and Social Issues — *David Laidler*

Economics research examines the allocation of Canada's human and other resources, the ways in which institutions and policies affect this allocation, and the distribution of the gains from their use. It also considers the nature of economic development, the forces that shape our regional and industrial structure, and our economic interdependence with other countries. The thrust of the research in economics is to increase our comprehension of what determines our economic potential and how instruments of economic policy may move us closer to our future goals.

One section from each of the three research areas — The Canadian Economic Union, The Politics of Canadian Federalism, and Federalism and the Economic Union — have been blended into one unified research effort. Consequently, the volumes on Federalism and the Economic Union as well as the volume on The North are the results of an interdisciplinary research effort.

We owe a special debt to the research coordinators. Not only did they organize, assemble and analyze the many research studies and combine their major findings in overviews, but they also made substantial contributions to the Final Report. We wish to thank them for their performance, often under heavy pressure.

Unfortunately, space does not permit us to thank all members of the Commission staff individually. However, we are particularly grateful to the Chairman, The Hon. Donald S. Macdonald; the Commission's Executive Director, J. Gerald Godsoe; and the Director of Policy, Alan Nymark, all of whom were closely involved with the Research Program and played key roles in the contribution of Research to the Final Report. We wish to express our appreciation to the Commission's Administrative Advisor, Harry Stewart, for his guidance and advice, and to the Director of Publishing, Ed Matheson, who managed the research publication process. A special thanks to Jamie Benidickson, Policy Coordinator and Special Assistant to the Chairman, who played a valuable liaison role between Research and the Chairman and Commissioners. We are also grateful to our office administrator, Donna Stebbing, and to our secretarial staff, Monique Carpentier, Barbara Cowtan, Tina DeLuca, Françoise Guilbault and Marilyn Sheldon.

Finally, a well-deserved thank you to our closest assistants: Jacques J.M. Shore, *Law and Constitutional Issues*; Cynthia Williams and her successor Karen Jackson, *Politics and Institutions of Government*; and I. Lilla Connidis, *Economics*. We appreciate not only their individual contribution to each research area, but also their cooperative contribution to the research program and the Commission.

IVAN BERNIER
ALAN CAIRNS
DAVID C. SMITH

PREFACE

In the overall structure of the research carried out by the Royal Commission on the Economic Union and Development Prospects for Canada, this volume is the third of four grouped in an area called "The Politics of Economic Policy." By definition, the politics of economic policy include three dimensions: the goals and ideas inherent in the art of politics; the shifts in the basic public-private and intergovernmental relationships of power; and the changes in the core structures and processes of policy formulation. The authors represented in the four volumes were asked, in keeping with the mandate of the Commission, to review key political trends and dynamics over the past three decades. Historical breadth was needed to allow the studies to speak intelligently about possible future lines of reform as well as current policy.

This volume provides a comprehensive political analysis of the evolution of economic regulation in three sectors vital to the basic infrastructure of the Canadian economy: airlines, telecommunications, and securities and financial markets. It is the first study of regulation in Canada to examine three major sectors concurrently and with historical breadth.

Richard Schultz and Alan Alexandroff show the transformation of regulation in the three sectors, moving from a policing mode to a promotional one, and then to a planning mode. This transformation is related to the expansion of goals and ideas both within each sector and across the three sectors. Once established, each form of regulation reinforces different kinds of political conflict among interests. In the planning mode, the character of political conflict takes on an increasingly "zero-sum" nature; that is, the gains of one interest are at the expense of another.

The changes examined are linked to an understanding of economic and technological imperatives in each sector that are leading us in the direction of de-regulation. The changes also explicitly relate to the triple role of the provinces in these regulatory realms; namely, as regulator, as owner of regulated enterprises, and as a representative forum for private interests of regional economic importance.

In the light of their findings, the authors examine four general options for the structural reform of economic regulation: the status quo, joint federal-provincial regulatory mechanisms, political regulation, and de-regulation. The status quo obviously refers to the planning modes that the authors identify in the three sectors. In joint regulatory mechanisms, the authors envisage a range of possibilities that could include a broadening of constitutionally concurrent fields or changes that could see, for example, provincial appointees represented on key national regulatory bodies. Political regulation refers to the greater use of bodies such as the Foreign Investment Review Agency (FIRA), which contained not only multi-valued negotiating criteria but was closely linked to direct ministerial/cabinet involvement. Finally, de-regulation refers not to a wholesale return to market dynamics, but to major steps that would lessen regulation.

Schultz and Alexandroff support reforms that lean toward greater de-regulation. They are careful, however, not to elevate de-regulation into a simplistic call for a return to the free play of market forces, nor do they extend its application to all regulation.

G. Bruce Doern

ACKNOWLEDGMENTS

In the course of working on this project, we have incurred a number of debts for which we wish to express our gratitude. The first is to the many individuals who, over the course of several years for this and related studies, gave generously of their time, knowledge and ideas. Their contributions are especially appreciated because they were made on the understanding that there would be no individual attribution. We recognize that this study would not be possible without their many kindnesses. We would also like to thank two anonymous referees for their comments and suggestions, which we believe improved the final version of this study. We are delighted that we can name two individuals whose support and guidance were essential: Bruce Doern and Hudson Janisch. Finally, we would like to thank Ian Scott and Brownlee Thomas for their assistance in the research for this study. Although both authors accept responsibility for the full report, it should be noted that Schultz wrote Chapters 1, 2, 3, and 5 and Alexandroff contributed to Chapter 5 and wrote Chapter 4.

RICHARD J. SCHULTZ
ALAN ALEXANDROFF
November 1984

Chapter 1

Introduction

One of the central components of the mandate of the Royal Commission is "to inquire into and report upon the long-term economic potential, prospects and challenges facing the Canadian federation and its respective regions, as well as the implications that such prospects and challenges have for Canada's economic and governmental institutions and for the management of Canada's economic affairs."[1] This aspect of the mandate is derived from what is, perhaps, the most compelling reason for the creation of the Commission, namely the need to assess Canada's ability to adapt to the changing nature of the world economy and, in particular, its capacity to compete effectively in that economy: The purpose of this research report is to relate the concern for our competitive capacity and our adaptability to the functions and operations of our regulatory institutions and processes. More specifically, the purpose of the report is to identify and analyze how the politics of regulation, associated with the functioning of the federal system, affect Canada's capacity to attain its economic objectives. Such an analysis will form the basis for an assessment of the policy and institutional responses directed at ameliorating any problems arising from the complex interaction between the regulatory and federal systems.

In this introductory chapter, our goal is to provide an overview of the remainder of the study. We begin by developing a definition of economic regulation that will both guide the study and establish the scope of its boundaries. The second part of the chapter seeks first to establish that economic regulation has been employed as a multifunctional instrument of government, particularly at the federal level, and then to identify some of the more significant analytical aspects of the functions of regulation. The section following outlines the central argument of this study, namely, that changes in the function of economic regulation cause changes in the politics of regulation. In particular, we focus on two aspects, namely the impact of changes in the function of regulation on patterns of interest representation and on patterns of relationships between regulatory issues and decision makers and other political issues and authorities. The first three sections of this chapter are essential background for the fourth part which describes and develops the basic hypothesis of the study which is that, as the function of regulation has evolved, intergovernmental conflict has either ensued or increased. Such intergovernmental conflict, it is our contention, is two dimensional: federal-provincial and interprovincial. The fifth, and concluding, section of this chapter will provide an overview of the three case studies that will be employed to illustrate our central hypothesis. In addition, the selection of the specific studies will be justified.

Definition of Regulation

The purpose of this section is to review the various meanings or definitions of the central concept, regulation, and to stipulate the definition to be used in the study. The purpose of this definitional review is to provide a clear and explicit focus for the research to be undertaken as well as to establish the scope of the study.

For more than a decade now, in both Canada and the United States, government regulation has been both a focus of concern and high on the public agenda for political, business and academic communities. Given all this attention, it is surprising that there is so little agreement on the definition of the central concept. To paraphrase the oft-quoted judicial comment on the subject of obscenity, it appears that, while we may not be able to define it, we all know regulation when we see it! The following compendium of definitions — some more rigorous attempts than others — indicates the difficulty of attempting to define "regulation":

- Regulation . . . is any constraint imposed upon the normal freedom of individuals by the legitimate activity of government.[2]
- Economic regulation [is] the imposition of rules by a government, backed by the use of penalties, that are intended specifically to modify the economic behaviour of individuals and firms in the private sector.[3]
- Regulation, if defined in the broadest possible way, could include virtually everything which the government undertakes, since most of what the federal government does provides benefits and imposes restrictions. Thus in the large sense, grant programs, research and development programs, tax code provisions, and the numerous benefits which the government provides for individuals have regulatory aspects.[4]

- Regulation, in the broadest sense is *the* essential function of government. Indeed, taxation and expenditures, the other two principal instrumentalities, can be thought of as special cases of regulation . . . . From this perspective, to examine government regulation is to examine the role and function of government itself — no small task![5]
- Economic regulation . . . is the imposition of rules intended to modify economic behaviour significantly, which is backed up by the authority of the state.[6]
- Regulation is the public administrative policing of a private activity with respect to a rule prescribed in the public interest.[7]
- Regulation is a process consisting of the intentional restriction of a subject's choice of activity, by an entity not directly party to or involved in that activity.[8]
- Regulation exists to affect the relationships in and results of private markets.[9]
- Regulation involves the . . . direct and coercive use of power over citizens.[10]
- Regulation attempts to restrict people's behaviour . . . .[11]
- Regulation refers to "governmental legislation or agency rules, having the forces in law, issued for the purpose of altering or controlling the manner in which private and public enterprises conduct their operations. Economic regulation generally refers to the control of entry of individual firms into particular lines of business and the setting of prices that may be charged. In certain situations, it includes the specification of standards of service the firms can offer.[12]
- By economic regulation we mean public intervention by way of non-market controls in a mixed but primarily market-oriented economy. More specifically . . . economic regulation [entails] a governmental role in the setting of prices for goods and services, in determining the entry of particular entities into particular economic activities and in fixing standards of service and ensuring that they are met by the regulated.[13]
- Regulation is what regulators do. (Anon., timeless)

As this list amply demonstrates, there is, in the various attempts to define "regulation," a confusing mix of intentions, consequences, objectives, tools, processes and targets. Our purpose in highlighting the tremendous conceptual confusion is not to bewilder those attempting to grapple with the subject of regulation — or, conversely, to excite the evangelical exegetes who would obviously have a field day with analysts working in a "conceptual quagmire."[14] Given the confusion, one can sympathize with those who choose simply to plunge ahead without a "serious effort" to define the subject matter of their research.[15] While there is no necessity for this research to undertake what so many others have failed to accomplish, namely enunciate a definition of regulation that could win widespread acceptance, nevertheless, an attempt must be made to stipulate the subject matter of the study. This is necessary not only to provide a focus for the study and to establish its boundaries but, even more importantly, to underline the specific public policy problems within the Commission's mandate which the research and the analysis of alternative responses seek to address.

For our purposes, economic regulation has the following central characteristics. First, it involves a government role in restricting or restraining the behaviour, i.e., the choices, of individuals or firms. Second, although the process of economic regulation can involve almost the totality of governmental instruments from moral persuasion to subsidies to taxes to public ownership, there is, at the heart of regulation what Lowi emphasized, namely, the coercive power of the state. In other words, regulation is most closely associated with government by "command and control" rather than by incentive. The third characteristic of economic regulation, for our purposes, is the focus on economic behaviour. Economic behaviour can be viewed broadly but, for our purposes, we will limit it to three specific areas: entry into (and exit from) a specific economic activity; prices (fares, tariffs, rates) to be charged; and conditions (standards) governing relations between regulated firms and those who purchase from them.[16] Of these three forms of behaviour, we consider the first two to be the most significant. Some degree or some variant of entry and/or price control are what we see as being the necessary conditions for an activity to be defined as economic regulation.

There are several points that need to be emphasized in this "non-definition" of economic regulation. In the first place, unlike some of the examples cited, we do not confine the universe of economic regulation to private sector firms or businesses; in an economic system in which Air Canada, Canadian National Railways, Canadian Broadcasting Corporation and Atomic Energy of Canada (not to mention equivalent provincial examples) are central economic actors, and subject to what we have defined as economic regulation, to do so would significantly distort reality. Secondly, like many others, although we emphasize governmental restraints or controls on the behaviour of actors as central to our definition of economic regulation, we are not implying that such actors automatically object to such a governmental role. Whatever the limitations of the predictive or universal explanatory theories of Stigler and others, there are too many examples of firms embracing economic regulation for such an implication to be valid. Thirdly, we do not link our definition with a specific form of government organization, i.e., the independent regulatory agency. Long before the first independent agency was created, governments were involved in economic regulation. The regime of "6 & 5," and now "4," which was imposed by governmental fiat over firms subject to regulation by such agencies, also cautions us against an unthinking linkage between a governmental activity and a governmental form. Despite that caveat, this report will concentrate on economic regulation involving independent agencies because there is a strong correlation between these two features, i.e., economic regulation by independent agency, and the growth of intergovernmental conflict. Finally, in our definition there is no automatic linkage between economic regulation and a specific function or objective. Mitnick, for example, in the sixth definition cited above (note 7), links regulation to the purpose of policing economic activity. In our view, although it is correct to contend that some regulation at some specific time was essentially a policing activity, nevertheless, to limit regulation to such a purpose imposes a conception of economic regulation far too static to find support in the historical record. That record clearly establishes that the proponents of regulation have deemed it to be both a dynamic and a multifunctional instrument of governance. An appreciation of this perspective is so fundamental to this research that the next section expands on it and explains its significance.

We must emphasize that, in our discussion of the employment of economic regulation as a multifunctional instrument, there is no assumption of the appropriateness or inappropriateness of such use. In other words, we make no normative judgment about the use of economic regulation in specific instances; ours is a more neutral exercise that seeks simply to establish how regulation has, over time, been used, and to discover its political consequences. Whether or not economic regulation should be used for such purposes is a question that we leave to the concluding chapter, where we discuss some of the costs and benefits associated with the various uses as well as some of the alternative responses to ameliorate the intergovernmental conflicts that we contend have been caused by such uses.

The Multifunctional Nature of Regulation

As we have just indicated, there is in some of the literature an assumption that economic regulation as an instrument of government has a fairly narrow and specific function or purpose, i.e., to police specific economic activities. By policing, analysts mean that the purpose of economic regulation is to ensure that the behaviour of regulated firms is confined to a restricted range of choices that society has deemed, usually via legislation, to be socially acceptable. Anything outside this range of choices is considered to be unacceptable behaviour and, as part of the policing role of regulation, regulators are empowered to order remedial action in the event that a regulated entity engages in proscribed behaviour.

It is our contention that limiting the function of economic regulation to policing is, for several reasons, unjustified. In the first place, there is nothing in any definition or conception of economic regulation that logically requires its function to be so restricted. Secondly, some of the criticism directed at individual regulatory agencies, as well as some of the theories developed to explain regulatory behaviour, have been predicated on the questionable assumption that policing is the regulatory function when, in fact, the agencies in question may be performing distinctly different functions that have been assigned to them. To cite a specific example, analysts should not automatically be surprised or shocked when airline regulators, rather than performing the function imputed by the analyst, attempt to protect the regulated firms from adverse economic forces. Most importantly, we believe that to concentrate on the policing function ignores what many have recognized and acted upon, namely, that economic regulation can be employed for a variety of ends or objectives. Indeed, it is our contention that economic regulation has proven to be multifunctional which accounts, in very large measure, for its attractiveness for some as a primary instrument by which governments seek to influence, direct and control economic, and consequently social, behaviour of firms and individuals.

Historically, the function of economic regulation has been both negative and proscriptive as well as positive and prescriptive. In addition to being a policing tool, it has been employed as a promoting and/or a planning tool. We have already described policing as having the objective of controlling what regulated firms could not do, hence its "negative" character. Regulation as promoting entails protecting or enhancing the economic well-being of the entities subject to regulatory control. If policing regulation is normally associated with natural monopoly or public utility types of regulation, promoting regulation is most common where entry into the industry, as in airlines and trucking, is licensed by the regulator. It should be emphasized that, just as with policing regulation where we make no automatic assumption that it is effective and socially beneficial, i.e., the regulator is not "captured" by the regulated, so also with promotional regulation, we do not assume that enhancing the health of the regulated via "producer protection" is socially beneficial. Such regulation, as many of its critics correctly contend, may simply be a means by which political authorities impose costs on, and transfer benefits to, various parties. On the other hand, particularly, but not necessarily, where there is a public enterprise involved, e.g., Air Canada, regulation may be used to play a putatively socially beneficial role by promoting a healthy airline. This, of course, is dependent on what constitutes "healthy" and an assessment of the costs and benefits of alternative instruments for attaining such a state.

Planning involves a much more ambitious, positive role for economic regulation. Regulation as planning involves a public role via a mix of entry and price controls as well as standard-setting in dictating objectives not only for regulated entities, but also for regulated sectors or industries as a whole, in establishing priorities among various objectives, assigning them weights, assigning responsibilities to individual entities for the attainment of specific objectives, coordinating their activities where necessary, and, as required, resolving disputes within the regulated sector.

It should be emphasized that the three different functions we have distinguished are not mutually exclusive. Furthermore, although we emphasize a developmental approach, there is no suggestion that with the emergence of a new function, the preceding role is terminated. In fact, both promotional and planning regulation are premised on policing regulation. The following example will serve to illustrate.

Broadcasting regulation in Canada provides a classic example of regulation as planning. Successive governments have established a broad-gauged set of public goals that both public and private broadcasters as participants in "a single system" are expected to attain. To do so, individual radio stations, for example, are assigned certain musical formats, i.e., roles, and they are protected to a certain extent via licensing, actually non-licensing, of potential competitors in their territory. Their licence, and concomitant protection, is presumably contingent on their attainment of public as well as private goals. Regular licence renewals offer opportunity for periodic evaluations of their performance. If a station does not live up to the conditions of its licence, or, alternatively, violates those conditions, as in the recent case of the Quebec City licensee, then the regulator can use its policing power to punish the regulated as it deems appropriate.

In addition to the "positive-negative" dimension, it is worth noting two other general characteristics by which the different functions of economic regulation can be distinguished. One pertains to the "decisional processes" usually associated with individual functions.[17] The other involves the scope of each regulatory function.

Policing regulation decision making is characterized by two basic attributes. One is its reactive nature. This feature is best captured by a statement from a 1919 decision of the Board of Railway Commissioners: "Where a regulative tribunal's jurisdiction comes, as it has always done, after the development of a rate situation, the function of that tribunal is to regulate, not to initiate."[18] As recently as 1966, the same board's successor emphasized that " . . . regulation is and must be to a large degree *ex post facto*."[19] The second characteristic associated with policing regulation decision making is its remedial or corrective character. Policing regulation was designed either to prevent unacceptable behaviour from occurring by such means as rate-setting or by requiring that specific actions be stopped and to correct grievances associated with regulated entities' conduct after they arose.

Promoting and planning regulation are less likely to embody reactive, remedial decision making. For its part, regulation as promotion is associated with a more activist gatekeeper role and, consequently, the regulator has more of an initiating role, especially vis-à-vis parties which may threaten the "health" of firms already regulated. As a concomitant of the responsibility to oversee the health, decision making for a promoting regulator is characterized less by grievance settling and more by generalized problem solving. Planning regulation involves an even greater movement away from reactive, remedial activity. It is far more likely to initiate regulatory activities and responses than the other regulatory roles. Similarly, its decision making will entail much more generalized, broader, problem-solving, policy-oriented activity.

The second general characteristic which can be employed to distinguish the different functions of economic regulation pertains to their respective scope. The scope of policing regulation is much more narrowly confined than that of promoting and especially planning regulation. One useful approach to conceptualizing and organizing a comparison of the scope of the three regulatory functions is found in the economic concepts of market structure, conduct/behaviour and performance.[20] By market structure we mean that the following aspects of economic activity may be regulated:

- entry and exit from sector;
- number of firms in sector;
- size of firms;
- product differentiation;
- vertical integration; and
- product diversity ("conglomerateness").[21]

By market behaviour or conduct, for our purposes, we include:

- pricing;
- costing;
- plant investment;
- advertising;
- employee relations;
- share transactions;
- customer relations;
- quality of service;
- environmental and safety protection;
- depreciation;
- corporate structure and relationships; and
- accounting practices.

Although there are some significant differences and changes in our use of the concepts of structure and conduct compared to the conventional usage of economists, the greatest departure involves the "performance" component. For economists, the concept of "performance" usually involves a "normative appraisal of the social quality of the allocation of resources. . . ." There is, for economists, a concern for evaluating performance against a set of standards or criteria for what constitutes "good performance."[22] For our purposes, the normative connotations of performance are both inappropriate and unnecessary. Our concern is with variations in the scope of the objectives or goals associated with the three different regulatory functions of policing, promoting and planning. A few examples may clarify the distinction:

Transportation Prior to 1967, the primary statutory objectives, as found in the *Railway Act* for the regulation of railway rates, were to ensure that rates were "just and reasonable" and that railways did not engage in "unjust discrimination" or "undue preference."[23]

In 1967, the declared objectives of transportation regulation, including railways, were to provide for "an economic, efficient and adequate transportation system. . . "Although railway rate regulation was ended for the most part, provision was made to ensure that individual Aldid not "prejudicially affect the public interest."[24]

Although the amendments were never enacted, for our purposes it is instructive to note that, in 1977, the federal government proposed that the existing policy objectives be replaced by the following statement:

> It is hereby declared that the objective of the transportation policy for Canada is to achieve a transportation system that
> a) is efficient,
> b) is an effective instrument of support for the achievement of national and regional social and economic objectives, and
> c) provides accessibility and equity for users. . . . [25]

Energy Prior to 1959, there was no statutory statement of standards, criteria or objectives governing the licensing of pipelines. The regulatory agency, the Board of Transport Commissioners, was authorized to "have regard to all considerations that appear to it, to be relevant . . . to a public interest."[26]

After 1959, the National Energy Board was required, prior to issuing a licence for a pipeline, to ensure that the pipeline satisfied "present and future public convenience and necessity." In so doing, the board was instructed to take the following into consideration:

- the availability of oil or gas to the pipeline;
- the existence of markets, actual or potential;
- the economic feasibility of the pipeline;
- the financial responsibility and financial structure of the applicant, the methods of financing the line and the extent to which Canadians will have an opportunity of participating in the financing, engineering and construction of the line; and
- any public interest that in the Board's opinion may be affected by the granting or the refusing of the application.[27]

Broadcasting Prior to 1967, there was no statutory statement of objectives governing Canadian broadcasting regulation. The closest approximation was found in a provision of the *Broadcasting Act* of 1936, which authorized the Canadian Broadcasting Corporation, then the regulator of private stations, to make regulations inter alia "to control the character of any and all programs broadcast by Corporation or private stations" and "to promote and ensure the greater use of Canadian talent by Corporation and private stations. . . ."[28]

After 1967, the *Broadcasting Act* contained the following statement of policy:

It is hereby declared that:

a) broadcasting undertakings in Canada make use of radio frequencies that are public property and such undertakings constitute a single system, herein referred to as the Canadian broadcasting system, comprising public and private elements;
b) the Canadian broadcasting system should be effectively owned and controlled by Canadians so as to safeguard, enrich and strengthen the cultural, political, social and economic fabric of Canada;
c) all persons licensed to carry on broadcasting undertakings have a responsibility for programs they broadcast but the right to freedom of expression and the right of persons to receive is unquestioned;
d) the programming provided by the Canadian broadcasting system should be varied and comprehensive and should provide reasonable, balanced opportunity for the expression of differing views on matters of public concern, and the programming provided by each broadcaster should be of high standard, using predominantly Canadian creative and other resources;
e) all Canadians are entitled to broadcasting service in English and French as public funds become available;
f) there should be provided, through a corporation established by Parliament for the purpose, a national broadcasting service that is predominantly Canadian in content and character;
g) the national broadcasting services should
   i) be a balanced service of information, enlightenment and entertainment for people of different ages, interests and tastes covering the whole range of programming in fair proportion,
   ii) be extended to all parts of Canada, as public funds become available,
   iii) be in English and French, serving the special needs of geographic regions, and actively contributing to the flow and exchange of cultural and regional information and entertainment, and
   iv) contribute to the development of national unity and provide for a continuing expression of Canadian identity;
h) where any conflict arises between the objectives of the national broadcasting service and the interests of the private element of the Canadian broadcasting system, it shall be resolved in the public interest but paramount consideration shall be given to the objectives of the national broadcasting service;

i) facilities should be provided within the Canadian broadcasting system for educational broadcasting; and

j) the regulation and supervision of the Canadian broadcasting system should be flexible and readily adaptable to scientific and technical advances;

and that the objectives of broadcasting policy for Canada enunciated in this section can best be achieved by providing for the regulation and supervision of the Canadian broadcasting system by a single independent public authority.[29]

Telecommunications Starting in 1906, the statutory objectives of telephone regulation were identical to those for the railways at the time, specifically, to ensure that rates were just and reasonable and that telephone companies under federal jurisdiction did not engage in unjust discrimination or undue preference.

In 1978, the federal government proposed a new statement of telecommunications objectives. The following are those applicable to telephone companies:

a) efficient telecommunication systems are essential to the sovereignty and integrity of Canada, and telecommunications services and production resources should be developed and administered so as to safeguard, enrich and strengthen the cultural, political, social and economic fabric of Canada;

c) all Canadian are entitled, subject to technologies and economic limitations, to reliable telecommunication services making the best use of all available modes, resources and facilities, taking into account regional and provincial needs and priorities;

d) telecommunication links within and among all parts of Canada should be strengthened, and Canadian facilities should be used to the greatest extent feasible for the carriage of telecommunications within Canada and between Canada and other countries;

* * *

n) telecommunication systems and services in Canada . . . other than the broadcasting undertakings referred to in paragraph (e) should be effectively subject to Canadian control through ownership or regulation;

o) the rates charged by telecommunications carriers for telecommunication facilities and services should be just and reasonable and should not unduly discriminate against any person or group;

p) innovation and research in all aspects of telecommunications should be promoted in order to improve Canadian telecommunication systems and to strengthen the Canadian industries engaged in the production of broadcast programming and the manufacture of telecommunication systems and equipment; and

q) the regulation of all aspects of telecommunications in Canada should be flexible and readily adaptable to cultural, social and economic change and to scientific and technological advances, and should ensure a proper balance between the interests of the public at large and the legitimate revenue requirements of the telecommunication industry.[30]

As these examples demonstrate, regulation as an instrument of government has not been confined to a narrow range of objectives. To the contrary, it has been employed to pursue almost any public policy goal imaginable.

For analytical purposes, this diversity does not permit an easy classification of regulatory goals. One approach that offers some utility, although it does not answer all the problems, is to distinguish between endogenous and exogenous objectives or goals. The former pertain to issues or aspects relating to the participants within an industrial sector, including relationships between buyers and sellers, while the latter relate to the employment or application of the industry for the attainment of other objectives. In the field of transportation, for example, Studnicki-Gizbert cites the improvement of the functioning of the transport system per se as an endogenous objective while the pursuit, via transportation policy, of regional or industrial development and interregional or intergroup income distribution are classified as objectives exogenous to transport.[31]

Our purpose in introducing the endogenous/exogenous distinction, which, it must be emphasized, is best understood as a continuum rather than as a dichotomous relationship, is based on the assumption that there are patterns in the relations among the different functions of regulation. Policing regulation is normally associated with fairly narrow, circumscribed, endogenous objectives whereas regulation as promoting and especially as planning entails a broadening of such objectives to include exogenous objectives. In the transportation or telecommunications sectors, for example, policing regulation would be expected to act as a surrogate for a competitive marketplace so as to restrict monopoly providers of a service from extracting monopoly or excessive profits. More ambitious but still policing regulation in those sectors, would seek to satisfy broader endogenous objectives such as regulating to ensure efficient provision of services. Planning regulation in such sectors, by way of contrast, entails a much broader set of objectives. Although such regulation would continue to be an instrument for the pursuit of endogenous goals, these would be supplemented and, possibly, reduced in priority by exogenous objectives such as regulating the industry in question in order to use it for the attainment of other goals such as regional development, national unity or technological sovereignty.

A summary method of integrating, for comparative purposes, the preceding discussion about the multifunctional use of economic regulation as measured by changes in the regulatory scope is offered by the following matrix:

We believe that employment of such a matrix permits a comparison, both over time and across agencies, of the employment by governments of economic regulation as a tool or instrument of government control and influence in specific sectors of the economy. In brief, it is our contention

FIGURE 1-1

Function of Regulation	Scope of Regulation: Structure	Conduct	Objective
Policing			
Promoting			
Planning			

that the three functions for which regulation has been employed are distinguishable in terms of the patterned relationships in the three measures of regulatory scope. Policing regulation, which is traditionally associated with natural monopolies and public utilities, has little concern for industry structure (normally this is taken for granted), concentrates on a limited range of firm behaviour and has minimalist, almost exclusively endogenous, policy objectives. Planning regulation, which is the other polar type, focusses explicitly on structural issues, subjects a considerably broadened range of industrial behaviour or conduct to regulatory control and pursues a much more complex set of objectives, including a mix of both endogenous and exogenous goals.

The Politics of Economic Regulation: The Argument

Thus far we have set out our definition of economic regulation and three analytical distinctions to characterize the multifunctional nature of such regulation as it has been employed. What needs to be established is the significance of the preceding to the concerns of the Royal Commission and, in particular, to those pertaining to the politics of economic policy making. We believe one can accomplish this easily, and we will do so in two respects. In the first place, we will identify what we believe to be the more salient implications of the evolution of the multifunctional character of economic regulation for the politics of regulation. Secondly, and central to the basic purpose of this research, we will identify the consequences of intergovernmental politics.

Prior to undertaking these tasks, it should be emphasized that this study does not attempt a comprehensive analysis of the politics of regulation. In particular, it does not seek to identify the sources of demands and pressures for changes in the function of economic regulation or to analyze the political processes that lead to any changes. Consequently, the study makes no assumptions, for example, about whether federal planning regulation was a response to either particular business or provincial demands or was generated within the federal government and imposed on other actors. Although we believe it to be important to undertake such an analysis, this study takes such prior political activity for granted.[32] Our concern is for the political consequences, particularly as they pertain to intergovernmental relations, of changes in the regulatory function.

Policy Determines Politics

A basic premise for this analysis is one increasingly common to policy analysis. Its most noted exponent is Theodore Lowi who contends that "policy determines politics."[33] It is our contention that if we equate the individual regulatory functions with a unique, or at least distinguishable, policy, then changes in the regulatory function cause profound changes in the politics of regulation.

From our perspective, given the definition of economic regulation advanced here, the underlying concern is its employment by government to influence or control corporate economic decision making. Consequently, the main criterion for distinguishing the three regulatory functions is the degree of corporate autonomy or, conversely, government control over corporate decision making associated with each function. Furthermore, we are most concerned about the degree of autonomy corporate decision makers are permitted in order to establish corporate goals and to make the strategic decisions necessary for their attainment. One approach for analyzing the degree of autonomy involves a distinction between the rules and the goals or outcomes for economic decision making. In our view, policing regulation focusses primarily on rules and far less so on outcomes, whereas the promoting and, especially, planning variants emphasize outcomes to a much greater extent, i.e., directing economic activities toward publicly determined outcomes or objectives.

When we employ the distinction between rules and outcomes, policing regulation entails a role for the regulatory authority in supervising relations between buyers and sellers of the goods or services of the regulated firm. The focus is primarily on establishing rules and ensuring that corporate behaviour respects these rules. Promoting regulation, however, entails not solely supervising the relations but in some respects managing the relations not only between individual firms and their customers, but also between and among firms in the same sector. The regulatory ambit expands to include not only rules for behaviour, but also a publicly determined outcome. Planning regulation involves all of the preceding but, in addition, entails a significant shift in emphasis toward establishing goals with a secondary emphasis on rules.

To return to our concern for relating the individual regulatory function to the degree of autonomy for corporate decision making, in policing regulation, regulated firms play the primary role in setting corporate goals and the related strategies for the development of their firms. Obviously, regulatory authorities may influence firm decisions, but they do not do so directly, except to prohibit both certain goals and specified forms of corporate behaviour. Within accepted behavioural boundaries, management prerogatives are paramount. In promoting regulation, firms and government are more integrated and closely linked in establishing goals and in directing both individual firms and specific industries such as trucking, airlines or broadcasting. It may be useful to make a distinction between two broad but nevertheless identifiable types of promoting regulation. The first can be labelled *private-interest promoting regulation*, which is characterized by the dominance of private sector interests over public interests. Under this form of regulation, which is closely linked with the various "capture" or "producer protection" theories, government regulation is employed to promote the interests of regulated private firms by protecting them from competition. Trucking regulation and, in the United States, airline regulation are excellent examples of this type of regulation. The second type is *public-interest promoting regulation*, in which public goals play a greater role, and some variant of the public interest may be dominant, in that government will use regulation to promote the economic well-being of a firm designated to be a chosen instrument. Usually, but not exclusively, the chosen instrument whose interests are being promoted will be a Crown corporation. Airline regulation in Canada from 1938 until 1964 exemplifies this form of promotional regulation.

In a planning regulatory regime, management prerogatives are substantially constrained, inasmuch as government emerges as the primary goal setter. With regulation employed as a planning instrument, there is a significant shift in the power to make strategic choices or decisions from corporate decision makers to regulatory authorities. The shift, of course, is relative, not absolute. Its significance for our purposes is derived from the fact that regulated firms not only lose some decision-making autonomy, they must, correspondingly, place a greater emphasis on seeking to influence or constrain public sector goal and strategy selection.

Although the distinction is somewhat overdrawn, from this perspective, policing and planning regulation are polar types (with promoting regulation, depending on the particular variant, falling somewhere in between) with respect to the degree of corporate autonomy/public control over corporate decision making. Policing regulation typifies *firm-led* or *firm-dominant* economic decision making, whereas the latter typifies *state-led* or *state-dominant* economic decision making.[34] For our purposes, the significance of a distinction such as this is the implication of a move from policing to planning regulation with respect to political intervention in the economy. Such a move means greater or enhanced employment of regulation as an instrument for political intervention in the economy, to shape and direct the ends of economic activity. Equally important is the obvious conclusion that an enhanced political role in the allocation of resources and in directing the production and distribution of goods and services means, by definition, a greater political role in determining winners and losers in economic activity. This fact, combined with a recognition that the sectors most commonly subject to economic regulation are those such as transportation, energy and communications, i.e., sectors involving the infrastructure of an economy with widespread economic and social ramifications, accounts in very large measure for the degree of political salience of the political process and institutions involved in regulatory decision making.

Our basic proposition is that changes in function of regulation result in changes in the politics of regulation. This is not to suggest, of course, that changes in the functions of regulation explain everything about the politics of regulation, but simply that they do account for some important aspects. Our contention is that there are distinctive patterns to the political processes and relationships associated with each of the regulatory functions. In particular, we believe it useful to focus on two specific dimensions of these political patterns in order to appreciate how changes in the regulatory function impact on the politics of regulation. One is the cast of characters in the process; the second is the interrelationships between regulatory processes and the regulatory arena and other political processes and forums. Let us now look at each of these in turn.

There is a relationship between the individual regulatory functions and the range and diversity of the actors or interests represented in the regulatory process. One method of characterizing this relationship is through the use of a *restricted/broadened* continuum. Participation in policing regulation is fairly restricted inasmuch as the participants are usually confined to those directly affected by regulatory decisions, i.e., the regulated firm and its customers. It should be noted, however, that the latter may be typically represented by a group or collective organization such as shippers' organizations and boards of trade in the case of railway shippers, and municipalities in the case of telephone subscribers.[35]

The pattern of interest representation in planning regulation, on the other hand, is considerably broadened and far more inclusive. This is, of course, a direct reflection of our argument that a shift from policing to planning regulation increases the political salience of regulatory issues, and, consequently, wider representation reflects the expanded ramifications of regulatory decisions. More actors or interests want to be represented because important decisions impacting on their well-being are being made or affected by regulatory authorities.

The changing function of regulation broadens interest representation for a number of reasons. In the first place, under policing regulation, interest representation is performed largely by omnibus, umbrella-type groups or organizations; with planning regulation, interests become more differentiated and less aggregated. This occurs because omnibus groups no longer find themselves able to reflect effectively the diversity of interests now affected by the differential impact of regulatory decisions. In the case of telephone regulation, for example, there has been an emergence of a wide variety of residential consumer groups representing the middle class, those under the poverty line and native users, to mention three, as well as groups representing the diversity of business subscribers such as small and large businesses, hospitals, hotels and universities. A related, but distinct, aspect of interest disaggregation pertains to the regulated firm itself. Under policing regulation and, particularly, promoting regulation, there may be a coincidence of interests for both management and labour resulting from the ability, in the case of the former, to pass on labour costs automatically or, in the latter case, to attain job security via anticompetitive entry restrictions. This coincidence of interests may be undermined in a regime of planning regulation. Consequently, labour may no longer perceive its interests as being adequately represented by management spokesmen, and it will choose to participate directly.

The second basic cause of broadened interest representation is obvious. Interests not previously affected by regulatory decisions, or which did not perceive themselves to be, may now find that with a shift in the regulatory function toward planning, their well-being is directly affected by what takes place in the regulatory arena. Consequently, existing but previously unrepresented interested parties, acting to protect or further their welfare, insist on being represented and on taking an active role in regulatory proceedings. Alternatively, hitherto unorganized, perhaps diffuse, interests may form into interest groups which seek representation in those proceedings. Transport 2000, organized to represent railway passengers, is an example of such an interest group.

There is a third source of broadened participation in regulatory decision making caused by changes in the regulatory function. That source is the public sector itself. As the regulatory function changes and, concomitantly, regulatory authorities take on greater prominence as a decision-making force, so other units of government may seek direct representation in order to protect policy objectives or bureaucratic and clientele interests which they now perceive to be threatened by regulatory action. Alternatively, regulatory arenas may take on prominence if governments choose to place greater priority on attaining their goals through the employment of regulatory instruments. This may encourage individual governmental units to pursue a role in the regulatory arena in order to further their objectives and interests or those of their clients or constituents.

The preceding argument, i.e., that changes in the regulatory function account for changes in the patterns of interest representation, is not meant to suggest that such changes are the sole cause. There is too much evidence that, even without an alteration in the regulatory function, more interests are seeking representation in the regulatory process. Our contention is, simply, that there is a direct causal link between changes in the regulatory function and broadened interest representation, but that other forces are at work accounting for such a development when the regulatory function does not change.

The significance of changes in patterns of interest representation is not in the expanded numbers of participants in the regulatory process, but in the impact of broadened representation on the politics of regulation. The most immediate impact is the potential cumulative effect on representation. As more groups participate in the regulatory process and make demands on regulators, other affected parties become aware of the importance of regulation and their actual or potential stake in the process. In brief, broadened representation serves to increase the political salience of regulation as an instrument of government.

One important aspect of this is that it may lead to demands for "no regulation without representation" on the grounds that, for regulatory decision making to have legitimacy, all affected parties must be represented.[36] One consequence of such demands is that, depending on the regulatory arena, conflicts can ensue over which interests are entitled to "standing," i.e., the right to be represented and to be heard. Even more important, given traditional concerns that there is an unequal distribution of resources in many regulatory processes (which can undermine the value of representation), conflicts can arise over mechanisms and procedures for representation, particularly of more diffuse, less organized interests. Debates over the creation of consumer-advocacy offices within governments and decisions to "tax" regulated firms to support interest representation illustrate such conflicts. In 1979, for example, the Canadian Radio-television and Telecommunications Commission (CRTC), in one of its first acts as regulator of telecommunications, announced that it was reversing a decision of its predecessor, the Canadian Transport Commission (CTC), and would award "costs" in certain circumstances to intervenors who "participated in a responsible way" and "contributed to a better understanding of the issues by the Commission."[37] An associated aspect of such a development is that governments or specific units of government may, for a variety of motives (such as to ensure balance or to seek allies), encourage, financially and otherwise, the formation of interest groups which subsequently seek to be represented in regulatory proceedings.

Perhaps the most significant impact of broadened representation involves the nature of conflict resolution over regulatory matters. Interested parties in regulatory decision making do not simply want a hearing; they want to be heard. More specifically, they want their views and their interests to be reflected in regulatory decisions, especially in matters where decision makers seem to be showing favouritism to particular interests, usually the regulated firms. Our contention is that broadened representation, which arises from changes in the function of regulation, makes the process of accommodation and the resolution of conflicts more difficult.

This contention runs counter to one of the more dominant views about the politics of regulation and, accordingly, requires some development. The view in question is Theodore Lowi's and is based on his definition of the "regulatory policy type." According to Lowi, regulatory policies are different from distributive and redistributive policies inasmuch as regulatory policies involve "a direct choice as to who will be indulged and who deprived."[38] In essence, Lowi is arguing that regulatory policies have a substantial zero-sum element to them. His examples — a single television channel and an overseas air route — characterize zero-sum decisions in that there can be only one winner; all other applicants must lose. In our view, Lowi's concept of regulation is misleading because it is far too narrow and one-dimensional. He fails to make a distinction between what we have labelled promoting regulation and the other two functions, i.e., policing and planning. We would argue that policing regulation was, and is, decidedly not zero-sum in its nature. From the outset, although policing regulation was premised on a largely bipolar conflict, the role of regulators as policemen was to balance the interests of both participants, the regulated firm and its customers. The requirement, for example, that rates or prices be "just and reasonable" was meant to apply to both parties. This did not mean that in regulatory conflicts involving the policing function there were not winners and losers but that it was not a simple either/or situation. Under promoting regulation, with the broadening of the scope of regulation to cover industry structure and designating the regulator to be guardian of the gates (granting licences for television channels and air routes), regulation most decidedly came to possess a zero-sum element. Moreover, the "zero-sum-ness" may increase with the move to regulation as planning if the public decision maker is confined, as is an independent regulatory agency, in its decision-making resources.

The zero-sum character of regulation may increase because of the broadened representation and concomitant growth in conflicting demands combined with the regulatory tools to satisfy those demands. It will be recalled that in our definition of economic regulation, we limited it to three specific areas of economic behaviour, namely entry, price and associated standards of service. The three tools, consequently, are licensing, rate setting and standard setting. The problem with these tools is that they are fairly blunt. They may be appropriate for resolving the essential bipolar conflicts in policing regulation, but it is doubtful that they have the necessary flexibility for the polycentric conflict resolution associated with the broadened representation characteristic of planning regulation. Such flexibility is needed to accomplish the bargaining and logrolling required to satisfy a sufficiently broad coalition of affected parties.

An increase in the zero-sum character of regulatory conflicts can have profound implications for the politics of regulation. It is generally recognized that the really difficult political problem is not that of distributing benefits and rewarding winners but of allocating losses and placating losers.[39] Zero-sum political conflicts, by their nature, thus confront decision makers with the problem of loss allocation. Moreover, if Thurow's contention is generally valid, that the "political process is least capable" of coping with loss allocation, it may be particularly relevant to the regulatory process. To the extent that regulatory authorities are not confined exclusively to the role of regulators, but can switch roles and, consequently, draw on other resources and on other policy instruments, then the growth of a zero-sum element is not necessarily an intractable problem. Public authorities who, in addition to their regulatory role, are prime participants in other political processes involving the imposition of taxes or the distribution of subsidies, may be able to resolve regulatory conflicts through their access to, and employment of, these other policy instruments. To the extent, however, that regulatory decision makers are restricted in their ability to confront the problem of loss allocation, then the losers in the regulatory process are faced with two choices. They can accept their losses, thus resolving any problems, or they can seek redress from other decision makers in other decision-making arenas. To do the latter is to effect significant changes in the patterns of relationships that exist between regulatory authorities and other public decision makers.

Another way of appreciating how changes in regulatory function impact on the politics of regulation is to focus on the relationship between the individual regulatory functions and the linkages between regulatory processes and arenas and other political processes and arenas. The changes in the linkages and the functions can be characterized by the use of another continuum with the two poles being *insulated* and *integrated*. It should be noted that, unlike the changes discussed in the preceding section, a movement from an insulated to an integrated process is conditional in the first instance upon the creation of a specialized regulatory institution. The distinction being drawn is not applicable when the actors playing a regulatory role are, simultaneously, occupants of other political roles in other institutions such as legislatures or government departments.

Typical policing regulation is associated with a political process that is largely, but obviously not totally, insulated from other political processes. In part, insulation is derived from, and dependent upon, the regulators' claim to a special or unique form of institutional competence vis-à-vis other public institutions. Thus, one of the major arguments advanced to justify hiving off the regulatory function for railways from cabinet in 1903 was the need for an impartial grievance-settling body which cabinet, as a partisan body, could not be. Simultaneously, the decision not to place this function in the hands of the judiciary to satisfy the impartial condition was defended on the grounds that the courts lacked the economic training necessary for the responsibility.[40] The irony of this argument was the fact that, in seeking to buttress the insulation of the regulatory authorities, the federal government at least drew a large proportion of its senior regulatory appointments in the transportation sector from legal and especially judicial sources.[41] A related tactic conducive to insulation was to emphasize the quasi-judicial role of the regulatory agency by making it a court of record and giving its members fixed, lengthy terms of office.

Insulation of the regulatory function from other political processes can also be sought through the legislative mandates conferred on regulatory authorities. Currie notes, for example, that the first regulatory agency in Canada, the Board of Railway Commissioners, "functioned only in comparatively narrow fields where its duties can be precisely defined by parliament or where the determination of what ought to be done can be fairly clearly arrived at by means of engineering and statistical data."[42] The regulator can reinforce his insulation by shunning any broader political conflicts. This can be done by giving a narrow interpretation to the mandate and by emphasizing the importance of precedent in decision making. Jackman, for example, noted that the Board of Railway Commissioners:

> . . . time and again emphasized that it is empowered to deal with transportation matters only. It refused to order experimental or developmental rates. . . . The board has refused to change rates to offset the effect of a tariff, and will not alter rates on the grounds of desirable public policy, because, it says, parliament is the proper place for such matters.[43]

Similarly, Darling, in his study of the politics of freight rates, emphasized the railway commissioners' strategy of concentrating on specific, narrowly defined issues and how the board fought a continuing battle not to be drawn into wider political conflicts.[44] One measure of "successful" insulation in the transportation sector, at least for that period which we would characterize as policing regulation, was the recourse to removal from the regulatory agency of particular issues. For example, regulation of the Crow's Nest Pass Agreement involving, as it did, immediately political issues, was removed from the railway regulator in 1925 by order-in-council and subsequently enshrined in legislation. Another measure was the periodic recourse to royal commissions to study the "railway" issue when political conflicts became too heated and appeared to threaten either the regulatory agency's capacity or its legitimacy.

As previously mentioned, the insulation of policing regulation was by no means total. The most obvious linkage between regulatory and other political decision makers was the "political appeal" mechanism included in the legislation creating the first regulatory agency. This mechanism provided for an appeal to the federal cabinet on any matter, whether of fact or law. Given the open-ended nature of such a provision, it would appear to undermine much of the preceding argument. We would disagree. While, on the face of it, the political appeal provision does seem to erode any substantial barriers between regulatory and other political decision makers, the record of its usage by the latter would tend to support our contention. In the first place, the appeal provision was enacted not, as it would appear, to give the cabinet final control per se, but rather to insulate the regulatory body from undue judicial interference. The draftsmen of federal regulatory legislation at the turn of the century had the U.S. experience as a guide. One critical aspect of that experience was the use by the railways of the judicial system to undermine much of the effectiveness of their federal regulator, the Interstate Commerce Commission. Accordingly, the Canadian draftsmen sought to give the regulator, and not the courts, the final determination of facts, and they limited the courts to appeals only on questions of law and jurisdiction.[45] To compensate for the restricted judicial appeal, the final version of the legislation provided for the political appeal route.

Secondly, and more importantly, successive cabinets during the policing era were evidently mindful of the need to defer to the regulatory authority. As Currie noted, cabinets had a "strong inclination to support the judgment of the board."[46] The cabinet itself noted in one of its appeal decisions:

> A practice has grown up not to interfere with an order of the board unless it is manifest that the board has proceeded upon some wrong principle, or that it has been otherwise subject to error. Where the matters at issue are questions of fact depending for their solution upon a mass of conflicting testimony, or are otherwise such as the board is particularly fitted to determine, it has been customary, except as aforesaid, not to interfere with the findings of the board.[47]

It is, perhaps, not necessary to dwell unduly on the fact that it was in the cabinet's best interests to support the regulator's decisions. Insulation served to protect both the regulator and cabinet. To the extent that it could "pass the buck" for unpopular political decisions to an "apolitical," impartial decision maker, cabinet did not have to bear political responsibility. The strength of the norm of non-interference is demonstrated by the fact that from 1904 to 1961, only six appeals, or 8 percent of the total, were accepted by the cabinet.[48]

Policing regulation was, however, a political function and so could not be completely insulated from other political processes. Dissatisfied parties at no time renounced the right to seek redress for decisions from other political authorities. The history of regulation provides ample evidence of efforts employing other political processes to overturn what were perceived to be unacceptable regulatory decisions. That same history, however, shows that, while not impossible, such results were not easily attained. One of the reasons for this was the relative insulation of the regulatory from other political processes. This insulation was a product of a wide range of forces: the institutional rationale for separate regulatory decision making, the organizational ethos that developed, the legislative mandate conferred on the regulators and, finally, an incentive system that encouraged other decision makers to respect institutional boundaries.

The shift from policing to promoting and, particularly, planning regulation had a significant impact on the linkages between regulatory authorities and other decision makers. Instead of being relatively insulated from such decision makers, regulators found themselves much more integrated within the larger political process. Instead of being relatively autonomous, regulators found themselves involved in much more complex interdependent relationships. While, in some respects, such interdependencies broadened the scope of their decision-making authority, they acted concomitantly to reduce regulatory autonomy.

The greater integration of promoting and planning regulation reflected a number of significant changes in the institutional linkages and roles. For one thing, a characteristic of both was that other political decision makers, such as cabinet collectively or individual ministers, normally reserved certain powers for themselves that, under policing regulation, were routinely conferred on regulators. In airline regulation after 1944, for example, the minister of transport, not the regulatory agency, was the licensing authority. This was also the case in the broadcasting sector from 1936 to 1968. Secondly, there was a decline in the importance of the legal profession and specifically the judiciary, as the major source of senior appointments. More members came from political and bureaucratic backgrounds.[49] Thirdly, there was a significant change in the legislative mandate of the regulatory agency. Rather than being confined to "comparatively narrow fields" with a fairly precise legislative definition of responsibilities, promoting and planning regulation has been characterized by open-ended mandates that give not only the vaguest of guidance, but also, in the process, confer considerably enhanced discretion on the regulatory decision makers.[50] Finally, reflecting the decline or, at least, the dilution of institutional specialization, planning regulatory authorities have found that other public organizations are allocated tasks identical to, or significantly overlapping, theirs. In the energy and communications sectors, for example, not only were the federal departments created after the regulatory agencies, but they were also given responsibilities identical in some respects to those earlier conferred on the agencies.[51]

Regulatory politics change significantly when the regulatory process is more integrated into wider political processes. In the first place, given the decline in institutional specialization, there is no intrinsic argument favouring deference on the part of other authorities. While the procedures employed by a regulatory agency may be distinctive, other political actors, particularly those in public bureaucracies with overlapping mandates, may claim equal, if not better, competence because of greater staff resources. For its part, the regulatory agency may aid in the decline of deference by rejecting the role of self-denial in favour of a more ambitious policy-making role. Alternatively, such a stance may not represent ambition but simply, to use Downs' phrase, "territorial sensitivity" to threats, real or imagined, to the jurisdiction of the agency.[52] Whatever the reason, the result is the emergence of a particular variant of institutional integration, namely bureaucratic competition. Such competition has profound implications not only for intragovernmental relations, but also for other participants. In a regime of policing regulation, notwithstanding the political appeal mechanism, the norm was for the regulator to be the ultimate decision maker within its area of authority. Under planning regulation, decision making may be regarded more as segmented or sequential. The notion that the regulator is only the first in a series but not the ultimate decision maker becomes the norm. One indication of this is the growth in the use of the appeal mechanism, whether by private petition or by other public authorities acting on their own initiative. Another is the emergence of "tandem proceedings" which are characterized by two sets of public decision makers coincidentally grappling with the same set of issues. Whatever the particular variant, the result is that parties, in a condition of integration, recognize that they are no longer restricted to a few arenas in the pursuit of their objectives.

The Intergovernmental Politics of Economic Regulation: The Hypothesis

In the preceding section, our objective was to sketch the basic argument that changes in the function of economic regulation cause changes in the politics of such regulation. More specifically, the argument is that, central to each of the three functions of regulation, there are variations in the degree of autonomy allowed corporate decision makers to set corporate goals and to establish strategic decisions. Changes in that degree of autonomy cause changes in the patterns of political processes and relationships. In particular, we said that there are causal relationships between the regulatory functions and the range of interests represented in the regulatory process as well as between those functions and the linkages between regulatory and other political processes.

Our concern in this report, however, is not with the broad political consequences of changes in the function of economic regulation, but with a particular subset of those consequences. We are concerned with the impact on intergovernmental relations of such changes. In particular, our purpose is to identify, within the specific scope of this study, the significance of the intergovernmental politics of economic regulation for the politics of economic policy making. Building upon the preceding dimensions, this section advances the hypothesis that there is a causal connection between intergovernmental conflict and the function of regulation. Such conflict increases as economic regulation performs less of a policing function and more of a planning function. We are not arguing that this is the only cause of such conflict; other factors such as partisanship, status concerns and personalities, to cite only three, play a role. Our purpose is to focus on the causal impact of changing regulatory functions on intergovernmental relations.

A starting point for analyzing this impact is to identify how changes in the federal regulatory function affect provincial governments. One useful method of doing this is to identify significant roles performed by provincial governments which federal regulation may influence or affect. More specifically, we must identify those impacts which are such as to cause or enhance intergovernmental tension and conflict and then stipulate why this is the result. To do this, we shall analyze the interrelationships between the three provincial roles and the patterns of interest representation and political institutional linkages associated with the individual regulatory functions.

For our purposes, there are three distinctive roles played by provincial governments which are relevant to this study. They are provincial government as interest representative, as owner of regulated firms and as policy maker. The first role is performed before regulatory decision makers, when provincial governments seek to represent, much like a pressure group, interested parties found within their province. Prairie governments, for example, long performed this role in the railway regulatory arena; more recently, Ontario and Quebec have participated routinely in federal telecommunications regulatory proceedings. The second role springs from the fact that provincial Crown corporations are often subject to federal regulation. Provincial electrical utilities are subject to federal regulation with respect to interprovincial and international aspects of their operations. Similarly, provincial educational broadcasters, airlines and passenger rail services are federally regulated. Finally, provincial governments now play a significant policy-making role. This role is significant, in the first instance, because of their constitutionally allocated powers which, over the years, have assumed great significance. It is a role that has been enhanced by the eradication of the so-called "water-tight compartments" and the emergence of the network of complex policy interdependencies — the "seamless web of policy" — with which both levels of government must cope today.

We contend that changes in the function of federal regulation can affect each of these roles seriously enough to cause intergovernmental conflict. Such conflict can arise with respect to the interest representative role because of the consequences of broadened group participation which we have suggested to be characteristic of planning regulation. Under policing regulation, provinces intervened largely on behalf of broad-based groups; indeed, such concerns of groups were often coterminous with provincial interests. In railway regulation, for example, provincial governments intervened on behalf of all shippers in their provinces. Similarly, Ontario and Quebec claim to participate in telecommunications proceedings, not on behalf of any narrow group, but on behalf of the citizens of their respective provinces. In a regime of planning regulation, the typical all-inclusive approach to interest representation is not easily accomplished. It is not possible, partly because of the process of group differentiation discussed earlier; omnibus groups cease to have shared interests and so break up. In part, the problem is that new interests, and thus new groups, enter the regulatory arena. As a consequence, intergroup conflicts and incompatibilities emerge.

The significance of this development is that what was once reasonably inexpensive for provincial governments can now become burdensome and politically disadvantageous. In the earlier period, provincial governments which intervened won, regardless of the specific regulatory outcome. They could take credit for defending provincial interests and still blame the "feds" for any adverse decisions. As the premier of Ontario bluntly acknowledged, "when Bell's rates go up it is nice to say that it is the Government of Canada who did it."[53] With the disintegration of omnibus groups, provincial governments can be forced, if they choose to intervene, to decide which groups they will support or will not. To cite one example of such difficult choices, in 1984, the Ontario government in telecommunications proceedings was confronted with the difficult dilemma of deciding whether to support the introduction of competition in the provision of public long-distance telephone services (the major immediate beneficiaries of which would be members of the business community) or to oppose such an action in order to protect the interests of residential telephone subscribers. Prairie governments faced similar choices in the debate over ending the Crow's Nest Pass Agreements. What is important for us are the consequences of choosing to represent some particular groups and thereby potentially alienating others. The most important consequence is that, having chosen, provincial governments will thus have a vested interest and an incentive not only to represent them, but also to pursue satisfactory outcomes for them in the regulatory process. This leads us back to the second conflict dimension discussed earlier, namely, the breakdown process and its greater integration into wider political processes. We will analyze this aspect below after we have discussed the impact of changes in the regulatory function on the other two provincial roles.

The second provincial role that is affected by changes in the function of federal regulation is that of owner of federally regulated firms. As indicated earlier, in most areas of federal regulation one finds provincial Crown corporations subject to the jurisdiction of federal regulatory authorities. The significance of this relationship is derived from the purposes for which provincial public enterprises were created. Although there is no generally agreed upon explanation accounting satisfactorily for the creation of public enterprises, federal or provincial, the fact is that, regardless of the specific purpose or rationale, provinces establish them to accomplish provincially determined policy objectives and to serve functions that provincial governments deem to be important. In other words, they are considered to be important provincial policy instruments. In a regime of policing regulation, where the primary role of the regulator is to set rules to govern the behaviour of the regulated firm, provincial governments must accept, however grudgingly, the legitimacy within federal jurisdiction of federal regulation. They can do so without serious problems because they maintain their role as goal setter for their public enterprises. A move to promoting and especially planning regulation, with the characteristic growth in the role of public authorities, in this case federal public authorities, threatens to undermine the provincial goal-setting role. In this respect there is little in principle that distinguishes provincial government opposition from private sector opposition to the employment of planning regulation by the federal government. Both affected parties reject the diminution of their decision-making capacity and autonomy and the growth of an enhanced, if not dominant, role for the federal government in setting corporate objectives. Such a situation may mean, in the case of provincial governments, that their "chosen instruments" are "captured" by the federal government and required to place a priority on goals that may conflict with provincially determined mandates. Even if the goals are not in conflict, federal regulation *qua* planning may threaten or impede the capacities of provincial Crown corporations by subjecting them to two lines of control and accountability, one provincial, the other federal. In the event that provincial governments can be expected to react negatively to a situation in which, at best, they share decision making for corporate objectives and, at worst, are relegated to the status of junior partners in their own public enterprises, one can confidently predict that intergovernmental conflict will ensue.

The potential for conflict arising from the provincial role as owner of Crown corporations is even more relevant to the general provincial policy-making role. As policy makers, regardless of the specific instrument to be employed, provincial governments have always sought to establish their own priorities and to control economic and social developments within their jurisdictions. In this regard it is worth noting that contrary to Evenson and Simeon, "province building," although, perhaps, now more pronounced and universal, is not a new phenomenon but has always been strong, at least within some provinces.[54] Indeed, for Ontario, province building as a prime imperative of policy making dates, as does nation building, from Confederation.[55] With specific respect to regulation, provincial governments, in their role as policy makers, have always demonstrated special concern about federal economic regulation. In large part, such concern is understandable because, as mentioned, economic regulation is most common in the infrastructure industries such as transportation, energy, and increasingly, telecommunications. Although the influence of these industries may have been exaggerated at times, they are deemed to be important because the development of other industries and sectors is believed to be conditional on their satisfactory development and performance. In addition, provincial governments as policy makers are concerned about the impact of federal regulation of one segment of an industry or sector of the economy on other segments or sectors. Provincial regulation of the trucking industry, for example, was affected by changes in federal regulation of the railways. Similarly, recent developments in federal telecommunications regulation have had immediate spillover effects for provincial regulation in the same sector.

Regulation as planning, we have argued, gives regulatory decision makers an enhanced, perhaps the dominant, role in the allocation of resources and in directing the production and distribution of goods and services. While provincial governments may or may not be prepared to rely on market forces or on firm-led economic decision making, it is reasonable to expect that they will challenge the idea of federal-led economic decision making by means of regulatory instruments. They want to be able to control as much as possible the mobilization and direction of resources within their territories. They want to control priority setting and to develop policy making and the formulation of strategies for implementing them. Although provinces are generally not sympathetic to federally imposed designs for economic development, this is an even more pronounced concern in the infrastructure industries where, because of the complex interdependencies that exist, by virtue of the use of regulatory instruments, provinces fear that federal imposition of exogenous objectives can have major repercussions for provincial priorities and policies well beyond the immediately regulated firm or economic sector.

Aside from their predictable opposition in principle to federal-led economic decision making, there are three specific reasons for provincial concerns. The first is the now commonplace and widespread provincial criticism that federal economic policy making is unfairly discriminatory in favour of some regions and industries, at the expense of others. This argument has long been routinely invoked, not without some justification, in battles, for example, over transportation and energy policies.

Secondly, in the past three decades especially, provincial opposition to federal economic dominance has been based on doubts about the capacity of the federal government to perform effectively as an economic decision maker. Provinces are simply not prepared to accept that the federal government possesses greater competence than they as justification for it having more power or influence over economic decision making. A concomitant of the rejection of federal pre-eminence has been the growth of a provincial role in economic policy making which has seen both the development of provincial economic plans and strategies as well as a demand that if the role of any level of government is to be expanded, it must be that of the provincial vis-à-vis the federal.[56]

A note of caution should be sounded, however, to guard against a misunderstanding of the foregoing. Although we have phrased the discussion in terms of federal-provincial relations, this should not be misconstrued so as to suggest that the "battle lines" are simply, or even primarily, drawn between the two levels of government. The reality is far more complex than this — particularly when it comes to analyzing the forces and motivations leading the federal government to a planning regulatory regime. While we do not attempt, as previously stated, such an analysis here, it is important to note that federal-provincial conflicts can result from the federal government's responding to demands from some provincial governments and regional interest groups to introduce alternatives to policing regulation. Darling, for example, provides a convincing analysis of how Prairie governments insisted that federal railway regulation be transformed from being neutral into being positively discriminatory — in their favour.[57] A similar process occurred in the 1970s when Western governments argued for a reversal of the railway deregulation of 1967 and the reinstatement of what we have labelled, although they did not use the term, planning regulation. A related aspect concerns the interprovincial aspects of regulatory conflicts. The political process we have described need not be confined to the federal-provincial context. Conflicts can arise between provinces when one provincial government employs regulatory instruments as positive tools of government in such a manner as to threaten the interests and policies of other provincial governments. One of the case studies in this report provides a useful illustration of this situation.

The third major reason why provincial governments can be expected to react negatively to planning regulation relates to the specific institutions and decision-making processes that have come to be associated with it. Although we earlier stressed that there was no necessary link between our definition of regulation and a specific form of government organization, the fact is that intergovernmental conflict in the regulatory arena is exacerbated by the central role of regulatory agencies such as the Canadian Transport Commission (CTC), the Canadian Radio-television and Telecommunications Commission (CRTC) and the National Energy Board (NEB).

The distinguishing feature of these agencies is their exceptionally high degree of independence within the federal parliamentary system. One measure of their independence is the tenure of the members of the agencies, which is comparable in kind, if not in length, to that conferred on members of the judiciary. Perhaps more important is the range of adjudicative and legislative powers that are delegated to the agencies combined, particularly, with the routine absence in their statutes of unambiguous goals and precise directions for their attainment.[58] As a result of their independence, federal regulatory agencies have come to play a central role in making not only the decisions about who will be the winners and losers in the regulatory process but also, and more importantly, what will be the basic policies in individual sectors.[59] In this respect, contemporary regulatory agencies are distinguished from their predecessors which, as we indicated above, were given reasonably precise legislative direction which served to structure and confine the exercise of their discretion. In addition, their predecessors also showed a degree of self-denial that some current regulators seem unwilling or unable to match. For all of these reasons, independent regulatory agencies have come to perform basic goal-setting as well as implementation roles.

It is important to acknowledge that the independence of these agencies is clearly relative and not absolute. There is a range of direct controls such as "political appeals" and directives as well as indirect controls such as budgets and appointments that serve to contain agency independence. Notwithstanding these controls, agency independence is clearly a major concern for provincial governments, particularly in the context of planning regulation. They are confronted, on the one hand, with a significant change in the function of regulation which has profound ramifications for them in their primary roles. On the other hand, they are faced with the fact that the initial, and often ultimate, regulatory decision maker is an independent federal agency which, in form and function, was originally conceived to be insulated from larger political processes.

The fact that enhanced public control for corporate decision making is delegated to independent decision makers within the federal government is, then, a major cause for concern among provincial governments.

It is worsened by the process by which regulatory agencies make decisions. The primary decisional process can be characterized as "trial-type," adversarial, quasi-judicial hearings.[60] This form of decision making may be appropriate for policing regulation with its emphasis on rules, but questions have been raised about its usefulness in dealing with the much more open-ended nature of issues associated with planning regulation. In the latter, the purpose is not reactive, remedial and issue-specific but proactive, problem-solving, general policy-oriented decision making. There is an even more specific political aspect of agency decisional processes. In such processes, to be recognized as participants, interested parties are expected to intervene in support of one of the contending parties in a hearing. This institutional imperative to choose sides compounds the problem discussed earlier, where conflicting groups compete for governmental support. The situation is not made easier for provincial governments by the public nature of the regulatory process, which contrasts sharply with the highly confidential, secretive world of most intergovernmental diplomacy in Canada.

Thus far, we have dealt only with the impact of the changing function of regulation on provincial governments as actors in the regulatory process. Changing the function in the direction of planning broadens significantly the impact on provincial governments and thus, the importance of their participating in that process. This provides the basis for expanded intergovernmental conflict over regulatory issues. Changes in the regulatory function also have an impact on the other central dimension, i.e., the pattern of relationships between regulatory issues and processes and other political issues and processes. Earlier, we argued that broadening the interests involved, in terms of numbers or political salience, could be expected to complicate the process of conflict resolution. In particular, we suggested that, whereas policing regulation was relatively insulated, one of the consequences of a move toward planning was the greater integration of regulation into the wider political process. Such integration, it was our contention, would reflect greater conflict over regulatory issues. The remainder of this section develops this point as it relates to provincial governments and intergovernmental relations.

There are two aspects to the greater integration of the regulatory process relevant to intergovernmental conflict. One, which is fairly narrow, relates to the nature of regulatory decision making; the other, and much broader aspect, is the integration of the regulatory agency into the wider political process. Insofar as the former is concerned with the increase in stakes as a result of planning regulation, affected parties have an incentive not to regard the regulatory agency as the ultimate or even primary decision maker but to treat it simply as the first in a series. In the case of provinces as participants, this incentive applies not only in their roles as owners and policy makers, but also as representatives. In this last capacity, given that they may have been compelled to alienate some supporters in their selection of groups to represent, provincial governments have an added incentive. Having made some potential enemies, they need to show that it was worth it by obtaining satisfaction for their "friends." Consequently, they cannot afford to treat the regulatory agency as the final word; they need, and will want, to pursue any and every avenue possible.

A related consequence of this development, particularly (but not only) if alternative routes such as political appeals are successful, is that this can undermine the claim to a special or unique form of institutional competence by regulatory agencies vis-à-vis other political institutions. By so doing, it can threaten the legitimacy of the agency as a decision maker.[61] Of course, it should be acknowledged that this is, perhaps, unavoidable when the role of the agency is transformed from that of a specialized, impartial grievance settler to one involving "an essentially legislative process of adjusting the competing claims" of interests, public or private, affected by agency decision making.[62]

The second intergovernmental aspect of the insulation-integration dimension related to changes in the regulatory function pertains to the more macro-level of the agency itself. One result may be the integration, not simply of decisions, but also of intergovernmental and regulatory issues and processes. In the first place, given the assumption that regulatory decision making is not as peripheral to provincial concerns as it once was, there is an incentive on the part of provincial governments to seek to influence the choice of decision makers. This may lead to a variety of demands, including a provincial role in their selection. It may also result in demands that decision-making responsibilities be shifted to other authorities within the federal government or to provincial authorities via delegation. Alternatively, it may result in demands for shared decision making either at the regulatory level by means of joint boards or at "higher" political levels such as intergovernmental conferences. A by-product of this type of demand is that it may lead to the "twin-tracking" of decision making which occurs when both the regulatory agency and the relevant federal department undertake to deal simultaneously with basically the same issue.

Of course, conflict requires two sides. The unstated, but surely obvious, premise for the preceding discussion is that the federal government will not, in the face of provincial demands, simply yield. If provincial governments respond because of the impact of federal regulation on them in their roles as representatives, owners and policy makers, it must be understood that this is, perhaps, an unavoidable consequence of the federal government's choosing to employ a specific policy instrument to satisfy the demands and imperatives of its own roles as representative, owner and policy maker. The result is intergovernmental conflict in its myriad forms as participants seek to insinuate or impose their viewpoints and choices on one another. In some respects, the intergovernmental conflict, inasmuch as it represents a clash of interests, is no different from public-private conflict over the nature and extent of public control over corporate decision making. In some very real respects, however, the two types of conflict are fundamentally different. The most important difference, perhaps, lies in the capacities of the conflicting parties to undermine, partially if not completely, the attainment of one another's goals. This is the central reality of policy making and implementation in the federal system in Canada today. It is not the fact of intergovernmental conflict which has formed a trilogy with death and taxes as unavoidables. It is the fact that satisfaction and attainment of one government's goals are heavily dependent on other governments, particularly, but not solely, across levels. This is the consequence of the emergence of a federal system whose dominant feature is that of separate levels of government sharing powers. Autonomy and independence at each level have given way to interdependence between levels and among governments. One objective of this study is to illuminate how and why these interdependencies have developed in one policy sector, economic regulation. Another objective is to suggest alternative responses to those consequences of interdependence which are negative and, as a result, threaten, in one sector, Canada's capacity to attain its policy goals.

Economic Regulation and Intergovernmental Conflict: Three Cases

The remainder of this study will test our hypothesis. In many respects, test is too strong a term. We have already acknowledged that changes in the regulatory function are not the sole cause for changes in the politics of regulation generally or in intergovernmental politics specifically. Given, therefore, the difficulty in weighing our causal variable compared to others, it is more accurate to describe the rest of this study as exploring or illuminating our hypothesis in order to provide a basis for an analysis of the policy implications and a discussion of some of the major policy options.

The exploration of our hypothesis takes the form of three case studies. The first is on airline regulation from 1938 to 1984. This is a case study of the evolution of regulation from promoting to planning and the emergence and development of intergovernmental conflict associated with that evolution. This case illustrates how provinces were willing to accept the promotional regulatory role but were opposed to federal efforts, beginning in the 1960s, to plan the airline system. Provincial opposition took many forms, the most important of which was, perhaps, the emergence of provincial airlines as chosen instruments in competition with Air Canada. Although intergovernmental conflict was just one aspect of the larger debate that has developed over airline regulation in the last few years, the conclusion of this case study is that such conflicts over both the aims of government regulatory policy and the roles of the individual government airlines played a major role in the decision to move away from a planning regulatory regime toward a more relaxed, significantly (but not completely) de-regulatory policy.

Telecommunications regulation is the focus of our second case study. Prior to the 1970s, policing was the primary role of regulation at both the federal and provincial levels. As a result of technological changes in both telecommunications and the computer industry, the basic premise of telecommunications regulation came under challenge. In contrast with similar developments in the United States, where the basic policy response was a move toward de-regulation, the Canadian response, at least at the federal level, was to call for a significantly enhanced regulatory role with regulation playing a planning function. Provinces which own or regulate telephone companies within their own jurisdictions found themselves confronting competitive pressures, on the one hand, and the federal proposal on the other, both of which challenged their regulatory regimes. Both would transfer decision-making power away from provincial governments. The result was an extended and acrimonious federal-provincial battle that took place in many arenas. One of the most important was the regulatory because of the actions and decisions of the independent federal regulatory agency. To date, there has been no resolution of this conflict which has inhibited the development of national telecommunications policies.

Whereas the first two case studies concentrate on intergovernmental conflicts which are primarily federal-provincial, our third study examines interprovincial conflicts that arise when provinces attempt to employ regulation as a positive, planning instrument of government. This case study involves the regulation of the securities industry by the Ontario and Quebec governments. In both provinces, securities regulation has evolved beyond narrow policing functions to become a major tool of economic management. In Quebec especially, economic development objectives have been undertaken with the purpose of restructuring capital markets and financial services industries under provincial jurisdiction. These economic and political objectives, combined with the pressures of technological change, have resulted in a jockeying for advantage in the environments in Ontario and Quebec. Although major complications have been avoided to date, the complex interaction of economic and technological pressures driven by policy-oriented provincial regulatory environments suggests the potential for a highly fractious interprovincial regulatory environment.

Securities regulation cannot be isolated from the larger national financial system, i.e., the complex of institutions, financial intermediaries, markets and regulators that constitute the national context transforming savings into investment. Consequently, in this case study, we attempt also to assess the larger national financial system and give some measure of Canada's ability to meet changing competitive industrial pressures in the world. Our concern is that, institutionally, the national financial system is ill-organized to bring Canada into the 1990s.

The three cases in this study were chosen, in part, because they represent three major types of jurisdictional relationships in Canada. The first case represents conflict in an area where it is recognized that the federal government had unchallengeable jurisdiction. The second case, on the other hand, involves an activity where, until recently, there was an acceptance of exclusive authority for both levels of government over undertakings within their jurisdiction. The third case provides an analysis of intergovernmental conflict that is not federal-provincial but rather, interprovincial, in an area where provincial jurisdiction has not been challenged. Although the jurisdictional variants involving other subject areas such as energy could provide useful additional case studies, we believe that the three studies undertaken provide a sufficient basis for exploring and illustrating our central hypothesis.

Chapter 2

Airline Regulation

Since its introduction in 1938, economic regulation of the Canadian airline industry has undergone several dramatic changes. At the outset, the primary function of regulation was to promote the interests of the nationally designated chosen instrument for air policy, the federally owned Crown corporation. This goal was pre-eminent for approximately three decades, at which point the federal government opted to introduce controlled competition on both mainline and feeder routes within Canada. In order to continue to protect the interests of its airline, the federal government moved from a promoting to a planning regulatory regime. In the same period, however, as the federal government sought to revise its airline policy, provincial governments began to identify airlines as a potential instrument for the attainment of provincial policy objectives. The result was a series of intergovernmental conflicts as provincial governments rejected the federal government's planning approach which sought to subjugate regional airlines to serving the interests of national carriers. Although the federal government attempted to reassert its superior interest and role, the outcome, after a decade of conflict, was a decision by the federal government to abandon not only its planning, but also its promoting regulatory role and to introduce a significant degree of airline de-regulation. This chapter will analyze these developments in order to demonstrate the interrelationships between regulatory regimes and intergovernmental conflict in the airline industry.

The High Point of Promotional Regulation: 1937–58

Economic regulation of the Canadian airline industry began in 1937–38. Prior to this time, although there was a national licensing system created for that purpose in 1919 under the Air Board and, subsequently, under the minister of national defence, the objective was not to limit competitive entry or to control pricing.[1] Airline regulatory policy changed significantly, however, after the 1937 creation of a federal Crown corporation, Trans-Canada Airlines (TCA), as a chosen instrument for the attainment of national air policy. The conventional viewpoint on this decision is that expressed by David Corbett: "Canada seems to have established a publicly-owned monopoly of scheduled inter-urban air services in a fit of absence of mind, as Britain is said to have acquired her Empire."[2] While this statement may be correct with respect to the public ownership of the airline, the evidence suggests that the decision to grant the airline a substantial monopoly was an act of very deliberate and conscious public policy.

In view of subsequent developments at the provincial level, it is worth noting the stated rationale for the creation of Trans-Canada Airlines advanced by the responsible minister, C.D. Howe:

> Canada is perhaps one of the few countries in the world without a scheduled air service. The air services from our centres of population to areas not otherwise served by transportation take second place to none, but we are woefully behind other countries in air services between centres of population. . . . Many Canadian citizens when travelling from one point to another in Canada find they have to use the airlines in the United States, and they have been very insistent in demanding the establishment of a direct Canadian service. Airmail stamps are sold in Canada and much of our mail is routed across the border, transported by the air services of the United States, and then brought back across the border at the point nearest to destination. The volume of this airmail is sufficient to warrant the establishment of a direct service in Canada. I believe such a service would prove of immense value for national purposes. Canada is a country of vast distances and sparse population, and the time needed to travel between the west and east is considerable under present circumstances. If that time could be cut in three or four by a new air service, the people living at the extremes of this country would be able to travel more frequently to the centres of government, business, and industry, and the interrelation of the country would thereby be facilitated.[3]

In short, the syndrome of "defensive expansionism" with its emphasis on both endogenous objectives such as an efficient air alternative to U.S. service and exogenous objectives such as national pride and integration and economic development, provided the rationale for the creation of a national airline.[4]

There is no need for us to comment on the decision to create a public as opposed to a private or mixed enterprise. Our concerns are with the purposes of the airline and the regulatory instruments for their attainment. The mandate of TCA was set out in its creating legislation in 1937:

> . . . to establish, operate and maintain airlines or regular services of aircraft of all kinds, to carry on the business of transporting mails, passengers and goods by air, and to enter into contracts for the transport of mails, passengers and goods by any means, and either by the Corporation's own aircraft and conveyances or by means of the aircraft and conveyances of others, and to enter into contracts with any person or company for the interchange of traffic . . . and to carry on its business throughout Canada and outside of Canada.[5]

What was not set out in legislation was that TCA would be granted a monopoly on the routes it was to serve. It was during the parliamentary debates that this became clear, when Howe explained that:

> This company will fly only the main artery of traffic across the country, and such other arteries of traffic as are designated by the government as being of national importance. It is not the intention to interfere with any existing operations. The company will not undertake other than inter-urban services. It will be given an exclusive contract to carry mails, passengers and express over the specified routes. . . .[6]

Included in the routes to be specified were not only inter-urban, particularly transcontinental, but also international routes.

The method by which the government proposed to grant exclusive contracts to TCA was the use of a regulatory agency which would engage in structural regulation so as to control competitive entry into the industry. There were three central aspects to the government's approach to the economic regulation of airlines. The first was giving responsibility for licensing entrants into the industry to the Board of Transport Commissioners, created in 1938. This agency was responsible under the *Aeronautics Act* to grant licences only if the "public convenience and necessity" for the licence had been established.[7] The second control was the general mandate given to the regulatory agency that it develop "the complementary rather than competitive functions of transport."[8] The most important control mechanism was the third, TCA's exemption from the "public convenience and necessity" requirements established for other airlines. According to the *Aeronautics Act*, the regulatory agency was required to ". . . upon application, grant to Trans-Canada Airlines a licence to operate a commercial air service under such terms and subject to such conditions as will enable Trans-Canada Airlines to perform any agreement made . . . between the Minister of Transport and Trans-Canada Airlines. . . ."[9] By means of these three controls, the status of the federal airline as a chosen instrument was assumed to be secure.

An incident six years after the creation of TCA demonstrated the extent of the federal government's commitment to regulation as an instrument for promoting the public airline. At issue in 1943 was an application to the Board of Transport Commissioners from TCA to complete its transcontinental route to link Victoria with Vancouver. This route was already serviced by Canadian Pacific Air Lines (CPA), a subsidiary of Canadian Pacific Railway, established in 1942. Despite the nature of the TCA–minister of transport agreement, the regulatory agency (acting on the principle that established licence-holders were entitled to keep their existing licences) ruled that TCA should be allowed to fly to Victoria, but to carry airmail and transcontinental passengers only. It was denied the right to pick up Victoria-bound passengers in Vancouver.

The government's response in defence of promoting the interests of TCA was immediate. Notwithstanding the fact that he did not have the legal authority to do so, Howe ordered the Board of Transport Commissioners not to consider any further applications for route licences.[10] This was followed by a prime ministerial statement reiterating the promotional function of airline regulation. In the House of Commons, Prime Minister King declared:

> Within Canada, Trans-Canada Air Lines will continue to operate all transcontinental systems, and such other services of a mainline character as may from time to time be designated by the government. Competition between air services over the same route will not be permitted between a publicly-owned service and a privately-owned service or between two privately-owned services.[11]

Subsequently, King reminded Parliament of the government's policy on international services:

> . . . Trans-Canada Airlines will continue to be the instrument of the government in maintaining all transcontinental air transport services and in operating services across international boundary lines and outside of Canada. . . . The government sees no good reason for changing its policy that Trans-Canada Air Lines is the sole Canadian agency which may operate international air services.[12]

To reinforce the government's policy, the Board of Transport Commissioners was stripped of its responsibilities for regulating the airline industry. A new regulator was created, the Air Transport Board, whose distinguishing characteristic was that, on licensing matters, it had only an advisory role. All licences to operate commercial air services were "subject to the approval of the Minister."[13] Finally, these actions were supplemented by a "divestment order" that required surface transport companies, i.e., CPR, to sell its airline interests within one year of the end of the war. This order was comparable to the restrictions proposed more recently in S-31, although this time, the objects of the order were to be provincial governments and, ironically, the demand for the order came in part from Canadian Pacific.[14] Speaking for the government, Howe defended the order on the following grounds:

> It is becoming obvious that ownership of airways by our two competing railway systems implies extension of railway competition into transport by air, regardless of the Government's desire to avoid competition between air services.[15]

After the end of the Second World War, the federal government postponed and then dropped its divestment order completely. In addition, in a series of decisions in the years from 1948 to 1957, the government authorized CPA to fly a number of international routes in the Pacific, South America and finally Europe, although it is important to note, not routes flown by TCA.[16] Notwithstanding these actions, at no time in the period from 1937 to 1957 did the federal government veer from its employment of regulation as an instrument to promote the interests of the public airline. It is important to emphasize that, while the government went to great lengths to serve this end, it did not see its role as one of planning the airline industry. Provided that other industry actors did not threaten TCA's position, the government left them alone, although subject to regulatory controls on entry. It was only after direct, albeit limited, competition with TCA was permitted that the federal government sought to employ regulation as a planning instrument. It is to this phase that we now turn.

The Emergence of Regulatory Planning: 1958–69

The period 1958–69 was characterized by a significant change in the function of regulation. Prior to 1958, airline regulation was essentially promotional; after that year, although not immediately, the federal government sought to employ economic regulation as a planning instrument. The objective was to use entry controls and licensing in order to assign responsibilities and specific roles for different categories of air services. Such planning was deemed necessary in order to protect the public airline in its continuing role as the chosen instrument of public policy. The specific concern was that, left to its own resources in the face of competition, the public airline would not be in a position to service the route network that had developed as a result of "routes being designated as being of national importance." Many of these routes, established more for political than for economic reasons, were not cost remunerative and could be offered only if cross-subsidies were made available from profits earned on other routes.[17] Although it was not appreciated at the time, planning regulation was (ironically) made necessary by the decision to allow the introduction of competition and market forces, albeit to a very limited degree.

The starting point in the decline of promotional regulation came in 1958, following the election of a Progressive Conservative government.

The new minister of transport announced his belief that "the time has come for the introduction of some measure of competition on our transcontinental routes."[18] Following the report of an independent consultant (who outlined very limited options for competition) and hearings by the Air Transport Board on applications for the right to serve transcontinental routes, the minister authorized CPA one daily flight each way between Vancouver and Montreal, provided that there were stops at Winnipeg and Toronto.

This initial breach in TCA's monopoly was significant. Ultimately, however, the more important breakthrough (from our perspective, in terms of its impact on the function of regulation) was the second pro-competitive decision of the government. This decision involved the regional airlines which, like CPA had not been allowed to compete with TCA on any of the inter-urban routes which were part of the latter's transcontinental network. Almost coincidental with CPA's application to compete with TCA, were those of two regionals to service the Montreal-Toronto route. Such applications were directly contrary to the government policy statement of 1943, cited earlier, which had guided airline regulation from that date. In 1961, the minister of transport announced the termination of that policy by accepting the recommendation of the Air Transport Board that one application be approved. This was immediately followed by a second decision that ended TCA's monopoly on a Quebec route.[19] Perhaps the most significant sign of change was the simultaneous announcement by the minister of transport that, henceforth, TCA licence applications would go before the regulatory agency just like those of other airlines.[20] This announcement, if implemented, would have ended the "special status" of TCA conferred in 1938 by making it subject to the "public convenience and necessity" test.

The new policy was short-lived, however. In 1963, a Liberal government was returned to office, determined to protect the public airline by reinstating TCA's regulatory "special status" and ending the pro-competition decisions. The former was easily accomplished as the government decided to reinstate the conditions of the *Aeronautics Act* and the Trans-Canada Airlines Contract. The latter was more difficult. The government had several choices. One was to reverse the decisions permitting CPA and the regionals to compete with TCA on inter-urban routes. Alternatively, it could have frozen competition at the level permitted as of 1963, i.e., on a few routes and to a very restricted degree. For reasons that are not known, and in any event need not concern us, the government rejected both these alternatives and opted to transform pro-TCA promoting regulation into a much more ambitious planning regulatory regime.

Airline regulation as planning involved a coherent, comprehensive attempt to structure the relationships between TCA and CPA as Canada's transcontinental air services as well as between these two companies and the five regional airlines: Pacific Western Air Lines, Transair Limited, Nordair, Quebecair and Eastern Provincial Airways.[21] To return to the framework introduced in Chapter 1, airline regulation as planning significantly refined structural regulation and also extended behavioural regulation to include aspects that hitherto had not been subject to regulation.

Furthermore, the regulatory agency was expected to play a much more proactive, policy-development role than it had previously.

With respect to the relationships between Air Canada, as TCA was renamed in 1965, and CPA, while rejecting the concept of equal treatment, the government opted to treat them as a unit. This was particularly true on the international level, for which the minister of transport established the following principle:

> In the international field, air services provided by Canadian air lines should serve the Canadian interest as a whole; these services should not be competitive or conflicting, but should represent a single integrated plan, which could be achieved by amalgamation, by partnership, or by a clear division of operations.[22]

Subsequently, to develop the "single integrated plan," the minister asked the two airlines to work out an accommodation on their own. Although we do not know how active a role the government played in this process, in little more than a year, the minister announced the outcome. The airlines agreed "that the most effective way to carry out this policy would be a clear division of their fields of operations so that outside Canada neither airline would serve any point served by the other."[23] In addition, they agreed to cooperate with one another on sales activities so that each would "represent the other to the best of its ability." Regardless of the government's role in working out the division of the world and the mutual assistance pact, it was pleased enough with the results to announce that henceforth, both would be regarded as the government's "chosen instruments in the areas of international operations allocated to each."

On the national level, agreement was more difficult to obtain. In his 1964 statement, the minister of transport had advanced the following principle:

> In the domestic main line field, while the principle of competition is not rejected, any development of competition should not compromise or seriously injure the economic viability of TCA's mainline domestic operations which represent the essential framework of its network of domestic services. In other words, there must not be the kind of competition which would put TCA into the red; and, in the event that competition continues, the air transport board should ensure an opportunity for growth to both lines above the basic minimum.[24]

In 1965, reflecting the difficulty in implementing this principle, the minister appointed an independent consultant to make recommendations. After receipt of his report, the government announced that it had "reached the conclusion that it is in the public interest to permit an increased role for CPA on the transcontinental route; but that at the same time, this role must be clearly defined in a manner which protects the future economic position of Air Canada. . . ." In particular, the government's policy statement emphasized the non-profitable routes Air Canada was required to serve as well as its impending capital requirements. These factors made it "necessary to ensure Air Canada a large portion of the transcontinental market . . . so that it can continue to maintain the less profitable domestic routes where necessary in the public interest; and to develop the funds necessary for the substantial expansion which faces it, both domestically and internationally."[25] Consequently, the government announced that CPA would be allowed to double its transcontinental capacity in 1967 and to increase its services until it provided 25 percent of the total transcontinental capacity by the year 1970. In addition, CPA would be allowed to service Edmonton and Calgary; although not on a non-stop basis linking them to Toronto or Montreal. In other words, the government opted for a system of regulated market segmentation in order to protect the public airline from the private airline on transcontinental routes. To ensure that the objectives of this policy would be met, such a scheme now required the government to protect not just one but two airlines against other competitors. This was the purpose of regional air policy.

The interdependent nature of national and regional air policies was well appreciated not just by the federal government; the implications were forcefully drawn to the attention of Air Canada and CPA as well. From the outset of the policy review process, the minister of transport recognized that, if his policy on mainline competition was to have any chance of success, "a reasonable role for regional carriers" had to be developed.[26] That he did not want to take full responsibility for this was made clear to the two major airlines when, in his 1965 announcement on international allocations, the minister stressed that he expected them "to assist in working out" regional policy.[27] The final policy demonstrated how far down the planning road the government, and the industry, had travelled as a result of the 1964 initiatives.

In his 1966 statement, the minister announced that the government had opted for very limited competition between the now-designated "two mainline carriers" and the regionals. Each would be assigned a specific role in air policy and the role for the regionals was "to supplement the domestic mainline operations of Air Canada and CPA . . . . They will not be directly competitive on any substantial scale . . . ."[28] To reinforce the point of role allocation, the minister emphasized that "regional carriers will be expected to operate on a regional basis and will not be authorized to expand as potential transcontinental carriers." This would not preclude regional-mainline carrier competition on specific segments. Although announced three years later, the route allocation was further refined by a subsequent minister of transport, Don Jamieson, who defined specific regions within which each of the five regionals would operate. They were:

1. *For Pacific Western Airlines*:
   British Columbia and Western Alberta.
2. *For Transair Limited*:
   The Prairie Provinces and Northwestern Ontario.
3. *For Nordair*:
   The remainder of Ontario and Northwestern Quebec.
4. *For Quebecair*:
   All of the Province of Quebec east of Montreal.
5. *For Eastern Provincial Airways*:
   The Atlantic Provinces.[29]

While an important indicator, route allocation is not sufficient in itself to justify the claim that regulation was now to be employed as a planning instrument. What should be persuasive, however, are the changes introduced for the role of the regulatory agency. In contrast to the traditional reactive role of the agency which we have suggested to be typical of policing regulation, the Air Transport Board in the new policy was assigned a proactive, initiating role with a significant overt policy-making component. The two mainline carriers were instructed, for example, to identify routes which might appropriately be transferred to regional carriers. The minister stressed that the regulator would have an active initiating role to play in this process, since it was "expected to bring forward cases where it believes review with a view to possible transfer should be initiated."[30] In addition, in order to encourage cooperation between the two types of carriers on joint fares and commission relationships, the board was authorized to "supervise progress and, if necessary, intervene to ensure that adequate progress is made."[31]

A third area of change involved the board's role in a new subsidy system. Not only would the agency be responsible for distributing subsidies, but it was also to play the central role in developing criteria for their allocation. In this regard it is worth noting, because they support our contention about the relationships between planning regulation and exogenous objectives, three of the five conditions that had to be met to justify subsidy payments. The broad, open-ended conditions, which in themselves exemplify the discretionary scope we have argued is typical of planning regulation, were:

- where a service is needed to a remote area which requires the maintenance of regular air service for its existence; and where other means of transport are inadequate or non-existent;

- where a developmental activity is involved and air service is essential to the support of that activity; and
- where a regular route operation appears to have a good chance of success but requires support during the initial period of growth.[32]

By far the most important indicator of the employment of regulation as a planning instrument (and of the concomitant changes in the role of the regulatory agency) was the responsibility assigned with respect to aircraft purchases by the airlines. Henceforth, these would be screened as part of the licensing procedure. The minister noted that "financial institutions which have been approached directly by carriers have not known where to obtain reliable information regarding carrier prospects; and that individual carriers have, upon occasion, acquired aircraft without due regard to the suitability of the facilities on proposed routes."[33] To protect both financial institutions and carriers, the minister announced that henceforth:

> The Air Transport Board and the Department of Transport will develop a scheme requiring all carriers operating on regular routes to report proposals for multi-engine aircraft acquisition before firm orders are placed. . . .
>
> The Air Transport Board will develop its capability for advising on financial aspects of re-equipment plans.[34]

Finally, the minister noted that, as part of its licensing process, the regulator would be authorized to exercise firmer control than it previously had over the financial structure of the regional airlines.

In short, it is our contention that the civil aviation policy enunciated over the period 1964 to 1969 transformed the traditional promotional role of economic regulation into a planning role. Relationships between the industry participants were to be rigidly defined, and structural regulation was to be employed to enforce those relationships. The scope of industry conduct to be regulated was significantly expanded to include some of the most basic functions of corporate management, such as financial structures and aircraft acquisition. Hitherto, decisions on these matters had been the prerogative of corporate decision makers; henceforth, regulatory authorities would play an enhanced role. In the process, the decision-making role of the regulatory agency was to be radically altered. The new air policy established the federal government, via the regulatory process, as the pre-eminent decision maker in the civil aviation field. The new policy was, we contend, a quintessential statement of state-led economic decision making in a sector. It was, in our terms, a clear statement of the government's intention to employ economic regulation as a planning instrument.

Planning and Its Challengers: 1970–84

It is not clear if, even under the most favourable of circumstances, the new aviation policy could have been successfully implemented. The fact is that circumstances were clearly not favourable: within ten years the policy was in shreds. Within fifteen years, after two abortive efforts to reinstate some semblance of the policy, the government abandoned the field and opted for a significant degree of de-regulation of airlines, although it chose to use the more neutral term, "liberalization." Whatever the label, it was the antithesis of regulation as planning. A number of factors account for the failure of the government's planning effort. It is our contention that one of the primary, if not the single most important, causes of that failure was the emergence of provincial governments as influential participants in the airline sector.

Prior to 1970, provincial governments were insignificant actors in the air transportation field. At one time, Saskatchewan operated a government-owned airline serving the northern part of the province but, aside from this minor role, provinces were largely irrelevant. There is no evidence, for example, that in developing the new air policy in the 1960s, the federal government solicited or even considered the views of provincial governments. All this changed after the announcement of the new policy. Provincial governments, emulating the example of the federal government, sought to employ air services as chosen instruments for the attainment of provincially established goals. This led them into contractual arrangements with airlines and, more importantly, acquisitions of regional airlines. The result was a series of intergovernmental battles and skirmishes fought out in federal-provincial conferences, regulatory hearings and in judicial proceedings. Provinces not only refused to be treated as irrelevant, they demanded, as well, a status in setting policy approaching that of the federal government. In its attempt to control the aviation sector in order to satisfy its policy objectives, the federal government found itself confronting provincial governments far more formidable in their opposition than private sector airline managements. The federal government had sought to impose its control, its definition of goals and objectives, on the airline sector. Intergovernmental conflicts, and their consequences, forced the federal government to acknowledge that it had lost control, at least insofar as the employment of regulation as a planning instrument was concerned.

The first important sign of the emerging role of the provinces came in the early 1970s with the Ontario government's decision to create an air service, "norOntair." This was not an airline but a contractual arrangement with a number of third-level air carriers whereby Ontario would underwrite the provision of air service "using modern and appropriate equipment to provide a high frequency of regularly scheduled flights designed for the convenience of the travelling public and continuity of service at minimum interlining."[35] The province conceived of this type of service as a method of promoting regional economic and social development. This is clear from material filed with the federal government which uses arguments remarkably similar to those involved to justify the creation of Trans-Canada Airlines:

> The norOntair service was initiated by the Government of Ontario as a component of the regional development mandate of the Provincial Government. It was considered that in northern areas the future air transportation systems are especially important to the development plans. Because of great distances and low population densities it was considered that air transport will have a great impact on the economic and social opportunities of the northern part of Ontario.[36]

In its first few years of service, Ontario had encountered no difficulties with the Canadian Transport Commission (CTC), or its Air Transport Committee (ATC), which had become the regulatory agency in 1967. The first problem occurred in 1973 when norOntair applied to add North Bay–Sudbury and Sudbury-Timmins to its routes. With respect to the former, the ATC rejected the application and concurrently authorized a private carrier to provide the service. In the committee's opinion, "the volume of local and connecting traffic between the [two] points . . . is not sufficient to justify unit toll service by two air carriers. . . ."[37] The regulator decided to defer a decision on the second route pending action by another private carrier.[38]

Ontario immediately appealed the decisions to the minister of transport, partly on the grounds that the ATC had "proceeded upon wrong principles and contrary to the evidence and disregarded established Federal Government policy."[39] The provinces, in response to a request from the minister of transport, had undertaken consultations with Air Canada on the applications and had reached an agreement "with respect to proposed patterns of service which are designed to complement the mainline network of services. . . ."[40] Consequently, it was quite confident that the applications would be routinely approved.[41] Moreover, the routes were of some significance to norOntair and particularly to the province, which provided the funding, inasmuch as these routes, within the complex of routes which norOntair served, were the ones which would most likely be profitable. Thus, they would be comparable to those routes most desired by Air Canada, i.e., routes which provided the basis for cross-subsidies to the non-remunerative, but socially and politically necessary routes. Such subsidies would reduce the demands made on the government of Ontario.

Ontario's appeal was successful. Within three months of the original decision, the minister ordered the CTC "without further delay and without further applications" to grant the licences. Despite the apparently minor issues at stake and the successful appeal, the norOntair episode was far from trivial. It served to raise substantial doubts in the minds of provincial authorities generally, if not about the new air policy, then about how they would be treated by the new transportation regulator in their efforts to promote provincial objectives and interests. It is important to note that with the passage of the *National Transportation Act* of 1967, the regulatory agency regained the decision-making power over airlines that had been lost in 1944. Henceforth, the regulatory agency was not simply an advisor to the minister of transport; it was given a degree of independent decision-making authority notwithstanding the provision for appeals to the minister or to cabinet. While the power of appeal was a significant constraint, observers noted the fact that there was no guarantee that any decision on appeal would be treated by the agency as a precedent. Consequently, provincial governments feared that the ATC might prove to be unsympathetic to their viewpoint and a significant hurdle for them. It must be recalled that the norOntair decision came at a time of widespread provincial opposition to federal transportation policies and especially to what was perceived as an agency far too independent and antagonistic to suit the provinces.[42]

These concerns came to the forefront in the second, but far more important, incident involving a provincial role in airline regulation, Alberta's purchase of Pacific Western Airlines (PWA).[43] In August 1974, the government of Alberta surprised the airline industry, the CTC, the federal government and, indeed, its own electorate with the announcement that it had purchased PWA. The purchase reflected the increasing importance that all provincial governments were attaching to air services, particularly to their role in pursuing broader developmental goals. PWA had been subject to one takeover bid earlier in 1974 to which Alberta had been opposed. According to Tupper, the government of Peter Lougheed was agitated about the possibility that control of PWA might "fall into the hands of interests who were indifferent or even hostile to Alberta's economic aspirations." This was viewed as a particularly serious problem because "an Alberta-owned PWA was essential to the maintenance of the province's hegemony in northern development matters."[44] All these arguments are remarkably similar to those employed by the King government to justify the creation of TCA.

The PWA purchase soon became a major intergovernmental (federal-provincial and interprovincial) conflict. For the federal government, the concern was that the purchase might undermine its capacity to satisfy national, interprovincial and interregional transportation needs as well as to ensure a regional balance in the adequacy of transportation services. Fundamentally, the federal government saw the purchase as a direct challenge to federal jurisdiction and control over transportation in Canada. It was feared that effective federal control would be lost, especially if the PWA purchase became a precedent for others, thereby, in the words of Senator Ray Perrault, "fragmenting airline services in Canada."[45] The federal government was concerned about provincial goals taking precedence over federal goals, particularly those just recently enunciated in the aviation policy statements. A particular aspect of this related to the capital needs and the availability of funds. The CTC, in 1976, completed a study which suggested that capital markets could be expected to be tight and competition for long-term debt and equity capital especially severe. This touched directly on one of the cornerstones of federal aviation policy, i.e., regulatory control over aircraft purchasing.[46] Although it is not clear how strongly felt this belief was, some federal authorities feared that provincial ownership of carriers under federal jurisdiction might undermine the federal regulatory system. It was argued that provincial governments might question the notion of subordination to federal regulatory agencies or demand "special status" within the regulatory system comparable to that held by Air Canada. More generally, federal authorities feared that provincial ownership of an airline might result in air policy, which hitherto had been immune, joining other transportation modes as a heated subject of intergovernmental conflict.

That there might be some validity to these federal concerns was suggested by the manner in which Alberta took control of PWA. Shortly after the purchase was announced publicly, the CTC informed the Alberta government that it had failed to comply with the *Air Carrier Regulations* and the *National Transportation Act* by not notifying the CTC of its intended purchase. These regulations give the CTC authority to prohibit such a purchase if it is deemed to be "prejudicial to the public interest." It is not clear whether Alberta had the recent norOntair incident in mind, but it claimed that these regulations were not binding on the province and therefore, it did not need approval. It is worth noting that, notwithstanding this argument, Alberta stressed that it accepted the federal government's jurisdiction and regulatory authority over air transportation. The issue was submitted to the judicial system. The Federal Court of Appeal ruled in favour of the CTC; however, the Supreme Court of Canada reversed this decision and ruled that Alberta, in fact, was not bound by the CTC regulations. Subsequent to the Supreme Court's decision, the government introduced amendments in the *Aeronautics Act* not only to close this loophole, but also to make any provincial government acquisition of an airline subject to prior cabinet approval.[47] It was notable, however, that with respect to federal concerns about the general applicability of federal regulatory authority, the chief justice cautioned the federal government about the threat posed by provincial ownership. Speaking for the majority, Chief Justice Laskin noted that "a comprehensive regime is already in place," and therefore, there was no need for special legislation.[48]

As noted earlier, the PWA purchase raised specific interprovincial political issues. One of the parties wanting the CTC to prohibit the purchase was the government of British Columbia. Its concern was heightened when PWA announced in 1976 that it was moving its headquarters from Vancouver to Calgary and some of its maintenance operations to Edmonton — a decision which Premier Bennett labelled "political and economic piracy."[49] Consequently, British Columbia applied to the CTC for an order prohibiting the moves. Alberta responded by claiming that the CTC had no jurisdiction over the matter. Although the ATC rejected Alberta's position, it also rejected British Columbia's application on the grounds that the province had ". . . not demonstrated that irreparable harm will be caused by the move."[50] British Columbia decided to appeal the decision to the commission but before the CTC could act, the federal cabinet, on its own "initiative," issued a restraining order that was to be operative until the Supreme Court had issued its decision. Alberta declared such an action to be a serious setback for its economic planning that "could have wide-ranging ramifications for any province wanting to invest in business."[51]

The specific issues involved in the PWA purchase were resolved when, as noted, the Supreme Court ruled that Alberta did not require CTC approval for the purchase. The federal cabinet allowed the headquarters move, and Parliament enacted legislation prohibiting any similar acquisitions in the future without cabinet approval. Cabinet had earlier rejected a proposal from the minister of transport that such acquisitions be prohibited by statute. The long-term consequences, however, were not resolved pertaining to potential intergovernmental conflicts over air policy and regulation, especially the concern in some federal circles that the federal government's influence and authority to control the development of the air system had been significantly lessened. If anything, the issues became even more complicated, and federal fears increased when PWA applied to the CTC to purchase Transair, the airline assigned the Prairie Provinces and northwestern Ontario under the regional air policy.

Transair developed serious financial problems and, according to Tupper, was on the brink of bankruptcy in late 1976.[52] The airline's requests for assistance were rejected by Air Canada, CPA and the Manitoba government. PWA then proposed to acquire 70 percent of Transair but not to merge the two airlines. PWA's offer, however, was conditional on its being granted access to routes in Saskatchewan which it did not serve and which Transair had been denied in 1975.[53] Such access was dependent upon Air Canada, which had opposed Transair's earlier bid. When PWA and Transair agreed to terminate the latter's routes east of Winnipeg, Air Canada withdrew any objections it may have had to the acquisition and to the plan to merge PWA's routes with Transair's.

Despite the very acrimonious battles between Ottawa and Alberta over PWA, which had ended only a few months before the PWA-Transair application, and despite the fact that the acquisition would restrict competition and was in direct conflict with the federal regional air policy, both the CTC and the federal cabinet permitted it to proceed. Nor were they able to prevent the subsequent complete merger of the two airlines which gave PWA an operating territory embracing all of Canada west of Winnipeg. The unwillingness of the federal government to intervene is understandable. It had no choice. If PWA did not have its demands met, it would have withdrawn its offer. The result would have been Transair's bankruptcy or, alternatively, pressure on Air Canada to salvage it. Either way the federal government would have assumed an enormous burden, political and economic. Having established itself as the planning agent for the airline industry, the federal government found that it had become a hostage, and what was particularly grating was that it had lost control to a provincially owned airline.

Despite its powerlessness in PWA matters, the federal government was determined to establish that it had not lost complete control over air policy and that it would not tolerate the possibility of a repetition of the PWA imbroglio. It had an opportunity to do so in the Skywest conflict.

This conflict represented another attempt by provincial governments, this time Manitoba and Saskatchewan jointly, to use air service as an instrument to promote provincial economic and social objectives. This time the chosen instrument was to be a jointly owned airline to be called Skywest. It was to offer, in particular, service linking Winnipeg, Brandon, Dauphin, Yorkton and Saskatoon. Service on this route had been lost when a subsidiary of Transair was given permission by the CTC to suspend its service.[54] Both Manitoba and Saskatchewan had opposed the suspension before the CTC and the federal cabinet, which denied their appeal. Consequently, the premier of Manitoba proposed a demonstration project, subsidized by the federal government, that would purchase aircraft and spares from a Manitoba-based manufacturer.[55] This proposal was taken up by the prime minister during the 1974 election campaign, when he promised in Winnipeg that the federal government would purchase the aircraft, a promise to which Minister of Transport Jean Marchand indicated in September 1975 the federal government was committed. As a result, the governments of both provinces announced that the service would be launched by March 1976. The assumption underlying this projection was that the ATC, in view of the intergovernmental agreements, would routinely grant the necessary licences.

Such approval was not granted. On December 1, 1975, the ATC met in Winnipeg to hear the application. That same day the committee decided to adjourn the hearing on the grounds that the information provided was insufficient to determine the merits of the application. In particular, the committee wanted copies of the intergovernmental agreements filed. The agreements, however, had not been signed by the federal government whose new minister of transport insisted that he would sign only when the carrier had a licence. In short, Skywest and the provincial governments found themselves in a classic Catch-22 dilemma.[56] After the review committee of the CTC denied an application to overturn the

ATC decision, the governments of Manitoba and Saskatchewan announced that they were not willing to proceed with the application, or the project, any further.

The central question, of course, is why did events take the turn they did? Why did the federal government reverse its commitment and then undermine the application? The answer is to be found in the agitation over the Alberta purchase of PWA. The Skywest negotiations, in the period 1973–75, overlapped with the Alberta purchase announced in August 1974 and Alberta's challenge to the CTC's authority to review the acquisition. The Skywest application thus emerged at the high point of federal concerns about losing control over aviation policy. Another provincially owned airline, however minor, could only complicate the problems for the federal government. In particular, it would be difficult to defend a prohibition, especially a retroactive one, on Alberta at the same time as the government was negotiating a licence for two other provinces. Supporting this argument is the proposal of the federal minister of transport, in January 1976, to the western governments that the project could be reinstated if a private carrier was allowed to operate the service. This proposal was rejected. The irony of the Skywest conflict was the fact that the routes in question were made part of the PWA-Transair purchase agreement of 1978. If Skywest had been allowed, Transair would have had no value for PWA. Denying Skywest, therefore, led directly to the creation of a much larger western, provincially owned airline and to a major breach in national policy. In asserting control, the federal government was contributing to its loss.

One important outcome of this conflict supports our contention that planning regulation breaks down the insulation of the regulatory process and its integration into larger political process. Air policy and regulation joined other transportation modes as subjects of provincial concern. Provinces began to talk about the necessity of a "Western Canadian Transport Commission" with, presumably, some role for the provincial governments in appointments and decision making.[57] British Columbia, in particular, stressed the need for proposals "that would build provincial government participation and authority into the structure of national policy-making."[58] Finally, the Manitoba Department of Industry and Commerce, which had been responsible for Manitoba's participation in Skywest, developed a position paper that proposed a new intergovernmental mechanism for processing air service applications. The proposal is found in Figure 2-1. This proposal carried the following explanatory note:

> It is suggested that applications affecting air services provided by all levels of carriers be referred by the federal regulatory authority to MOT and the provinces for comment. Notice of application would be published and interventions requested from interested parties. The application would be heard by an "Examiner" or by full regulatory authority both of which

include provincial advisors if desired by the provinces affected. Provision is made for the Minister of Transport to allow an expedited temporary operating authority where interest requires a decision in a shorter than normal time. In any event, if no decision is made by the regulatory authority within 30 days of presentation of the examiner's report on the conclusion of a public hearing the carrier is free to start service on a temporary basis and the license must be confirmed within 60 days unless the regulator has compelling reasons why, in the public interest, the application should be denied. Normal appeal procedures would be open to all parties on all decisions.

In brief, Manitoba was suggesting a process similar to that under the Air Transport Board after 1944, with the addition of provincial governments as decision makers. This was a far cry from what the federal government had envisaged when it opted for a planning role.

The federal government's troubles had not yet ended. The cause of the next conflict, surprisingly, was Air Canada, which in 1978 stunned the aviation industry with its offer to purchase Nordair, the Quebec-Ontario regional airline. This purchase was not only a significant blow to the regional air policy but, in many respects, because of the intergovernmental turmoil it set off, it may also have contributed more than any other factor to the demise both of the policy and to federal efforts to plan the aviation sector. The intergovernmental conflicts involved the provinces of Ontario and Quebec, both of which decided that a provincially based, if not owned, airline was needed. In fact, one outcome was the purchase by the Quebec government of Quebecair, the Quebec-based regional airline.

FIGURE 2-1 Mechanism for Processing Air Service Applications

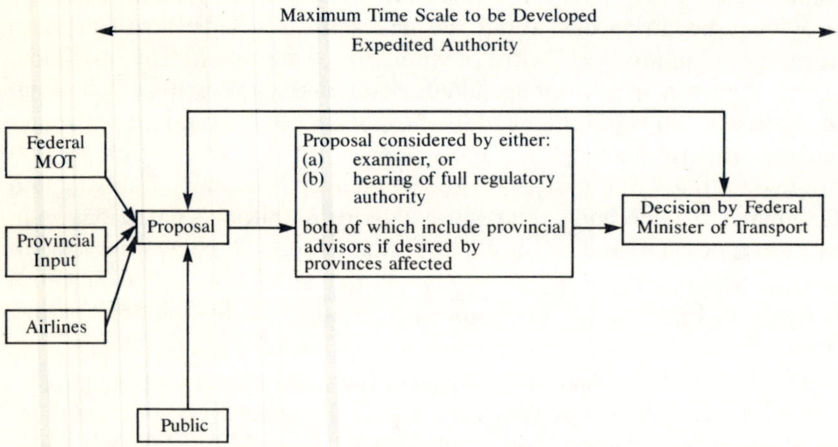

Source: Manitoba Department of Industry and Commerce, 1976.

This episode began, as indicated, when Air Canada sought permission, in 1978, from the ATC to purchase 86 percent of the outstanding shares of Nordair. This was granted, although by a seriously divided committee.[59] The next step was up to the federal government. It could have overturned the decision if it so chose, but it did not. Instead, the minister of transport informed the CTC that "the Government proposed to acquire all of the issued and outstanding shares of Nordair Ltd. that were acquired by Air Canada and, in turn, sell the shares back to private enterprise."[60] Three months later, the minister further informed the commission that it would not acquire the shares but that it would continue to look for a private sector buyer.[61] It was expected that this process would be completed within a year.

This expectation, which was optimistic, did not assume that the governments of Ontario and Quebec would become involved in the bidding war that ensued. Ontario, for example, proposed that there be an Ontario-based regional carrier that would take over the Ontario routes of Nordair, the provincial operations of Air Canada, link up with norOntair and include as owners, Air Canada, private interests, and a minority provincial government interest.[62] Subsequently, Ontario shifted its position to support a joint bid from Quebecair of Montreal and Great Lakes Airlines of London to buy Nordair. Under this plan, all three airlines would disappear to be replaced by two new regional airlines — Air Quebec and Air Ontario.[63] The central rationale behind Ontario's position was its insistence on a regional airline based in Ontario. The Ontario minister of transport was opposed both to the idea (apparently favoured by his federal counterpart) that there be one carrier for Eastern Canada and to the possibility that the Ontario service would be controlled by Quebec-based interests. The federal government rejected the Quebecair–Great Lakes bid because it did not favour either the breakup of Nordair or the possibility of further provincial control of airlines. According to press reports, the federal minister of transport would not agree to any takeover of Nordair unless Ontario and Quebec interests, preferably private, held 40 percent each, with Air Canada continuing to hold 20 percent.[64]

The government of Quebec was even more forceful in pressing its demands than Ontario. Quebec wanted no less than Ontario and, in fact, preferred that control of Nordair remain in Quebec. The provincial government's determination was demonstrated by its actions involving Quebecair. After the federal government rejected the joint bid to purchase Nordair, with the support of Air Canada, Nordair itself offered to buy all of the shares of Quebecair, which was a privately owned airline. Quebecair immediately rejected the offer but, even more importantly, the Quebec government purchased $15 million worth of non-voting convertible shares in Quebecair. The move was justified by Quebec's minister of economic development on the ground that the province "wants the airline controlled by Quebec interests."[65] Subsequently, the Quebec minister of transport stated that the Nordair offer was rejected "because Quebec had no guarantees [that] air service to remote regions of the province would be maintained. Via Rail, for example, cut train services to some regions by 50 percent. Air service is essential. We have to have guarantees it won't be withdrawn."[66] Although both the federal minister and the CTC indicated that this action might be contrary to the *Aeronautics Act* amendment passed after the PWA purchase and therefore illegal, both Quebecair and the government of Quebec dismissed the concerns and did not submit the purchase to regulatory scrutiny. The federal authorities did not rigorously pursue the matter. It was later learned that Quebec had gained effective control of Quebecair at the time, although technically the original majority shareholder continued to be the controlling shareholder. Quebec had vetoed the Nordair bid, but the price of its veto was $15 million and an agreement to buy out two of the other shareholders after two years. This was done in June 1983.[67] Thus, a direct result of Nordair's purchase by Air Canada was the emergence of another provincially owned regional airline. Air Canada finally sold its shares in Nordair to private interests in Quebec in 1984.

Intergovernmental factors also played a role, albeit less primary, in the final blow to the regional air policy. This involved Eastern Provincial Airways (EPA), the regional airline serving the Atlantic Provinces. In 1980, both CPA and EPA applied to the CTC for permission to serve the Halifax-Toronto route. For CPA, this would complete its transcontinental route network in accordance with the 1966 policy statement and with the announcement, in 1977, that the government favoured removing any restrictions on CPA in its relationship to Air Canada. On the other hand, as the ATC noted in its decision, "a policy impediment stands in the way of adding Toronto to EPA's licence."[68] The impediment was the 1969 regional air policy statement. Consequently, the ATC having "been guided by existing government policy on commercial air services," approved CPA's application and denied that of EPA.[69]

There was a larger impediment to the CTC's decision and that was intergovernmental and other political forces. The hearing on the route had generated one of the largest sets of interventions that the committee had encountered. Over 80 parties intervened, approximately two-thirds of whom did so on EPA's behalf. Most significantly, EPA was supported by a number of local MPs, Liberal and Conservative, the Atlantic Provinces Economic Council, and Premier John Buchanan, representing the Council of Maritime Premiers. One of the most common arguments used by both EPA and its supporters in defence of the application was that EPA needed the route in order to subsidize some of its existing services.[70] This community of supporters was not content to let the decision stand and appealed it to the federal cabinet. Unlike the CTC, cabinet recognized no "policy impediment" and revoked the decision. Halifax-

Toronto was granted to EPA and, as a consolation prize, CPA was awarded Montreal-Halifax. The ultimate irony, however, was to come. In 1984, CPA purchased EPA. Where ten years earlier there had been five regional airlines, and none provincially owned, now there are only three, two of which are owned by provincial governments.

The Demise of Federal Planning: 1977–84

It was not immediately apparent that the federal government was prepared to abandon its planning role. In fact, available evidence, while contradictory, suggests another attempt to assert control. Among the signs that suggested a move away from planning were the substantial policy changes concerning Air Canada and CPA. The Air Canada changes were part of a new legislative mandate for the airline. Three changes in particular stand out. The first was that Air Canada's "special status" in the regulatory process was removed; henceforth, the airline's licence applications would be subject to the "public convenience and necessity" test of the Air Transport Committee.[71] This is an action ordered by the Conservative government in 1961 but overturned when the Liberals regained office in 1963. Of equal significance is that, while there was no statement that its role as instrument of national policy was ended, the airline was instructed to "have due regard to sound business principles, and in particular the contemplation of profit."[72] As Langford notes, although the indications were confusing, the idea seemed to be that "Air Canada should be an efficient and safe profit-making airline competing on a more or less equal footing with other carriers."[73]

The correctness of this view is suggested by the third major change which is found in the directive provisions of the new act. Prior to the new legislation, the government could impose routes and services on the airline which were designated "of national importance" without providing compensation where such routes or services were not profitable. The protection from competition on the profitable routes was the quid pro quo. Under the *Air Canada Act*, while the government was authorized to issue directives for economic, social or other policy reasons, it was required to pay compensation to Air Canada in the event that losses were incurred as a result of Air Canada's compliance with the directives.[74] Of equal importance to the Air Canada changes were those affecting CPA. In 1979, the government announced that the capacity restrictions on CPA's competition with Air Canada were removed. Henceforth, Air Canada and CPA would be able to compete freely, although the CTC was expected to monitor activities to prevent undue competition that might be prejudicial to the public interest.

Despite these changes which "liberalized" regulatory control over Air Canada and CPA, there were other, more powerful indications that planning had not completely lost favour in Ottawa. In 1977, federal officials drafted a new air policy statement which was discussed with industry and provincial representatives. Consultation with the latter was a significant change from the previous decade when provincial governments were ignored. In 1977, the federal government conceded that provinces have interests in air policy and "that's why we consult them."[75] Both groups, however, rejected the proposed policy as being "too restrictive," and the government decided to shelve the issue for the time being. In 1981, the Department of Transport tried again and released a paper containing a "proposed domestic air carrier policy." Although a senior departmental official described the proposals simply as "an attempt to fine tune the status quo," few observers agreed.[76] Most saw the proposed policy as an attempt by the federal department to regain control over the airline sector by imposing a fairly rigid classification of roles on individual airlines. There would be controls on the length of flights permitted regional carriers as well as restrictions on the type of aircraft certain carriers could use.

The radically changed circumstances were reflected in the treatment of the policy paper. Earlier statements, after cabinet agreement had been obtained, were simply announced and affected parties, including the regulatory agency and the airlines, were expected to abide by their terms. In 1981, air policy had become so controversial that cabinet could not even agree on what had been minimized as "an attempt to fine tune the status quo." As a result, cabinet opted to refer the policy statement to the House of Commons Standing Committee on Transport for public hearings. Not only did most of the provinces participate, but two other units of the federal government testified in opposition to the proposals.[77] In fact, the majority of industry as well as other intervenors was critical.[78] The parliamentary committee, reflecting this consensus, concluded that it "is persuaded that the prospect of competition is the principal inducement to efficient performance in the airline industry." Accordingly, it favoured "a regime that should increase competition within a regulated environment."[79] Although this was far from a call for substantial de-regulation, it was a significant move away from the planning approach favoured by the Department of Transport. This was acknowledged a year later by the minister of transport who stated that he could not accept such a proposal.[80]

His successor, however, was more receptive. In May 1984, the federal minister of transport unveiled a "new Canadian air policy" which signalled the end of the unsuccessful attempt by the government to plan the airline industry.[81] He contended that "the present regulatory system is no longer required . . . " and proceeded to indict it on the grounds that it had:

- hindered innovation in services and pricing;
- reduced the flexibility of airline managements to pursue new market opportunities and to adjust their operations to minimize costs;

- hampered the ability of airlines to respond quickly to change, because of undue delays in regulatory decisions;
- required airline management to devote excessive time and energy to essentially unproductive regulatory considerations; (and)
- complicated airline planning, to the extent that regulatory decisions have often been difficult to predict. . . .[82]

The policies that had produced such conditions, he concluded, were "obsolete" and consequently all "existing policies defining air carrier roles" were repealed.[83] In addition, he declared that licence restrictions on airlines which reflected regulatory efforts "to fine-tune the relationship between demand . . . " and competition will be eliminated on routes in southern Canada.[84] For the geographical demarcation, see Figure 2-2.

FIGURE 2-2 Geographic Scope of Liberalization

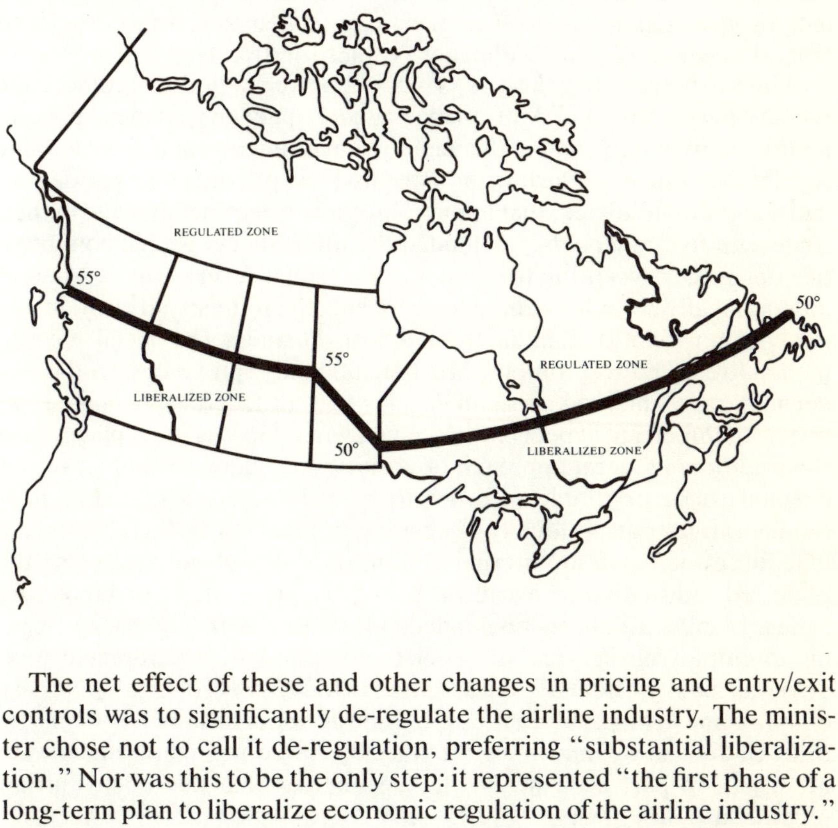

The net effect of these and other changes in pricing and entry/exit controls was to significantly de-regulate the airline industry. The minister chose not to call it de-regulation, preferring "substantial liberalization." Nor was this to be the only step: it represented "the first phase of a long-term plan to liberalize economic regulation of the airline industry." Regardless of how the policy is characterized, it amounts to the termination of airline planning in Canada. Indeed, except for the protection afforded for northern Canada, the new policy reflects the termination of promotional regulation as well.

Conclusion

It would be inaccurate to claim that the intergovernmental conflicts over air policy that emerged in the last decade were the sole cause of the 1984 decision to de-regulate the Canadian airline industry significantly. Other factors clearly played a role, especially the U.S. de-regulation beginning in 1978 and the subsequent "hemorrhaging" of Canadian traffic to U.S. border points such as Burlington, Vermont; Buffalo, New York; and Bellingham, Washington. In addition, partisan and personal motives on the part of the then Minister of Transport, Lloyd Axworthy, were doubtless instrumental. It is our contention, however, that no other single reason played as important a role as that of intergovernmental conflict. To the extent that airline de-regulation represented "an idea whose time had come," the decade of conflicts and the numerous setbacks for the federal government, as well as the many stalemates, were crucial to federal acceptance, and willingness to act, on that fact.

While it is true that the use of economic regulation to promote the healthy development of Air Canada had an impact on provincial governments, it was only when the federal government sought to employ regulation to plan the airline industry that the provinces responded to, and sought to influence, that impact. Provinces became involved in their representative role as they defended the interests of specific communities desiring, or wanting to protect, a particular level of air service; of individual airlines who wanted to serve specific routes; and even, in one case, of an aircraft manufacturer whose business provincial governments attempted to promote. Most significantly, provinces, in the last decade, have emerged as significant owners of federally regulated airlines. An important aspect of provincial ownership was the replication of the traditional federal approach of wanting to acquire or protect routes deemed to be profitable in order to be able to cross-subsidize non-remunerative, but politically necessary, routes. As in the case of the federal airline, such an internal system of cross-subsidization was the preferred alternative to a call on provincial treasuries for direct subsidies. Finally, provinces responded in their role as policy makers seeking to employ air service as a social and economic development tool. This was most particularly the situation in the case of Alberta's purchase of PWA, but it was also central for Ontario in norOntair. The demands from Quebec and Ontario for provincially based regional airlines were premised, in part at least, on the assumption that this could further provincial policy goals.

The federal move to planning profoundly influenced the politics of airline regulation. As we suggested in Chapter 1, a major consequence was felt in the patterns of interest representation and participation. Prior to the emergence of planning, the central participants were the federal government and industry management. After the 1964 move to a much more enhanced, comprehensive role for the federal government, many more groups sought to influence aviation policies and decisions. For our purposes, the most important new participants were the provincial governments. They became involved not only to pursue their own policy and political objectives, but also because other participants sought their support for demands made on the federal government. This was most obvious in the process of route selection as well as in the acquisition or establishment of carriers.

The second major political consequence was in the relationship between the air regulatory process and other political processes. While it is important to note that air regulation, prior to the planning period, was never characterized by total insulation from the political process because of the pre-eminent role of the federal government, after 1964 such regulation became even more integrated. The regulatory agency, despite having regained a significant decision-making role in 1967, found itself being treated as simply the first stage in the decision-making process. Appeals from regulatory decisions directly affecting provincial governments became the norm. Indeed, on at least two occasions, provincial governments ignored the regulatory agency. More importantly, to the extent that provincial governments perceived the regulatory agency as a significant obstacle to the attainment of their objectives, they sought to link the agency with wider intergovernmental issues and processes. Provinces sought direct representation on the agency; alternatively, some proposed that the agency's role be supplanted by intergovernmental decision making.

The wider representation of interests and the closer integration of the regulatory with other political processes had a significant impact on federal aviation policy and the employment of regulation to attain the goals of that policy. Prior to 1964, the federal government was clearly in control and able to dictate, and impose, its objectives on the airline industry. What is crucial, however, for an understanding of that period is to see that the federal government's objectives were limited and easily attained. They were to promote a healthy national Crown airline which would not make major demands on the federal treasury. After 1964, the federal government sought the same objective but to do so, it was forced into a planning role, casting a broadened range of industry participants and playing a much more direct supervisory role in their decision making. Before 1964, the federal government was responsible for the health of only one airline; after that year, it was responsible for the industry as a whole. By assuming a planning role the federal government, which expanded the scope of its control, found within a decade its control significantly lessened. This was the paradoxical result of radically transforming the politics of regulation so as to include provincial governments as central participants.

Chapter 3

Telecommunications Regulation

This chapter analyzes an unsuccessful attempt by the federal government to introduce a planning role for economic regulation of the telecommunications carriage industry and the consequent intergovernmental battles. For most of this century, regulation of telecommunications has been confined largely to a policing role, regardless of level of government. Starting in the 1960s, the telecommunications industry began a dramatic period of technological and economic change, change that called into question the fundamental premises and principles of the regulatory systems. In particular, such changes as occurred challenged the traditional relationships between and among the providers of telecommunications services, especially the telephone companies, their subscribers and governments.

Almost coincidental with the onslaught of technological change, the federal government began to reassess its traditional public policies and instruments. The result of this reassessment was a commitment to a new policy approach that not only expanded significantly the federal role in telecommunications but sought specifically to employ regulation of the industry, not in a policing, but in a planning capacity. Those provincial governments that traditionally had exercised almost exclusive responsibility for telecommunications found themselves fighting on two fronts, the technological and the intergovernmental, to protect their decision-making power. This chapter, while not ignoring the first, concentrates on the second front in order to illustrate our basic hypothesis that changes in the function of regulation cause intergovernmental conflicts. The chapter consists of three sections, the first of which provides essential background information on aspects of the telecommunications industry most relevant to our purposes. The second and third sections analyze the nature of intergovernmental relations from the perspective of two periods, the pre-1968 policing era and the post-1968 period of attempted federal planning.

The Canadian Telecommunications Industry and Regulatory Structure

Prior to an analysis of the intergovernmental conflicts, their development and causes, it is in order to provide some background information on some of the central aspects of telecommunications in Canada. In particular, it is necessary to focus on those aspects of the industry that are relevant to the policy issues central to the politics of telecommunications. Accordingly, this section provides information on four major aspects: the size; the ownership; their individual regulators; and pertinent financial aspects of the carriers. In addition, it is germane to discuss two other features, namely, the jurisdictional distribution of responsibility for regulating the telecommunications carriers and the unique organizational form by which many of the long-distance services are provided in Canada, i.e., Telecom Canada.

Although there are more than three hundred telephone companies and other telecommunications carriers in Canada, 19 companies dominate the industry, in that they provide approximately 99 percent of the services. The details of these companies, including their names and their share of the market as of 1982, the last year for which we have data, are found in Table 3-1.

As can be seen from this table, there are considerable variations in the size of these companies. Bell Canada, for example, has approximately 52 percent of the market as measured by total operating revenues, and the nearest company in size is B.C.Tel which represents 12 percent of the market. It is also instructive to note that the members of Telecom Canada represent almost 88 percent of the telecommunications carriage market in Canada, as measured by total operating revenues.

The second aspect of the industry is the nature of carrier ownership. Here we find a wide variation including privately owned, publicly owned, foreign-owned and joint public-private enterprises. In addition, there is an interesting mix of cross-ownership relationships. Table 3-2 provides the detailed information. Based on the information found in Tables 3-1 and 3-2, we can see that privately owned carriers represent almost 75 percent of the market while publicly owned and joint ventures represent approximately 21 percent and 4 percent respectively. Janisch may well be correct when he suggests that ownership per se may be "relatively unimportant because of the overriding nature of common telecommunications objectives," at least insofar as corporate manage-

TABLE 3-1: 1982 Telecommunications Carriage Market by Company

	Total Operating Revenues	Share
	($ millions)	(%)
Bell Canada[a,b]	4,359.3	51.9
B.C.Tel[b]	1,009.4	12.0
AGT[b]	825.3	9.8
CNCP Telecommunications	302.2	3.6
SASK TEL[b]	295.7	3.5
MTS[b]	244.6	2.9
Maritime Tel & Tel[b]	235.9	2.8
NBTel[b]	191.5	2.3
Teleglobe Canada	170.2	2.0
"edmonton telephones"	151.1	1.8
Québec Téléphone	139.6	1.7
Newfoundland Telephone[b]	109.6	1.3
Télébec Ltée	80.9	1.0
Telesat Canada[b]	59.0	0.7
NorthwesTel	48.9	0.6
Terra Nova Tel	33.2	0.4
Island Tel[b]	26.5	0.3
Northern Tel	21.1	0.3
Thunder Bay Telephone	16.0	0.2
Total	8,320.0	99.1

Source: Revised from Canada, Department of Communications, *Canadian Telecommunications: An Overview of the Canadian Telecommunications Carriage Industry* (Ottawa: Minister of Supply and Services Canada, 1983), p. A2.

Note: Because of rounding, columns may not add up to the total indicated.

a. Telecommunications operations only.

b. Members of Telecom Canada.

ment is concerned.[1] It remains to be seen, however, whether or not ownership, i.e., public or private, is as important a factor with respect to intergovernmental relations in telecommunications as it was in the airline sector. One indicator that ownership did matter, at least in one instance, was the action taken by the province of Nova Scotia in 1966 when Bell Canada acquired a controlling interest in Maritime Telegraph and Telephone (Maritime Tel & Tel). The province, unwilling to accept the idea that Maritime Tel & Tel would be controlled "out of province" passed an amendment to the Maritime Tel & Tel statute limiting Bell's voting power to 1,000 shares.[2] Figure 3-1 provides the same information found in Table 3-2 but presented in a format highlighting the territorial dimension of the ownership of Canadian carriers.

The third basic set of facts to be known about Canadian telecommunications carriers is the identity of their individual regulators. This information is found in Table 3-3. It is worth noting that Teleglobe Canada is not regulated but reports to the federal minister of communications. Similarly, SASK TEL was not regulated by a separate agency until after 1982 when Saskatchewan created a regulatory agency, the Public Utilities Review Commission. As we shall discuss in more detail

FIGURE 3-1 Ownership of Canadian Telecommunications Common Carriers

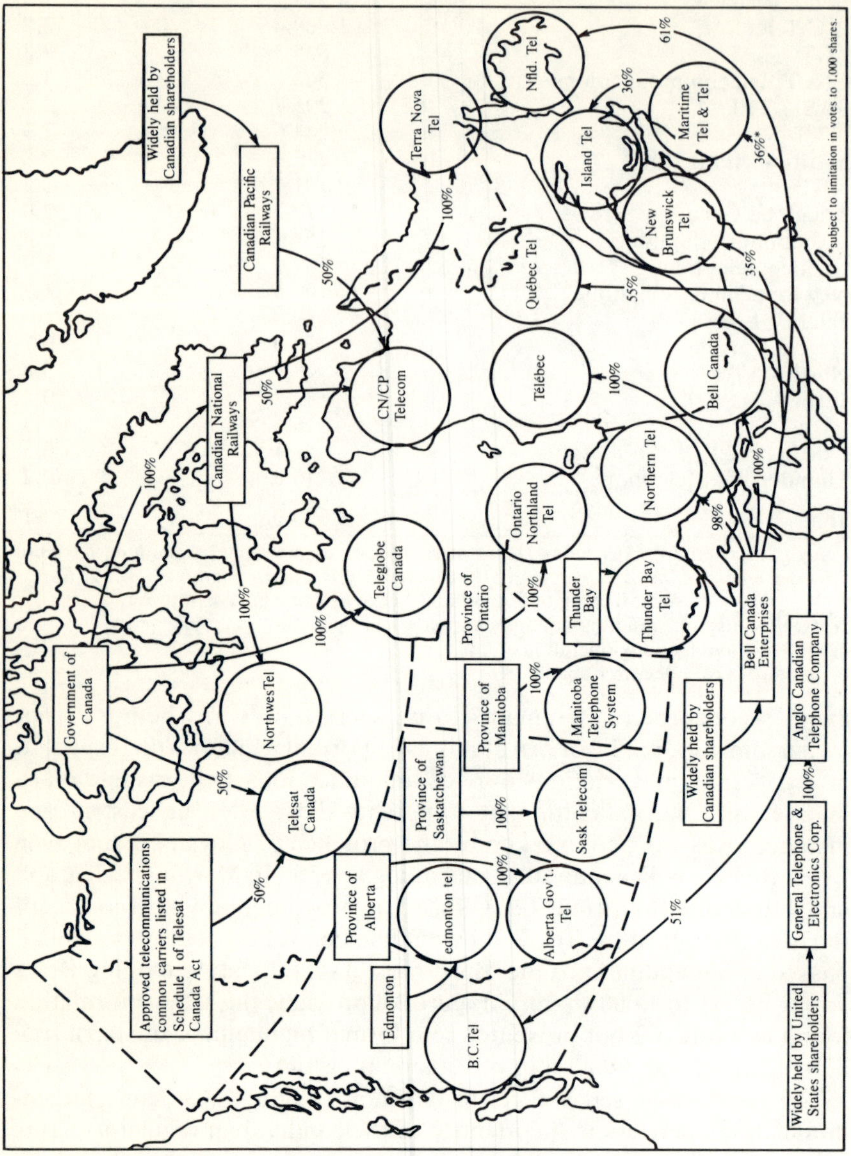

Source: H.N. Janisch, "Telecommunications Ownership and Regulation in Canada: Compatibility or Confusion?" Paper prepared for the 12th Annual Telecommunications Policy Research Conference, Airlie, Virginia, April 23, 1984.

TABLE 3-2 Ownership of Canadian Telecommunications Carriers

Company	Type of Ownership — Principal Shareholder
AGT	Province of Alberta (100%)
Bell Canada	Investor owned (Bell Canada Enterprises — 100%)
B.C.Tel	Foreign investor owned (through subsidiary of GTE of United States — 51%)
CNCP Telecommunications	Joint Venture (Government of Canada through CNR and Canadian Pacific — each party 50%)
"edmonton telephones"	City of Edmonton (100%)
Island Tel	Investor owned (Maritime Tel & Tel — 36%)
MTS	Province of Manitoba (100%)
Maritime Tel & Tel	Investor owned (Bell Canada Enterprises — 36%)
NBTel	Investor owned (Bell Canada Enterprises — 35%)
Newfoundland Telephone	Investor owned (Bell Canada Enterprises — 61%)
Northern Tel	Investor owned (Bell Canada Enterprises — 98%)
NorthwesTel	Government of Canada (through Canadian National Railways — 100%)
Québec Téléphone	Foreign investor owned (through subsidiary of GTE — 55%)
SASK TEL	Province of Saskatchewan (100%)
Télébec Ltée	Investor owned (Bell Canada Enterprises — 100%)
Teleglobe Canada	Government of Canada (100%)
Telesat Canada	Joint Venture (Government of Canada — 50%; approved telecommunications common carriers listed in Schedule 1 of *Telesat Canada Act* — 50%)
Terra Nova Tel	Government of Canada (through Canadian National Railways — 100%)
Thunder Bay Telephone	City of Thunder Bay (100%)

below, Telecom Canada is not itself regulated. When we combine the information provided in Tables 3-1 and 3-3, we can see that the federal government regulates approximately 68 percent of the telecommunications sector, as represented by total operating revenues, with the provinces regulating almost all of the remaining 32 percent. As a percentage of total telephones, the CRTC regulates almost 70 percent of the industry.[3] There are some very important provincial variations. The three Prairie Provinces and the four Atlantic Provinces regulate almost all telecommunications within their jurisdictions, while Quebec and Ontario regulate less than 3 percent and 1 percent of the industry respectively. These relatively small figures, however, hide the fact that both provinces regulate approximately 50 independent telephone companies.[4] Only British

TABLE 3-3 Canadian Telecommunications Carriers and their Regulators

AGT	Public Utilities Board of Alberta
Bell Canada	Canadian Radio-television and Telecommunications Commission (CRTC)
B.C.Tel	CRTC
CNCP Telecommunications	CRTC
"edmonton telephones"	City of Edmonton
Island Tel	Public Utilities Commission of Prince Edward Island
MTS	Manitoba Public Utilities Board
Maritime Tel & Tel	Nova Scotia Board of Public Utilities Commissioners
NBTel	New Brunswick Board of Public Utilities Commissioners
Newfoundland Telephone	Newfoundland Board of Public Utilities Commissioners
Northern Tel	Ontario Telephone Services Commission
NorthwesTel	CRTC
Québec Téléphone	Régie des services publics du Québec
SASK TEL	Saskatchewan Public Utilities Review Commission
Télébec Ltée	Régie des services publics du Québec
Teleglobe Canada	Not regulated
Telesat Canada	CRTC
Terra Nova Tel	CRTC
Thunder Bay Telephone	Ontario Telephone Service Commission

Columbia lacks any significant degree of jurisdiction, in terms of both size and numbers, over carriers operating within the province. Figure 3-2 provides an overview of the territorial dimension of the regulation of telecommunications carriers in Canada.

In themselves, the preceding data do not suggest a basis for intergovernmental conflicts except for the fact that three provinces do not

FIGURE 3-2 Regulation of Canadian Telecommunications Common Carriers

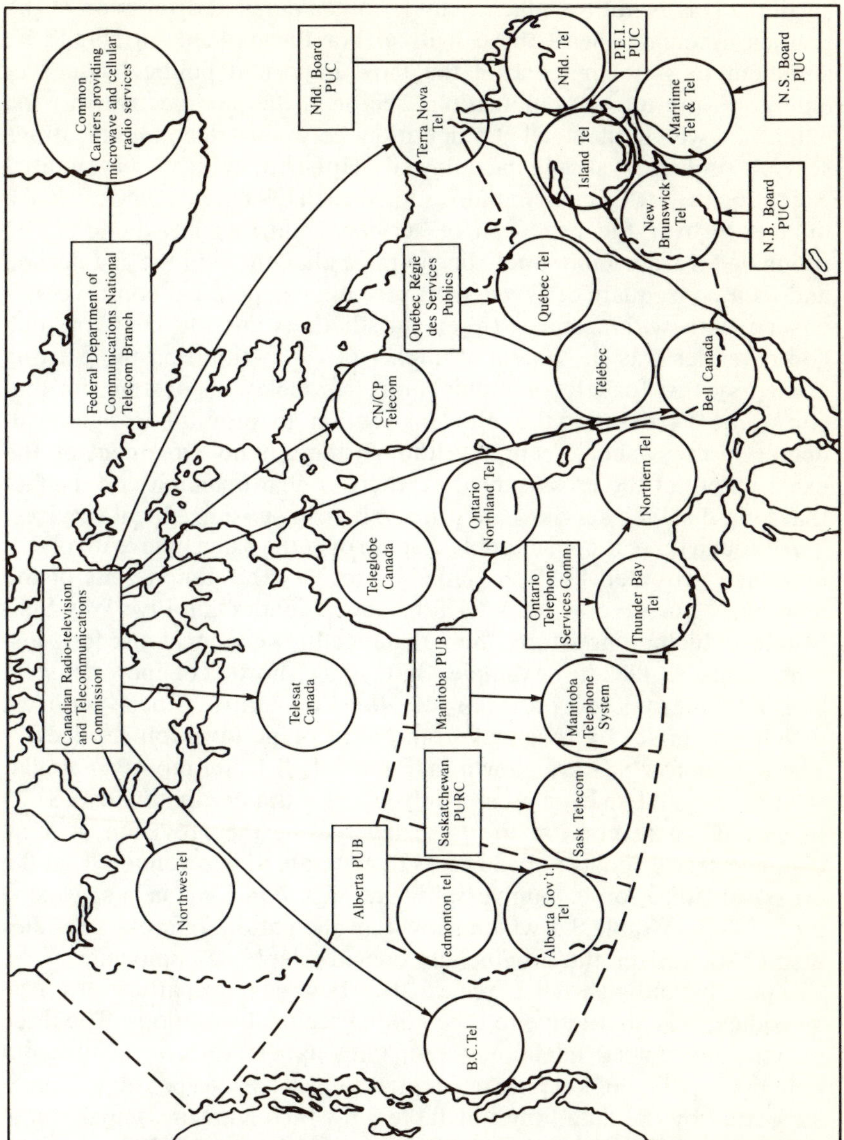

Source: H.N. Janisch, "Telecommunications Ownership and Regulation in Canada: Compatibility or Confusion?" Paper prepared for the 12th Annual Telecommunications Policy Research Conference, Airlie, Virginia, April 23, 1984.

have jurisdiction comparable to the other seven over major carriers operating within their jurisdiction. To develop such a basis, it is necessary to provide information on aspects of the costs and revenues of the carriers. This is not the place to undertake a detailed discussion of the politics associated with these figures. For the moment, it should be sufficient to state that one of the most important political issues to emerge in the telecommunications sector in the past decade was the extent to which, if at all, competition between telecommunications service providers should be allowed. Hitherto, with a very limited exception in CNCP Telecommunications, each telephone company had a monopoly over the provision of service within its jurisdiction. The rationale for such a monopoly began to be challenged in the last decade and as a consequence, as we shall see, intense political controversies ensued both within and between jurisdictions. At the heart of such controversies was the potential impact of competition on the existing pricing system for telecommunications services. This system, for reasons to be discussed in the following section, incorporates a significant degree of cross-subsidization. Although there is no agreement on the exact extent of the cross-subsidies, there is near unanimity on the fact that long-distance services are priced so as to subsidize local services.

Although there is considerable dispute over the exact figures involved, evidence provided by Bell Canada suggests the dimensions of the amounts.[5] For several years, Bell has been conducting Five-Way Split Studies which demonstrate the imbalance between local and long-distance rates. In 1982, for example, Bell "had a shortfall of approximately $1.2 billion from the provision of Non-Competitive Local services, which was offset by revenues from Non-Competitive Toll services."[6] The figures for 1983 are shown in Table 3-4. B.C.Tel reports a similar relationship and an even greater subsidy. It estimates that it costs $2.23 to earn $1 in revenue at the local level while the provision of long-distance service costs only 36 cents to generate $1 in revenue.[7] That the cross-subsidization is a universal phenomenon in Canada is suggested by the data in Table 3-5 which show that the pattern of cross-subsidies also characterizes the provincially owned telephone companies.

Notwithstanding what is regarded to be a general pattern of cross-subsidies, it is instructive to take note of regional variations. The three provincially owned telephone companies appear to have instituted a deliberate policy of keeping residential rates as low as possible. This is suggested by the data found in Table 3-6 which allow a comparison of different residential rates charged across Canada as of 1982.

Given the existing pattern of cross-subsidization and the fact that the provision of such subsidies is dependent on long-distance revenues, it is important to appreciate the degree or extent of dependency of the carriers on long-distance rates. In 1982, for example, Canadian telephone companies as a whole received 53 percent of their total operating

TABLE 3-4 Bell Canada's Estimated Revenues and Costs by Service Category, 1983

Category (1)	Revenues (2)	Costs (3)	(2) – (3)	(3) ÷ (2)
		($ Millions)		
Local service (non-competitive)	1,389	2,630	(1,241)	1.89
Toll service (non-competitive)	1,988	626	1,362	0.32
Competitive network	386	317	69	0.82
Competitive terminal	878	834	44	0.95
Common	99	333	(234)	
Total company	4,740[a]	4,740		

Source: Response to Interrogatory, Bell (CRTC), May 22, 1984 — 22 IC — as found in Steven Globerman, "Economic Factors in Telecommunications Policy and Regulation," paper prepared for IRPP Conference on Competition and Technological Changes: The Impact on Telecommunications Policy and Regulation in Canada, Toronto, September 25–26, 1984, p. 32.

a. Versus $4,710 for non-consolidated telecommunications revenues.

TABLE 3-5 Net Revenue and Expenses by Lines of Service for the Year 1982 — SASK TEL

Category (1)	Revenues (2)	Costs (3)	(2) – (3)	(3) ÷ (2)
		($ Millions)		
Local	52.3	102.9	(50.6)	1.97
Toll	179.4	54.8	124.6	0.31
Optional	25.9	24.0	1.9	0.93
Unregulated	35.3	26.8	8.5	0.76
Common	2.8	79.4	(76.6)	
Total	295.7	287.9		

Source: Steven Globerman, "Economic Factors in Telecommunications Policy and Regulation," paper prepared for IRPP Conference on Competition and Technological Changes: The Impact on Telecommunications Policy and Regulation in Canada, Toronto, September 25–26, 1984.

revenues from long-distance rates. It is even more important, for our purposes, to acknowledge the provincial/carrier variations which run from a low of 49.5 percent for Bell Canada to a high of 65.5 percent for SASK TEL. Table 3-7 provides the percentages for all the members of Telecom Canada.

These figures, however, do not tell the whole story of toll dependency because they include both interprovincial and intraprovincial revenues.

TABLE 3-6 Comparison of Residential Basic Service Rates in Canadian Telephone Companies, 1982: Main Individual Residence

Stations	SASK TEL Proposed	B.C.Tel[a]	AGT[b]	MTS	BELL	Maritime Tel & Tel	NBTel	Newfoundland Telephone	Island Tel[c]
250	$ 5.70	$ 6.95	$ 5.35	$ 4.00	$ 6.60	$10.70	$ 9.80	$ 8.75	$ 8.70
750	5.70	6.95	5.60	4.25	6.60	10.70	9.80	8.75	8.70
1,750	5.70	7.50	5.60	4.75	7.10	11.10	9.95	8.75	9.40
4,250	7.10	8.00	5.80	5.05	7.40	11.50	10.25	9.90	9.40
15,000	7.10	8.55	6.40	5.65	8.05	11.90	11.10	10.85	10.95
30,000	7.10	8.55	6.40	6.05	8.35	12.35	11.45	11.90	11.60
60,000	7.10	9.10	6.40	—	8.90	12.35	12.05	11.90	—
110,000	8.30	9.60	6.75	—	9.60	12.80	—	—	—
Regina	8.30								
Saskatoon	8.30								
Victoria		10.15							
Vancouver		12.25							
Calgary			7.30						
Edmonton			9.00						
Winnipeg				6.75					
Montreal					11.45				
Toronto					12.35				
Halifax						12.80			
Saint John							12.05		
St. John's								11.90	
Charlottetown									11.60

Source: Saskatchewan Telecommunications Rate Schedule Application 1983 as found in R. Brian Woodrow and Kenneth B. Woodside, "Players, Stakes and Politics in the Future of Telecommunication Regulation in Canada," paper prepared for IRPP Conference on Competition and Technological Changes: The Impact on Telecommunications Policy and Regulation in Canada, Toronto, Sept.25–26, 1984, Table VI.

a. Application before CRTC
b. Application before Alberta PUB
c. Application before PEI PUC

TABLE 3-7 Percentage Toll Revenues (Interprovincial and Intraprovincial) of Total Operating Revenues of Telecom Canada Members, 1982

	(percent)
SASK TEL	65.0
AGT	64.0
MTS	59.2
Newfoundland Telephone	58.9
Maritime Tel & Tel	56.5
NBTel	55.8
B.C.Tel	55.0
Island Tel	54.0
Bell Canada	49.5

Source: Telecom Canada, Statistics 1982.

Although there are no published figures available that disaggregate the toll revenue category, industry sources have suggested that there are wide variations among the companies. For some, interprovincial toll revenues can contribute from 30 to 45 percent to the total revenues, while for others, Bell Canada being the most often mentioned, a much larger proportion of revenue is derived from intraterritory toll services.[8] The significance of these and the preceding figures is derived from the existing distribution of regulatory responsibilities. A change in that distribution, such as giving the federal government more authority over interprovincial rates and services, raises provincial objections based on concerns that the existing subsidy system may be challenged as a result of such a change.

There is a final aspect of the revenue picture of the telephone companies that is directly relevant to the policy issues that have emerged. As the preceding information suggests, the present pricing system for telecommunications and, in particular, the cross-subsidization practices are heavily dependent on long-distance toll revenues. In recent years, there has been a growing awareness, or at least acknowledgment, that toll dependency is itself part of another dependent relationship. In telecommunications, as in many other businesses, all customers are not equal; some are more important than others. For the telephone companies, the significance of this is the fact that large portions of overall toll revenues are derived from a small concentration of business subscribers. SASK TEL reported that 7 percent of its business subscribers provide 54 percent of its toll revenues while for NBTel, 3 percent of its business customers provide 53 percent of total business revenue. As a further indication of the exceptionally high degree of concentration, NBTel acknowledged that 20 business customers alone in New Brunswick accounted for 32 percent of total business revenues.[9] The Atlantic provinces' telephone companies collectively reported that 5 percent of business subscribers contributed 60 percent of total business revenues.[10] B.C.Tel provided even more startling evidence of concentration when it stated that ". . . one tenth of one percent of B.C.Tel's business subscribers generate over 20% of the Company's interexchange [i.e., long-distance] revenues."[11] Figure 3-3 provides evidence on the overall concentration of B.C.Tel's business interexchange revenues.

FIGURE 3-3 B.C.Tel Business Interexchange Revenue Distribution

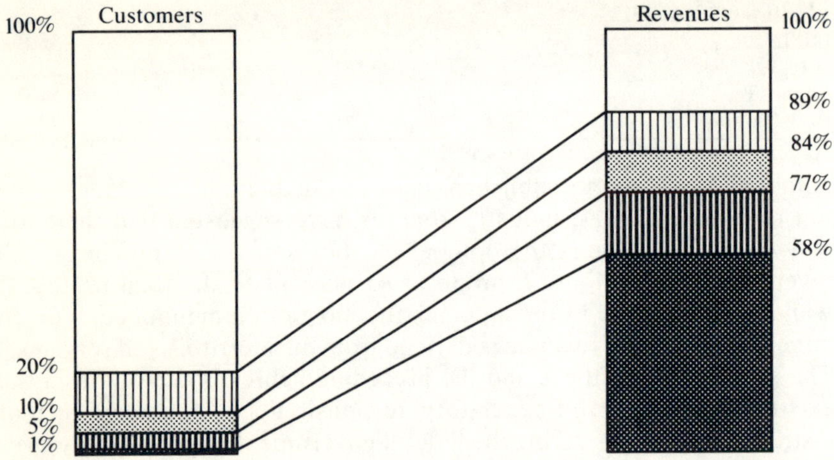

Source: B.C.Tel, *Memorandum of Evidence, CRTC Telecom Public Notice 1984 – 86, Interexchange Competition and Related Issues*, April 1984, Appendix 1, p. 1.

Until recently, these figures on revenue concentration as well as the others have had little political significance. Indeed, one measure of this is the fact that until very recently, much of this information was not even compiled. This was because the pricing systems and the underlying principles of the telephone companies, public and private, and the public policies, explicit or implicit, which authorized them were not even questioned, let alone challenged. The principles and the public policies are currently under challenge. In particular, there is concern about the willingness of major sources of revenue to continue to contribute such an overwhelming share. In the event that such sources are able to withdraw all or a significant portion of their contribution, telephone practices and public policies must respond. The stakes, both within provinces and interregionally, are enormous, and this fact provides the intergovernmental dimension to telecommunications issues today.

There are two major anomalies in the information just provided. The first pertains to the allocation of jurisdictional responsibilities between the two levels of government. Telecommunications clearly does not reflect the "territorial principle" associated with Canadian federalism: "what goes on within a province should be provincial; what is interprovincial or international should remain federal."[12] Instead, we have allocation by company, not by territory or function. The federal government regulates seven companies, two of which have been declared "Works . . . to be for the general Advantage of Canada," while the provinces or in the case of "edmonton telephones," a municipality, regulate the other major companies.[13] It is important to emphasize that regardless of level, the government that regulates a company regulates all the telecommunications carriage of that company with some minor exceptions that need not concern us here. By this we mean that the CRTC, for example, regulates Bell Canada's intraprovincial, interprovincial and international rates and services as does Saskatchewan for SASK TEL or New Brunswick for NBTel.

With the exception of a direct challenge to federal jurisdiction over Bell Canada, launched by a municipality in 1905 and confirmed, and some indirect challenges involving labour relations, for example, until recently, there has been no other legal challenge to either federal or provincial jurisdiction nor any attempt, particularly by the provinces, to have their jurisdiction confirmed judicially. This is somewhat surprising because academic legal commentary is unanimous in suggesting that, at a minimum, federal jurisdiction extends beyond the companies it now regulates to encompass the interprovincial and international operations of all telecommunications companies and, at a maximum, the federal government has exclusive jurisdiction over all telecommunications services and facilities comparable to its jurisdiction in broadcasting and aeronautics.[14]

Jurisdictional issues, however, have emerged in the past few years. Although governments have been willing, as Buchan and Johnston note, to "'let sleeping dogs lie' in a legal sense," the federal government, starting in the early 1970s, proposed to make functional changes in jurisdictional allocation.[15] These proposals, and provincial responses, were central to the intergovernmental conflicts to be discussed below, and we shall leave it until then to provide more detail. More recently, two industry participants, namely CNCP and "edmonton telephones" have sought to invoke federal jurisdiction over aspects of their relationships with Alberta Government Telephones (AGT). In October 1984, the Federal Court Trial Division ruled that AGT fell under federal jurisdiction because "it is a non-local undertaking as described in section 92(10)(a) of the *Constitution Act*, 1867."[16] However, the court also ruled that AGT is a provincial Crown agent and, therefore, not within the jurisdiction of the CRTC because it has Crown immunity within the existing *Railway Act*. Although this decision, if it stands on appeal, will allow the three Prairie provinces to continue to exercise jurisdiction until the *Railway Act* is amended to remove their immunity, it does mean that the four Atlantic telephone companies come under the CRTC's jurisdiction. CNCP has indicated that it intends to appeal the court's ruling on the Crown immunity issue.[17]

If federal jurisdiction is upheld, the decision will have profound implications for both the regulation of telecommunications and intergovernmental relations in this area. For our purposes, it is sufficient to note that the uncertainty over jurisdiction and the subsequent challenges clearly coloured the nature of the intergovernmental conflicts that ensued in the past decade.

The second major anomaly involves Telecom Canada or the Trans-Canada Telephone System (TCTS) as it was known until 1983.[18] Telecom Canada, which was created in 1931 to provide an integrated cross-Canada long-distance system, describes itself as "a cooperative organization comprising ten of Canada's major telecommunications carriers responsible for building, operating and maintaining the country's long distance voice, data and image communications facilities."[19] There are three key features of Telecom Canada to be noted. The first is that, as an organization, it has no employees of its own but relies on staff lent from the member companies. Secondly, it is run by a board of management on which each member is represented and, most importantly, unanimity is required for all decisions. In other words, each member has a veto. The most important decisions pertain to the long-distance rates charged by member companies for Telecom Canada routes which are governed by the Revenue Settlement Plan. Finally, Telecom Canada itself is not regulated by any government. Each member files the Telecom Canada rate schedule with its regulatory agency which submits it to the degree of scrutiny that it chooses. It is of some significance that, until recently, all regulators have tended to accept such rates as filed because of the need for uniformity and because of the unanimous agreement of the member companies. Consequently, the members of Telecom Canada have for years played what is, in effect, a major policy role by setting national long-distance rates in Canada and by allocating revenues accruing from such rates. Obviously, any change in the regulatory status of Telecom Canada or its members vis-à-vis long-distance rates causes a corresponding change in the policy role as well as in the beneficiaries of that role. As we shall see, this has been a prime source of concern for most provincially regulated telephone companies and consequently a point of serious friction in intergovernmental relations.

Telecommunications Regulation as Policing: Pre-1968

Although economic regulation of telecommunications in Canada can be said to have begun in 1892 when Bell Canada's Special Act was amended to require cabinet approval for increases in existing rates, such regulation in its fullest sense began in 1906 when responsibility for the regulation of telephone companies within federal jurisdiction was given to the Board of Railway Commissioners.[20] Shortly thereafter, provincial governments established or empowered regulatory agencies to regulate telephone companies within their jurisdiction with Saskatchewan, as noted earlier, being the sole exception to this trend until 1982.[21] Although different terms were used, with some variations in the powers granted to the regulators and in their exercise, there is general agreement that such regulation, regardless of jurisdiction, was essentially the same.[22] In our terms, the function of economic regulation was primarily to police the telephone companies. Indeed, such regulation prior to the 1960s can be said to represent the purest form of policing regulation.

To return to the concepts employed in Chapter 1, telephone regulation ought to be characterized as a policing function because of its decisional processes and especially because of its scope.

With respect to decisional processes, there can be no doubt that telephone regulators saw their role as reacting to, rather than initiating, actions by the telephone companies. In its first hearing on a Bell Canada rate-increase application, the board declared: "where a regulative tribunal's jurisdiction comes, as it always has done, after the development of a rate situation, the function of that tribunal is to regulate, not to initiate."[23] Two years later, this position was further elaborated by a commissioner who stated:

> It is not one of the functions of this Board to initiate a tariff for this or any telephone, or railway company. Its duty, generally, is to examine and pass upon, approve, or reject, tariffs proposed, having regard to whether, in the opinion of the Board, such are just and reasonable. . . . True, the Board has the power to reject, or amend a tariff, or direct another, but no duty is cast upon the Board to mould one suitable to various conditions and areas of traffic, dependent upon a multitude of conditions, as to which the Board has no evidence before it.[24]

As late as 1966, the board stated that ". . . regulation is and must be to a large degree *ex post facto*."[25] A measure of the consistency of the federal regulators' position on this is the fact that only once in the period 1906 to 1968 did the board, on its own motion, initiate an investigation or a hearing.[26]

Another basic characteristic of regulatory decisional processes that justified the claim to a policing function was its remedial nature. Regulators saw their role as providing relief or correcting specific problems, not in managing the firms or the industry. In 1927, for example, the federal regulator declared that "the function of the Board is one of corrective regulation, not of business management." In support of this position the board quoted a U.S. Supreme Court decision which stated that "the Commission is not the financial manager of the corporation, and it is not empowered to substitute its judgment for that of the directors of corporations . . . unless there is an abuse of discretion in that regard by the corporate officials."[27] In 1965 the board noted that it "has consistently held that its powers are regulative and corrective, and that they are not managerial. Thus it is necessary for the Board to review the company's actions from time to time . . . and to take whatever corrective action for the future may be necessary."[28] In 1970, the Canadian Transport Commission used these words almost verbatim to describe its role in exercising jurisdiction over the telephone companies.[29]

To provide the most persuasive evidence as to the policing function of telecommunications regulation prior to 1968, we need only examine the scope of such regulation. To do this we will employ the concepts of goals, structure and conduct of corporate behaviour introduced in Chapter 1.

Federal and provincial regulators had one major goal: ". . . to prevent carriers from using their monopoly position to extract excessive profits . . . ."[30] In this respect, although it is routinely stated that regulation is a substitute for competition, this is only partially true for telecommunications. More precisely, regulation in this industry pursued only a subset of the goals that are conventionally associated with competition. In particular, regulators did not perceive it to be their function to promote economic efficiency, progress or growth which are common goals ascribed by economists to a competitive system. If these goals were influenced by their efforts to control excessive profit taking, it was a happy coincidence but not a set objective. Given the regulatory goals in other sectors such as airlines and broadcasting, it is significant to note that there was no hint of exogenous goals for the regulatory system. As John McManus has noted, and his words are equally valid for provincial regulators, ". . . the record of the Board is clear evidence that the telecommunications firms under its control are not treated as 'chosen instruments.' There seems to have been little political pressure in the past towards achieving national policy goals through this industry."[31] The only possible challenge to this system arises from the system of cross-subsidies that developed in the pricing of telephone services. Although initially and for most of this period, as we shall discuss below, this system had an economic rationale, it has in more recent years assumed a broader public policy role, more akin to an exogenous objective in our terms.

In keeping with their very limited goals, regulators had little authority over the structure of the industry. In part, this was due to the fact that by 1906, when economic regulation effectively began, the principle of a territorial monopoly for each carrier had become established. Although there was, in the first 25 years after the introduction of the telephone, some competition between telephone companies in the same or overlapping territories, the industry quickly assumed the characteristics of a natural monopoly which it was to demonstrate until the 1960s.[32] Consequently, entry into the industry was not an issue and thus, when economic regulation was introduced, it was accepted that there was no regulatory role in shaping industry structure in this aspect. Nor was it assumed that the regulator had any role in preventing vertical integration, another central aspect of industry structure. This issue was relevant primarily to the regulation of Bell Canada and B.C.Tel, but the regulatory agency was given no jurisdiction over vertical integration per se. As the Board of Railway Commissioners stated in 1921, it was given no general supervisory power in regard to intercorporate relations.[33] This view was adopted by all of its successors, the last of which as late as 1970 made the following statement:

> The Canadian Transport Commission possesses no regulatory authority over the corporate structure of a regulated company or over its ownership. It may take the financial structure of a regulatory [sic] company into account, but only in relationship to its duty with respect to reasonable rates and charges; free from unjust discrimination or undue preference.[34]

One qualification to the preceding involves the regulator's supervisory role over the interconnection of non-competing systems. In 1908, the Board of Railway Commissioners was empowered to order interconnection of such systems and to establish terms for revenue allocation. A second qualification pertains to mergers and acquisitions. All regulatory agencies had some jurisdiction to determine if any mergers or acquisitions were in the public interest, although the federal regulator did not have such authority over Bell Canada. There is little evidence, except in some of the Atlantic Provinces, that they used this power to impose their view as to the appropriate structure of the industry. Most acquisitions, particularly those by Bell Canada, were routinely approved by provincial agencies if only because they promised significantly improved service for subscribers of the acquired companies. The only major exception was noted above, i.e., the action by the Nova Scotia legislature to limit Bell Canada's voting power within Maritime Tel & Tel. Finally, although there was one application in the 1950s that raised the possibility of entry into the industry, it was only in the 1960s that this emerged as a potentially significant issue. Such entry could involve alternative equipment (terminal interconnection or "foreign attachments" as they were then called) or alternative service providers (system interconnection). In 1968, at the end of this period, the federal regulator was given a supervisory role over the terms and conditions for terminal interconnection.[35] This was the beginning of a significant regulatory role in structural issues.

The clearest evidence of the policing role is to be found in the scope of regulatory control over corporate behaviour. The very precise limits of that control are summed up in a term used by the Canadian Transport Commission to describe the extent of its responsibilities: "toll jurisdiction."[36] As far as the CTC was concerned, its primary jurisdiction was to police the pricing behaviour of the telephone companies subject to federal regulation, seeing to it that telephone tolls were "just and reasonable" and free from "unjust discrimination or undue preference." The federal regulator had additional policing powers, particularly over system interconnection as noted above; and over capital stock issues.[37] It is instructive to note that the federal regulator routinely insisted on the very strict limits of its jurisdiction. It claimed, for example, that it had no "authority over the nature and quality of the services offered."[38] It also denied that it had control over the investment plans or construction plans of the carriers or over "the technical characteristics of telecommunications facilities."[39] As indicated above, the federal regulator denied it had jurisdiction over structural aspects of intercorporate relations, but it did assume that it should police such relations so as to determine that the interests of both shareholders and subscribers were not adversely affected. Consequently, in every rate case since 1919 the board and its successors have reviewed the prices charged the parent firms by their subsidiaries to see that they were not excessive.[40]

The policing role of federal regulation is demonstrated not only by the severely constrained scope of behaviour subject to scrutiny, but also by its reactive nature. We have already discussed this above, but it is worthwhile to note it again in this context. Although the regulators stressed their responsibility to police carrier pricing behaviour, they also emphasized that, unless specific forms of behaviour were deemed to be unacceptable, they would respect the prerogatives of corporate management. The regulatory agency, for example, opted not to interfere with management's right to define local calling areas unless discrimination resulted. Similarly, it left to management the discretion to develop the distinctions between residence and business subscribers. Finally, management, not regulator, decided to price on a flat rate rather than a measured basis for local exchange service.[41] In short, federal regulation was quintessential policing regulation with corporate management the primary economic decision maker and the regulatory agency concerned about a limited set of outcomes and supervising corporate behaviour to ensure that it abided by the rules to produce such outcomes.

It is difficult to characterize provincial regulation over a 70-year period, given the diversity of the provinces. Some authors have contended that, as long as corporate management stayed within the boundaries of acceptable behaviour, provincial regulators would respect and defer to management prerogatives.[42] According to this view, provincial regulation with its emphasis on just and reasonable rates served a policing function. Janisch and Huber, however, suggest that in the Atlantic Provinces at least, regulators played a more active, positive role as well. They point out that the provincial regulatory agencies were given a broader supervisory role over telephone companies than their federal counterpart. Moreover, they cite evidence concerning regulatory-mandated extension of service and regulatory encouragement of industry consolidation to support their view that regulators performed, on occasion, what we have described as a planning function.[43] In the Prairie Provinces, it is also worth noting that, while regulatory agencies did not play a planning role, provincial governments (through their ownership of the telephone companies) did seek to employ the telephone system to satisfy broader social and economic policy goals. However, the difference between such goals and those pursued by the private telephone companies in the rest of Canada may reflect only differences of degree and not of kind, given the generalized commitment to universal service.[44]

There are a number of general observations, relevant to more recent developments, that must be made about this period of telecommunications regulation. The first is that, notwithstanding the existence of regulation, however confined the regulatory role, the period was marked by the infrequency of regulatory proceedings. Given that the federal regulator defined itself in terms of a "toll jurisdiction," it is notable that between 1906 and 1968 there were only five rate proceedings for each of Bell Canada and B.C.Tel, and, for both companies, four of the proceedings were in the 20 years following 1949. The situation was not very different at the provincial level. According to a former official of Alberta Government Telephones, "until 1958 we had virtually no regulation in Alberta and our first rate hearing was not held until 1966."[45] In the Atlantic Provinces, Janisch and Huber report a total of 13 general rate cases prior to 1969, an average of four per company over the previous 60 years.[46] Before conclusions about regulatory "capture" are drawn, it is important to note that this period was not one in which the telephone companies would need to turn to their regulators for rate relief. It was in this period that telephone service witnessed the greatest growth as measured by availability of service. Such growth enabled the companies to develop significant economies of scale, which more than matched their revenue needs, except for the few instances when rate increase applications were filed. Another contributing factor was technological change, which further reduced the cost burden. Finally, the development of the TransCanada Telephone System and its revenue settlement plans, particularly in the 1950s and after, aided the financial position of the carriers such that the need for rate increases was minimized.

In the second place, it is also important to note that although prior to 1968, regulators were reactive, it is not accurate to assume they were passive to the demands of the telephone companies. At the federal level, McManus, while acknowledging the tendency to respect managerial prerogatives, cited a number of examples where the regulator challenged and changed corporate proposals.[47] Similarly, at the provincial level, there is evidence, particularly in the Atlantic Provinces, that the regulatory authorities did not simply rubber-stamp carrier requests nor did they hesitate to intervene, when requested by subscribers, on questions of quality of service. In Newfoundland, for example, the Board of Commissioners of Public Utilities rejected in 1965 an application for a general rate increase on the grounds that service was inadequate, and it was "unable to conceive of reasonable rates for inadequate service."[48]

Moreover, despite the paucity of proceedings, there is no evidence that the primary regulatory goal, namely the prevention of excessive profits, was not attained. In fact, the available evidence suggests most clearly that it was. Tables 3-8 and 3-9 demonstrate that the rate-of-return guidelines to which the then eight Telecom Canada companies were subject were effective as measured by both gross rates and return on net worth.

A third major observation pertains to the development of the Canadian telecommunications system prior to 1968. This system is generally acknowledged to be one that, in terms of availability, reliability, range of services and employment of advanced technology, has few equals. Moreover, one of the most distinctive features of this system, given the multitude of components, is that it is nationally integrated. For our purposes, the significance of the quality of the existing system is that it is the result of corporate, not government, decision making. The only qualification to this involves the indirect role that provincial governments played in the Prairie Provinces as owners of the telephone companies. The key point, though, is that quality of the telecommunications system reflected firm-led decision making. The achievements are all the more remarkable at the national level, for it has been corporate executives who have created the nationally integrated system through the TransCanada Telephone System (TCTS), now Telecom Canada. In the words of McManus, "the telecommunications industry in Canada is the only industry since the fur trade to have voluntarily constructed a link between East and West to the North of the Great Lakes without government intervention of some kind."[49] Prior to the creation of TCTS, national long-distance traffic had to go through the United States. TCTS's basic functions were to plan the construction of the system (ensuring, especially, compatibility), to unify rates and service offerings, and to divide revenues from traffic involving non-adjacent territories. As Carl Beigie has noted, "each of these functions is essential, and if the TCTS or something capable of performing these functions at least as well had not existed, it would have been impossible for Canada to maintain a position among the world's leaders in telecommunications services with its present ownership structure."[50]

The fact is that TCTS did exist as a result of industry initiative and consequently, corporate executives were responsible for planning the development of the system. Their achievements, which have been described as the product of "private sector cooperative federalism," could not have come easily. The disparate nature of the individual members as measured, for example, by size of company, extent of territory, regional differences and ownership, combined with the fact that the decision-making system required unanimous consent, must

TABLE 3-8 **Gross Rates of Return, 1956–68: Percentages**

Year	Newfoundland Telephone	NBTel	Maritime Tel & Tel	Bell Canada	MTS[a]	SASK TEL	AGT[b]	B.C.Tel
1956	10.6[c]	10.7	12.0	10.3	7.0	10.2	—	11.8
1957	9.3[c]	9.2	11.6	10.4	7.1	8.3	10.6	10.1
1958	9.3[c]	10.2	11.7	10.2	6.4	7.8	8.4	8.5
1959	8.9	11.8	11.9	11.7	6.3	8.3	7.5	11.2
1960	9.2	11.7	12.2	11.7	6.7	8.6	8.0	11.4
1961	9.4	11.3	12.5	11.9	6.6	9.8	7.7	12.3
1962	8.7	11.0	13.1	12.2	7.0	10.3	8.4	12.1
1963	7.7	11.2	11.6	12.1	7.1	10.2	7.9	12.5
1964	5.7	12.0	11.7	12.5	7.0	10.7	7.7	12.9
1965	6.6	12.3	11.7	12.8	7.6	11.7	7.6	13.6
1966	7.5	12.8	12.8	12.8	8.4	12.0	7.4	13.3
1967	11.7	12.6	13.0	13.0	8.5	12.5	8.9	12.7
1968	12.1	12.7	12.9	13.0	7.9	12.4	10.4	12.7

Source: Carl E. Beigie, "An Economic Framework for Policy Action," in *Telecommunications for Canada*, edited by H. Edward English (Toronto: Methuen, 1973), p. 151.

Note: Numerator consists of net operating income, inclusive of income taxes and exclusive of other taxes, and depreciation allowance. Denominator consists of gross plant and equipment.

a. Fiscal year from April 1 to March 31.

b. Fiscal year from April 1 to March 31 in the period 1956 to 1966; January 1 to December 31 in 1967 and 1968. The rate of return for the period April 1 to December 31, 1966 was 5.2 percent.

c. Numerator excludes all taxes other than income.

TABLE 3-9 Return on Net Worth, 1956–68: Percentages

Year	Newfoundland Telephone	NBTel	Maritime Tel & Tel	Bell Canada	B.C.Tel	MTS[a]	SASK TEL	AGT[b]
1956	7.9	6.6	8.1	7.0	7.6	8.7	16.1	—
1957	7.0	5.4	7.3	6.2	5.8	12.9	10.2	20.3
1958	7.4	5.8	7.7	6.2	4.9	3.6	6.4	12.7
1959	6.8	7.2	7.5	7.4	7.3	3.6	8.7	8.5
1960	7.0	7.5	7.8	7.2	6.8	3.6	11.6	9.7
1961	7.2	7.2	8.2	7.2	7.2	3.1	17.5	8.0
1962	5.4	7.0	8.0	7.2	7.0	4.7	19.8	10.5
1963	3.9	7.0	7.3	7.0	7.2	3.5	22.4	5.9
1964	0.5	8.0	7.5	7.4	7.5	1.1	25.4	3.1
1965	1.9	8.3	7.4	7.7	7.9	7.0	31.4	0.6
1966	0.7	8.2	8.9	7.5	7.8	12.9	30.6	(4.3)
1967	9.3	8.3	8.7	8.1	7.8	14.5	32.1	(0.3)
1968	7.2	7.8	8.5	8.2	8.2	8.1	28.5	11.0

Source: Carl E. Beigie, "An Economic Framework for Policy Action," in *Telecommunications for Canada*, edited by H. Edward English (Toronto: Methuen, 1973), p. 151.

Notes: ( ) = negative. Numerator consists of after-tax net income. Denominator consists of net worth (book value). For the three government-owned carriers, net worth has been estimated from initial capital investment plus retentions of net income for reinvestment.

a. Fiscal year from April 1 to March 31.

b. Fiscal year from April 1 to March 31 in the period 1956 to 1966; January 1 to December 31 in 1967 and 1968. The return on net worth for the period April 1 to December 31, 1966 was (13.3%).

have required as much diplomacy and skilful negotiation as is required in intergovernmental relations.

A further point that arises from the pre-1968 period concerns the system of cross-subsidies that developed. The existence of this system which, as noted, involves subsidies from business to residential users, urban to rural users and long-distance to local exchange users, does not challenge, in one important respect, our contention that in this period the policy objectives of regulation were very limited. In particular, our argument was that there was no significant use of regulation to pursue exogenous objectives, i.e., to employ the telecommunications system to satisfy policy goals external to that system. At first glance, a system of cross-subsidies would seem to contradict this assertion. The fact is, however, that such subsidies are premised on economic objectives. Discrimination between buyers of a service, in this case telephone subscribers, who exhibit different demand elasticities, is a widely accepted method of increasing the total number of subscribers. By increasing the number of subscribers, the overall cost of providing the service can be made affordable.[51] Thus, the growth of subscribers in the period prior to 1968 (and it was largely in this period that telephone service became universally available in Canada) was dependent on the system of cross-subsidization that was basic to the pricing of telephone service.

It does not follow, however, that a practice introduced for economic reasons cannot be transformed to satisfy other objectives. As we shall see, this is what has occurred with the telephone cross-subsidy system. Whatever its original rationale, it is now defended as well, or even primarily, on welfare grounds as a means of satisfying social policy objectives be they income assistance, maintenance of rural communities or regional development.[52] Moreover, what is particularly germane to our purposes is the interregional, intercompany aspect of the subsidy system. The present pricing system for long-distance services and the related Revenue Settlement Plan of Telecom Canada provides subsidies from users of one system for those of others. This is particularly true in the case of allocation of revenues for Canadian-American traffic where the bulk of this traffic originates within one territory, namely Bell Canada. Consequently, any suggestion of tampering with the pricing system can be expected to result in political conflicts not only among different subscribers, but also among different companies and their respective regulators. Such conflicts did not arise, by and large, in the pre-1968 period; to the extent that they did, they were resolved through the private corporate bargaining process within TCTS. After 1968, the conflicts became increasingly public and political.

The final point to be made about this period is one that the perceptive reader will have already noted. There has been no mention of intergovernmental politics, let alone conflict, involving the telecommunications industry prior to 1968. This is easily explainable: there were no conflicts and no need for intergovernmental relations. The telecommunications sector may have been one of the last vestiges of "watertight compartments" in Canadian federalism. Although by 1970 this view was already dated, the CTC reflected the pre-1968 reality when, in response to the telecommission request for comment on "the existing federal and provincial regulatory structure in Canada, and the interrelationships of its components," the commission submitted that it did not understand the last phrase:

> Federally incorporated companies are regulated by the Canadian Transport Commission and provincially incorporated companies are regulated by provincial regulatory bodies. The division of jurisdiction is quite clear and is exercised by the separate regulatory bodies.[53]

Prior to 1968, any of the interdependencies, the externalities and spillovers that arose from the nationally integrated telecommunications system were handled, and handled successfully, by telecommunications corporate decision makers. The success of the industry in the years leading up to 1968 in developing an efficient, economical, advanced and politically non-controversial (publicly at least) telecommunications system undoubtedly contributed to the self-confident assumption that what was true of the private sector could be true of the public and that "federal and provincial interests in telecommunications are complementary rather than conflicting, and afford ample opportunity for constructive cooperation by all governments in Canada."[54] The naïvete of this statement was soon apparent. Constructive cooperation was dependent in large part on decision making by corporate executives which, in turn, was dependent on the policing function of regulation. Any attempt to change that function could only lead to intergovernmental conflict as subsequent developments clearly demonstrate.

Telecommunications Regulation and the Attempt to Plan: 1968–84

The use of 1968 as a cutoff date is clearly arbitrary. Some of the forces leading to federal efforts to attempt to introduce a significant governmental planning role for the telecommunications sector were present earlier. Others did not gain any serious momentum until after 1968. Furthermore, although we shall contend that the planning exercise was a primary factor in causing the intergovernmental conflict (the only constant in a dramatically changing industry in the past 16 years) other forces were at work as well. In fact, the high degree of insulation of the industry from political forces and processes, so characteristic of telecommunications prior to 1968, and the correspondingly dominant role played by corporate officers in directing the development of the industry would have been eroded regardless of the intergovernmental conflict. Technological and economic forces contributed significantly to this process. Indeed, it is perhaps unlikely that the intergovernmental conflict would have been as acrimonious or as extended if such forces had not acted as catalysts. On the other hand, we would contend that the federal government's attempt to introduce federal planning in the telecommunications sector, while not sufficient to cause the intergovernmental conflict, was a necessary condition. This planning activity occurred at two levels, the departmental and the regulatory. In this section we shall analyze how such activity caused and provided the subsequent motor force for the intergovernmental conflict, but before doing so, it is necessary first to discuss briefly the impact of technology and economics.

In a number of respects, 1968 represents a watershed year in telecommunications. In the United States, it was the year of the "Carterphone" decision, one which, along with the "MCI" decision one year later, not only unleashed the forces of competition in telecommunications in the United States but also, in the process, began an extensive debate over fundamental principles that hitherto had determined both the provisioning of telecommunications services and the public policies that authorized them.[55] This debate soon washed over the borders of the United States into Canada and, indeed, into most of the industrialized western world.[56]

Prior to the "Carterphone" and "MCI" decisions in the United States, telecommunications policy had been based on a few integrated assumptions.[57] One of these has been that only one company can economically serve a single area and therefore, telephone service is best provided on a monopoly basis. A related assumption is that a single company should be responsible for providing end-to-end service. The third assumption is one just discussed, namely, that the pricing of telephone service should be based on value-of-service rather than cost-of-service pricing principles. The "Carterphone" and "MCI" decisions, and subsequent ones, subjected these assumptions to considerable reassessment. "Carterphone" led to the rejection of policies prohibiting the attachment of equipment other than that provided by the telephone company. Customers in the United States, encouraged by manufacturers and retailers as a result of "Carterphone," were able to attach a host of devices ranging from their own phones to mobile equipment and answering devices and, most importantly, switchboards and word and data processors that communicate with others. In fact, the American success of Northern Telecom is in no small measure due to the de-regulation of terminal equipment in the United States.[58]

The "MCI" and subsequently, the broader "specialized common carrier" decision led to the acceptance of competition among service providers, especially in the provision of long-distance services. In the

United States today, customers can choose among several companies. In addition, as a result of technological developments, a subset of customers, namely large users, can, and have chosen to "by-pass" the existing telephone network completely to provide their own long-distance services.[59] Such customers can use satellites, microwave, cellular mobile systems and broadband cable to serve their needs.

The most significant consequence for public policy is that the erosion of the traditional monopoly provision of both transmission and equipment undermines the principles of value-of-service pricing. Competition is largely, if not wholly, incompatible with such a system of pricing. Consequently, the cross-subsidization practices could not be continued in their traditional form. The challenges to such practices, however, have led to significant political battles in the United States pitting states against the federal government, Congress against the Federal Communications Commission and region against region.[60] Similar battles have ensued in Canada.

Coincidental with the turmoil embroiling the principles and practices of telephone regulation in the United States was another, perhaps even more revolutionary force that would have equally profound ramifications for Canada and Canadian policy makers. That force was the integration of communications and computers. This integration builds on the transformation in telecommunications resulting from satellite technology, fibre optics, lasers, electronic switching and digital technology along with equally important advances in computer technology and science. The convergence that results has been largely responsible for the belief that we are currently in the throes of an "information revolution" which will radically transform our societies and economies.[61]

These twin forces, the re-evaluation of telecommunications principles and the convergence of communications and computers, have been responsible, to a much larger degree for the dramatic shift in public policy in Canada, primarily at the federal level, toward the telecommunications sector. Prior to 1968 this sector, we have contended, was largely taken for granted; after 1968 it was to be given a "governmental embrace."

There were two key aspects to this embrace. The first was that as a result of the recognition of telecommunications as a vital, indeed, possibly lead sector of the social and economic infrastructure, it became commonplace to emphasize a significantly expanded range of telecommunications policy objectives. Indicative of this view was the popularity of the rhetoric which described telecommunications as "the nervous system of society" and as "the railways of the future." Equally important was the second aspect of this embrace: if telecommunications were so critical, their uncontrolled development could pose serious dangers to the Canadian economy and society, especially if external forces (particularly from the United States) gained undue influence. The measure of this aspect is found in the host of federal government sponsored studies which, in the words of two federal public servants, all reflected ". . . the same anxieties about the vulnerability of Canada to the information revolution."[62] Inevitably, therefore, we witnessed another episode of "defensive expansionism" as the federal government decided that, whatever the merits of the telecommunications system as it existed, it was too important to be left in the hands of its present managers. If telecommunications systems and services were so vital to the future development of Canada, according to this line of thinking, the federal government must assume, as it had in broadcasting, railways and airlines, the dominant role in shaping and planning that future. Unfortunately, in developing this approach, federal planners showed insufficient appreciation of the intergovernmental hurdles that would have to be overcome.

The first major indication of federal ambitions came in 1968 with the creation of the Department of Communications.[63] In some respects, despite its novelty, this was a rather innocuous act. Certainly there was nothing in the statute to indicate any major shift in the federal government's approach. The statute was a mere two pages and assigned the minister of communications federal powers not already assigned to other ministers. There was a short statement of the minister's functions which were to be rather mundane. He was, among other things, to:

- coordinate, promote and recommend national policies and programs with respect to communications services for Canada . . . ;
- promote the establishment, development and efficiency of communications systems and facilities for Canada; and
- assist Canadian communications systems and facilities to adjust to changing domestic and international conditions.[64]

The legislation was more notable for what it did not contain — neither new powers for the minister nor, especially, a statement of public policy that would govern the exercise of the federal government's powers in this field.

Such a statement would have been appropriate given that the government gave every indication that the creation of the new department heralded a new approach to telecommunications and particularly its role in this industry. In introducing the legislation, Prime Minister Trudeau noted that "we can foresee that the whole field of communications will be of growing importance to Canada and require increasing federal government involvement."[65] The proposed objective of that involvement was identified by the first minister of communications when he stressed the role of the planning section in the department:

> The purpose of planning will not be regulation for regulation's sake but regulation, where and when needed, for the public good. We intend to evolve a national communications plan and a national communications

policy to integrate and rationalize all systems of communications whether those of today such as telephones, microwave relays, telex, TWX, telegraph and the Post Office, or those of tomorrow: communication satellites; sophisticated information retrieval systems linking computers which exchange and store information of all kinds; waveguides; lasers, and on up to the "wired city" of tomorrow.[66]

This was a clear statement of the government's intention to plan the telecommunications system and to employ regulation as the primary planning instrument. Subsequently, in 1977, when the government introduced legislation detailing a comprehensive policy statement, the centrality of regulation remained constant. In this bill, the government declared that ". . . the telecommunication policy for Canada . . . can best be achieved by providing for . . . the regulation of telecommunications undertakings over which the Parliament of Canada has legislative authority."[67]

There are two important aspects to this declaration of the government's intentions. The first is that at no time in the debate did any member of the government attempt to explain, in any detail, why planning — and planning by the federal government in particular — was necessary. There was no detailed statement of deficiencies in the present system. The minister limited himself to the comment that "telecommunication legislation and regulation as it now exists is, to a considerable degree, uncoordinated and in certain areas inadequate."[68] Nor was there any effort to justify the emphasis on regulation as the primary instrument for attaining the government's objectives.

Despite the radical nature of the federal government's plans for the telecommunications industry and their implications for both carriers and most of the provincial governments, there was no immediate provincial response. In larger part, any response was delayed by the government's decision to undertake a comprehensive study on the present state and future prospects of telecommunications in Canada.[69] The intergovernmental conflicts began, or at least became public when, following the completion of this study, the government released a position paper entitled "Proposals for a Communications Policy for Canada."[70] This paper made it clear that, henceforth, exogenous objectives would dominate communications policy. It stated that the objectives of such policy should be to:

- safeguard, enrich, and strengthen the cultural, political, social and economic fabric of Canada;
- contribute to the flow and exchange of regional and cultural information;
- reflect Canadian identity and the diversity of Canadian cultural and social values;

- contribute to the development of national unity; and
- facilitate the orderly development of telecommunications in Canada, and the provision of efficient and economical systems and services at just and reasonable rates.[71]

There was a significant inconsistency, however, in the federal proposals. At the same time that it was proposing to use the telecommunications system, via regulation, to pursue a host of external objectives, the federal government was also suggesting that it might favour the introduction of competition. It did so when it suggested that some services "might perhaps better be provided in the public interest under competitive conditions."[72] In addition, the policy paper intimated that new entrants might be permitted because this "kind of competition can be regarded as a valuable stimulus to innovation and the use of new technology in response to developing needs of users." Furthermore, following the lead of "Carterphone," the paper suggested that the federal regulatory body could be empowered to allow interconnection of subscriber-owned equipment.[73]

These two components, an expanded set of objectives federally imposed, and the introduction of competition, were guaranteed to provoke widespread provincial opposition. As additional stimulus were the federal comments on the existing system for regulating interprovincial long-distance rates and services. The green paper noted that:

> Since there has been no co-ordinated authority over the several undertakings that together provide telephone service to all parts of Canada, the recognition of a "national dimension" in the network as a whole has been left largely to the discretion of the TransCanada Telephone System.[74]

The position paper, while acknowledging that "a commendable degree of coordination and standardization has been achieved by TCTS . . . ," then asserted that "there has in the past been little opportunity for expression of the public interest, in a national sense, in the orderly development of telephone systems in Canada."[75] The need, therefore, was "to ensure a proper equilibrium between national and regional interests in the regulation of all telecommunications carrier services."[76] As in 1969, no specific definition of the "national dimension" or "the public interest in a national sense" was provided. Nor was there any attempt to justify changes of the magnitude proposed by providing evidence of the inadequacies of the present regulatory system.

Given the radical restructuring of the regulatory responsibilities involved, as well as the reorientation in the basic objectives of regulation, combined with the failure to provide any serious explanation of why change on the scale proposed was necessary, the universal provincial opposition could hardly have surprised the federal government. At least a year before the policy paper was issued, an interprovincial conference of communications ministers had approved a resolution stating that interconnection was a provincial, not a federal, responsibility. When the federal government called a federal-provincial conference in 1973, the conflicts burst into the open. The provinces' approach was to demand jurisdictional changes, i.e., to deny the federal government any significant decision-making power. For its part, the federal government refused to discuss such matters and sought to confine the discussion to administrative mechanisms and consultative procedures. This conference, the first of its kind, broke up within a few hours.

Nor was there much success at subsequent conferences in 1975. In the meantime, the federal government had issued a new policy paper which, while not abandoning the essential federal positions, sought to placate the provinces with more formal consultative arrangements.[77] This accomplished little. Provinces invoked a rationale for provincial jurisdiction similar to that of the federal government. Communications policy was vital to the provinces, they argued, because they "have responsibilities in the social, cultural, educational and economic spheres." Federal proposals were unacceptable not only because they "denigrate responsibilities historically exercised by a number of provinces, but also because they "do not recognize increased provincial decision-making." Building on these arguments, the provinces put forward a "provincial consensus position" which called for not only an acceptance of the status quo for those provinces which regulated carriers, but also a transfer of jurisdiction over Bell Canada and B.C.Tel to Quebec, Ontario and British Columbia. In addition, "questions such as development plans of federally regulated carriers, standards, frequency spectrum management, use of satellites and intercarrier competition" would be submitted to a federal-provincial conference subject to federal-provincial agreement. The federal government rejected these proposals because they "would effectively remove the Federal Government from a substantial role in telecommunications."[78]

With the collapse of the July 1975 conference, intergovernmental negotiations on telecommunications issues effectively ended. It is true that there were two intergovernmental conferences as well as numerous bilateral meetings, ministerial and official, in the years following. It is also true that there were several intergovernmental working groups and task forces which met and issued reports in the post-1975 period. It is also the case that in 1977 and 1978, the federal government gave first reading, on three occasions, to legislative proposals which, on the face of it, incorporated all the features to which the provincial governments had taken objection. Finally, it is true that, in the 1980 round of constitutional discussions, the subject of communications was on the agenda. The provinces advocated a position essentially the same as their 1975 joint position, which the federal government rejected, although it also suggested that it was willing to accept a two-tier system of regulation, whereby all provinces would regulate intraprovincial telecommunications with the federal government having jurisdiction over interprovincial and international telecommunications matters. The provinces summarily rejected this proposal. Despite all this activity, which seemed to have taken on a life of its own, there was little movement. The provinces assumed that they had successfully defeated any federal desire for planning. This appears to be the case despite the 1977–78 legislative proposals to which the provinces did not even react (unlike the case in 1969), assuming that its policy statement was largely rhetoric and that the government's heart was not in its proposals. That this was a correct assumption was established by the failure of the government, despite its majority, to proceed beyond first reading on three occasions.

To suggest that intergovernmental negotiations effectively ended in 1975 is not to argue that intergovernmental conflict ceased. In several important respects it increased. The difference, however, was that now the source of the conflict was not the planning proposals of the federal department but the policing and planning activities of the federal regulatory agency. Complementing the decline in the federal government's fervour for planning as a cause of reduced intergovernmental tension was the search by the provincial governments for allies within the federal government, particularly in the Department of Communications against what many of the former adversaries came to regard as a common foe, the federal regulatory agency, the Canadian Radio-television and Telecommunications Commission (CRTC). The CRTC had emerged as a significant actor in the telecommunications sector in 1975, when jurisdiction over telecommunications was transferred to it from the Canadian Transport Commission.[79]

The CRTC was not a popular agency among provincial governments prior to the 1975 transfer. In fact, of all federal regulatory agencies, it was the least popular because it was perceived to be the least sympathetic to provincial interests or claims.[80] It did little after 1975 to assuage provincial concerns. In 1976, after a federal-Manitoba agreement had been signed on the subject of cable hardware ownership, the CRTC issued decisions which reminded the signatories that it was bound by its statutes, not intergovernmental agreements.[81] In 1977, the CRTC ruled that Telesat Canada's application to become a member of the TransCanada Telephone System would not be in the public interest. This application came only after Telesat had completed difficult negotiations with the other members of TCTS and had obtained the federal government's approval. The CRTC decision caused concern for all members of TCTS, but it particularly irked the provincial governments, which owned three of the members of TCTS, because they saw it as a further example of CRTC intrusion into policy matters. While the decision was successfully appealed to the federal cabinet, the CRTC's response did little to encourage either provincial governments or the members of the TCTS. The commission issued a press release declaring that it was "convinced that as a minimum, a much fuller review of the operations, finances and practices of TCTS and its individual members will be required than has ever been the case before."[82] Within a year, the commission ordered a wide-ranging hearing on TCTS rates, which is discussed below.

In 1975, when the legislation was before the House of Commons creating the new CRTC, the minister described the move as mere "housekeeping" introduced to tidy up the federal regulatory system.[83] That the regulatory agency did not perceive the action in the same light, and that the provinces now faced a much more formidable, and obdurate, proponent of regulatory planning, became very evident within a few short months of the proclamation of the act of transfer. In July 1976, in a public statement ostensibly on "procedures and practices," the CRTC declared that the public interest requires that telecommunications services "should be responsive to public demand over as wide a range as possible, and equally responsive to social and technological change."[84] Although no change had been made in its enabling legislation, the CRTC proclaimed that it would not be bound by its predecessor's rather narrow interpretation of its "toll jurisdiction":

> The principle of "just and reasonable" rates is neither a narrow nor a static concept. As our society has evolved, the idea of what is just and reasonable has also changed, and now takes into account many considerations that would have been thought irrelevant 70 years ago, when regulatory review was first instituted. Indeed, the Commission views this principle in the widest possible terms and considers itself obliged to continually review the level and structure of carrier rates to ensure that telecommunications services are fully responsive to the public interest.[85]

The full extent of the reorientation of federal regulation needs to be appreciated. In terms of decisional processes, the CRTC, in its 1976 statement and in subsequent decisions, indicated that it would not be simply reactive but that it intended to play an initiating role. It proposed, for example, not to rely on rate applications alone but to hold general "issue hearings" on such matters as service quality and priorities, interconnection and intercorporate relations.[86] In 1978, the commission solicited applications from cable licencees for permission to use their systems to provide non-programming services.[87] Both of these actions also show that, rather than assuming a remedial role, the commission conceived a more appropriate role for itself as being issue oriented, problem solving. Subsequently, in its decision making on individual applications, it provided a number of examples that demonstrated such a role. These included:

- the development of quality of service standards;
- the study of the adequacy and location of pay telephones;
- the requirement that Bell Canada undertake a feasibility study on budget telephone service;

- the requirement that Bell propose a program for the installation of digital technology and direct distance dialling in remote communities;
- the introduction of affirmative action programs concerning staffing and language usage for northern communities;
- the requirement that Bell study the merits of a separate rate structure for remote northern areas that would include social and economic considerations relevant to the area; and
- the request that Bell review various approaches to establishing rate structures for contract primary service which recognize the distinction between small and large businesses.[88]

More generally, in the scope of its decision making, the CRTC indicated that it was rejecting a predecessor's view that its role was to regulate "particular companies and not utilities in the abstract."[89] The CRTC's approach, while not "utilities in the abstract," was a shift away from firm-specific regulation and was now more clearly industry- or system-oriented. This approach was undoubtedly derived from its broadcasting mandate which required it to regulate and supervise not simply individual companies, but also members of a "single system."[90] The CRTC also demonstrated that, unlike its predecessor, it would pursue not only a wider set of distributional objectives via regulation, but other goals as well, such as intra-firm and system efficiency and productivity.

A number of comments need to be made about the preceding claim that the CRTC infused regulation with a planning objective. In the first place, in some respects, the CRTC's expansive view of its regulatory role was, in the jargon of the economist, simply designed to distinguish its product from what went before it. According to this argument, the CRTC rhetoric should be distinguished from its behaviour. While there is a certain element of validity to this view, the record does show that CRTC regulation is, in many respects, fundamentally different in process, scope and objective from that of its predecessor. To the extent that this claim is accepted, it is argued that CRTC regulation does not so much constitute planning as it does updated policing, more in tune with the demands of the times. Again, there is considerable merit in this position. Clearly, as some provincial agencies had demonstrated more than a decade earlier, consideration of quality of service and investment programs as part of a determination of "just and reasonable" rates is not undue interference in managerial prerogatives, however traditional, nor do they in themselves constitute planning. The fact is, however, that these were neither isolated nor incremental extensions of regulatory scope. The CRTC, acting under the *Railway Act* of 1906, rejected the traditional limited, negative, proscriptive role of its predecessor and assumed an expanded, positive and prescriptive role. For us, this constituted more than a change in degree. Telecommunications regulation was fundamentally transformed from a policing into a planning instrument.

Our objective, of course, is not to criticize such a transformation but to relate it to our basic thesis, i.e., that it increased intergovernmental conflict. In itself, such a change would not have significant, direct impact on provincial governments. Nor would it, in principle, cause anything but possible expressions of sympathy for their federally regulated brethren from provincially regulated telephone companies. However, the fact is that the change in federal regulation in both aspects, i.e., more activist policing as well as planning, did have significant direct and indirect impacts on both provincial governments and provincially regulated telephone companies. Consequently, whereas the 1968–75 period was dominated by provincial efforts to prevent or control federal departmental planning efforts, in the post-1975 period, the focus of concern and conflict shifted to federal regulatory planning.

Provincial governments and provincial telephone companies began to worry almost immediately about the new federal regulatory regime and its implications for them. In 1976, CNCP filed an application for interconnection to Bell Canada's telephone system similar to that awarded to "MCI" in the United States in 1969. This was approved in 1979.[91] In 1980, following an application by Bell Canada, and then in 1982, upon its own motion, the CRTC liberalized the regulations governing the attachment of customer-owned equipment to the systems of federally regulated carriers.[92] Perhaps even more important for provincial interests was the announcement, in 1978, that applications by Bell Canada and B.C.Tel for increases in TCTS rates would be subject for the first time to a full public hearing. It is worth noting that, although only federally regulated carriers were directly involved, the CRTC in its list of issues to be examined did not propose to confine the scope of the hearing to them. The seven issues to be addressed were:

1. Whether the settlement procedures employed by the TCTS member companies are fair and reasonable and in the best interests of subscribers and the public.
2. Whether the rates charged on a cross-Canada basis for each of the TCTS services, including those of Telesat Canada, are just and reasonable.
3. Whether the terms or restrictions upon which services or facilities are offered by the TCTS members, including Telesat Canada, are reasonable and do not confer an unjust advantage on any person or company.
4. Whether the relative treatment by TCTS of competitive and non-competitive services is just and reasonable.
5. Whether the TCTS construction program is reasonable, and whether the information generated and employed in the planning of TCTS facilities and services is appropriate and sufficient.
6. Whether TCTS including Telesat Canada, is sufficiently responsive to

the demand for the transmission of programming and other information services at a reasonable cost.
7. What the information requirements of the regulatory agency should be in regard to future TCTS rate cases.[93]

Although there was no unanimity among the provinces, most of them expressed great concern about these regulatory initiatives. As representatives of provincially based interests, provincial governments shared the concerns of their telephone companies about the possible erosion of telephone revenues that, they claimed, would result from these decisions. Whether they owned the telephone companies or simply regulated them, provincial governments claimed there would be a negative impact on provincial telephone systems and, particularly, on the cross-subsidization system for local and rural telephone subscribers. As policy makers, either directly or indirectly via provincial regulation, provincial governments feared that they would have to bear the costs that federal regulatory actions were imposing on them. Aside from potential revenue losses and the political repercussions, provincial governments were concerned, as were their telephone companies, with the spillover effects for their jurisdictions of federal decisions regarding policies on system interconnection and terminal attachment. The fear was that the route of diffusion for competition was from Washington and the Federal Communications Commission through Ottawa and the CRTC to provinces and their regulatory agencies. Although this has not proven to be the case with system interconnection which, to date, is limited to federally regulated carriers, it has happened in varying degrees in the area of attachment of customer-owned equipment despite the most persistent efforts on the part of some provinces to prevent such practices.[94]

The most important reason for provincial opposition to federal regulatory actions was their fear that control over the development of basic policies affecting all telecommunications carriers, not simply the federally regulated, was passing into the hands of the federal government. In other words, they perceived that what had been an industry in which corporate (public and private) executives had exercised dominant control was being transformed into a federally controlled industry. This was a particularly important concern for the Prairie Provinces which owned their telephone companies; it was no less a concern for the Atlantic Provinces, and, indeed, it was a concern for the three provinces whose major carriers were subject to federal regulation and over which they exercised no control. Quebec, for example, opposed the CNCP application partly because it "risked compromising the aims of Quebec in the development of communications."[95] The only significant breaks in provincial opposition to federal decisions came, first, in the CNCP application, which British Columbia supported, while Ontario, reflecting the political cross-pressures it was confronting, endorsed partial acceptance because "complete denial would constitute an unsatisfactory reconciliation of the public policy goals."[96] The second break came in the TCTS decision where Ontario, Quebec and British Columbia, presumably because they believed subscribers in their provinces to be the source of monies for cross-subsidies, argued against them.

Given the consequences that provincial governments believed would befall them in their various roles as a result of federal regulatory decisions, especially with the emergence of federal dominance in policy making for the industry as a whole, they were particularly concerned that such a role should be exercised by an independent federal regulatory agency. The record of negotiations had given the provinces considerable confidence that they could prevent federal planning at least at the political level. Having won the battle at this level, they found it most troublesome that they might lose the war to an independent agency. They fought back on two fronts. Before the regulatory agency, they urged either denial of any application that might significantly change the status quo or they sought to persuade the agency that it should abstain from deciding on the issues. This position was most clearly advanced by the spokesman for the governments of the Atlantic Provinces in the CNCP case and concurred in by all the provinces except British Columbia and Ontario:

> We express our deep concern that your Commission is placed in the position of hearing and deciding a matter fundamental to the public interest while our governments, provincial and federal, are discussing but have not resolved policy respecting intercarrier competition. That the regulation of all telecommunications carriers in Canada are performed by the ten provinces and the federal government and therefore national policy must consist of harmonious and compatible federal and provincial policies. . . . [97]

In response, the CRTC adopted the position that, while it should be mindful of the impact of its decision on other jurisdictions, it had a "duty to decide" and to fail to do so would not be "desirable in the public interest or indeed lawful."[98]

When this tack failed, indeed simultaneously, the provinces sought to arrive at intergovernmental agreements. As mentioned previously, a certain abatement of intergovernmental conflicts came at about the same time as these major applications began to emerge or to be heard. The two levels of government sought to develop, through negotiation, acceptable policies on such matters as competition and terminal attachment but without any significant degree of success. They were more successful on another directly related matter, namely, the independence of the regulatory agency to make public policies. Provinces had long argued that such a policy-making role was singularly inappropriate, and they were joined in this position by successive federal communications ministers.

As early as 1973 in the green paper, the federal government had announced its intention to subject the CRTC to a greater degree of political control on policy matters. As time passed, this intention became even more resolute in the face of CRTC actions and decisions that intruded on intergovernmental negotiations. By 1976, the federal minister was echoing the provincial line that it was not "acceptable for a non-elected body to create major irritants in our relations with Government to have no control over them."[99] Consequently, agreement was reached that the cabinet would be authorized, in new telecommunications legislation, to issue binding "policy directives" to the CRTC. Despite this agreement, the federal government was unable, as indicated, to proceed with its legislative proposals and the CRTC, by its precedent-making decisions on system interconnection, terminal attachment and then interprovincial rates and services, annexed a large part of the policy-making territory.

One final point needs to be made regarding CRTC decisions and their policy impacts. We have contended that, in the post-1976 period, intergovernmental conflict was particularly intense because provincial governments feared that the federal regulatory agency was going both to supplant the industry and to pre-empt the provincial governments (and the federal government) as the primary, indeed dominant, policy maker. In short, they feared not only federal dominance but particularly, the dominance of an independent federal agency in decision making. It is true that they would have objected to such a development even if the federal regulatory objective was only to update its policing role because of the inevitable spillover for their jurisdictions and so for them in their various roles. What made the conflict more intense, however, was their collective fear that the CRTC, which had been given a planning, managerial role for the broadcasting sector, intended to assume, with or without a new legislative mandate, the same role in telecommunications. Based on the record of its policy statements and initiatives vis-à-vis federally regulated carriers on matters which had had little spillover effect for them, provincial carriers and provincial governments were convinced that they faced the spectre of federal planning when the CRTC turned to applications of industry-wide significance. In the decisions that caused most provincial concern, the CRTC indicated that it had considered a broad range of policy objectives such as "innovation in the telecommunications industry, and in Canadian business generally," "efficiency in telecommunications systems" and "optimal allocation of resources taking account of geographic differences," nevertheless, the grounds for such decisions could be construed as constituting a policing regulatory role.[100] The point to be made, of course, is that for provincial governments, regulatory planning, real or spectre, was a threat to be fought.

Conclusions

When one examines the telecommunications industry from a public policy perspective, three general conclusions stand out for most of the past century. The first is that corporate, not public, executives dominated decision making. If there was ever an industry that was completely firm-led in its development, it was telecommunications. Secondly, regulation was introduced to satisfy very explicit and restricted public policy objectives. The function of regulation was to prevent monopoly providers of telephone service from extracting monopoly profits from their subscribers. In our terminology, the function of regulation was to police the telephone companies. Thirdly, there were no intergovernmental disputes or conflicts involving the telecommunications sector. Telecommunications services were regulated in watertight compartments, perhaps the last industry in Canada to be so treated.

All of this changed dramatically in the period beginning in 1968. Before this time, telecommunications had been a peripheral responsibility of a regulatory agency. In 1968 the federal government created a Department of Communications with a mandate to create "a national communications plan and a national communications policy to integrate and rationalize all systems of communications. . . ." The federal government proposed to give telecommunications a "governmental embrace" so as to employ the industry to pursue a broad range of public policy objectives. Moreover, it proposed to use regulation as its planning instrument in order to attain these goals.

For the most part, prior to 1968, provincial governments, like their federal counterparts, ignored the telephone industry. The industry was performing admirably, and provincial regulatory agencies appeared to be effective policemen. In terms of their roles as representatives, as owners and as policy makers, the telecommunications industry posed few problems for provincial governments. The federal planning proposals threatened all of this. By proposing to supplant corporate decision makers as the primary goal setters for the industry, the federal government threatened the interests of provincial governments. For the three that owned telephone companies, federal proposals threatened to undermine their financial health and, hence, their capacity to achieve the public policy goals set by their owners. This was of equal concern for those provinces which did not own but which regulated telephone companies. These provinces felt compelled to represent both the interests of the telephone companies and the interests of subscribers who had benefited from industry policy making, especially the majority: the residential telephone users. Finally, although provincial governments had made few demands on the industry in their roles as policy makers, federal proposals, if implemented, would effectively pre-empt such a possibility.

The watertight compartments burst in 1968, creating a flood of intergovernmental conflict. The conflicts became particularly acrimonious and difficult to resolve when, with the apparent weakening of the federal government's resolve to plan the industry in the face of universal provincial opposition, the federal regulatory agency appeared to be willing to pick up the torch in defiance of the provinces and, at times, its own government. If provincial governments were not prepared to countenance federal government-led decision making for the telecommunications industry, the possibility that the agent of such decision making would be independent, to a significant though not absolute degree, was anathema to them. The result was that the regulatory process was embroiled in the intergovernmental process with neither being significantly improved.

It must be emphasized that 1968 was important in another key respect. It represents the emergence of external forces, technological and economic, which would call into question existing public policies and political relationships in the telecommunications sector. The 1960s thus represented the need to re-evalute and reconstitute public policy in telecommunications. In 1984, at neither the federal nor the provincial level have we witnessed the emergence of such policies in Canada. Sixteen years after promising a plan and a policy at the federal level, telecommunications is still regulated by the 1906 *Railway Act*. The provinces are no better off. Telecommunications thus represents a case in which intergovernmental conflict over federal regulatory planning not only misdirected our policy efforts, but also sapped our political will. Instead of the "wired city," we are left with the Gordian knot.

Chapter 4

Capital Markets, Regulation and Industrial Adjustment

Introduction

In contrast to most primarily industrialized states, capital or securities markets in Canada are, for the most part, regulated below the national level.[1] Regulating at the provincial level, however, does not suggest any diminution in the importance of capital markets for channelling capital to private and public industrial interests. In fact, as we shall show, Canada, much like the United States and the United Kingdom, and in contrast to other industrialized countries such as Germany, France and Japan, depends on capital markets to create investment and provide for industrial adjustment.

Capital markets and their regulators, however, represent a part of a larger institutional structure — the national financial system.[2] By this term we mean the complex of institutions, financial intermediaries, markets and regulators that constitute the means of transforming savings into investment. It is difficult, if not impossible, to examine securities markets and regulation without describing in some manner the larger national financial system. This broader approach to examining securities regulation is dictated, in part, by contemporary events. At present, there are three public inquiries concerned with aspects of the national financial system which may have a strong bearing on securities regulation: the Ontario Securities Commission (OSC) hearing in the fall of 1984 on financial services, particularly on the issue of ownership of the securities industry;[3] the Ontario government task force, established in January of 1984 to examine the financial industry and the advisability of maintaining separate institutions to service the capital markets;[4] the federal government's MacLaren Committee on the changing functions of institutions such as banks and near-banks and the need for revision of federal regulatory regimes.[5] These task forces and hearings are themselves the result of efforts by financial industry actors to diversify and provide services that have, until now, remained the preserve of distinct segments of the financial services sector. Thus, events make it increasingly impractical to examine just securities markets and their regulators.

An examination of the national financial system in general is important, in order to assess the critical institutional component of a nation's capacity to meet changing world competitive industrial pressures. John Zysman has argued persuasively in his recent book, *Government, Markets and Growth*, that national financial systems are an institutional parameter setting one critical limit on a nation's capacity to reindustrialize.[6] As he puts it, "The arrangement of the markets for finance helps shape the choices a government confronts, thus influencing the policies it adopts and the political process by which industrial change occurs."[7] Increasingly, industrial adjustment is the central element of national economic survival. It would be remiss, therefore, to ignore the wider context of capital markets and securities regulation.

Having said this, however, let us hasten to add that a thorough examination of the entire national financial system is beyond the scope of this chapter. At best we can only highlight certain aspects of this enormously complex institutional environment. Our tentative conclusions must be seen in this light; greater certainty must await a far more detailed examination of all the structural and process elements of the national financial system, something well beyond the scope of this chapter. Nonetheless, as will become evident, many of the same forces that are at work in the larger national financial system are chronicled in securities regulation and in our other two case studies.

This case study chapter, then, is really divided into two major sections. The first broadly describes Canada's national financial system. Using Zysman's three contrasting models of national financial systems, we compare Canada's financial services sector, market, mixed regulatory environment and direct governmental financial programs and institutions with other industrialized countries. When viewed against Zysman's three ideal type constructs of national financial systems — credit-based price-administered systems, credit-based institution-dominated systems and capital-market-based systems — the Canadian system fits more closely the capital-market-based financial system. It thus appears closer to the American financial system than either the French and Japanese credit-based price-administered systems or the hypothesized German bank-dominated credit-based system. Nevertheless, the Canadian capital-market-based system shows certain deficiencies that make Canada's system appear less capital-market-based than the U.S. structure. In fact, the institutional government-business-economic linkages create distortions and inconsistencies. In turn, such distortions and inconsistencies suggest difficulties in coping with industrial adjustment in Canada.

The identification of Canada's national financial system as capital-market-based provides the rationale for the chapter's second focus — the capital markets and securities regulation. Though the financial services industry is a mixed regulatory environment, the capital markets direct (the dealer and agency markets and the brokerage industry) have been provincially regulated for a significant period. Both Ontario and Quebec, which maintain the most developed markets and regulate the bulk of dealers and brokers, have developed highly sophisticated regulatory regimes. Securities regulation in both provinces is supervised through provincial regulatory agencies: the Ontario Securities Commission (hereinafter the OSC), the Commission des valeurs mobilières du Québec (hereinafter the CVMQ) and specialized regulatory organizations (SROs). Though securities regulation takes place at the provincial level in contrast to our other case studies, our examination in this chapter reveals similar patterns of regulatory evolution: analysis of provincial capital-markets regulation reinforces many of the conclusions reached earlier in our airline and telecommunications analysis.

Much as at the federal level, economic regulation has become a major tool of economic management. Provincial economic regulation has evolved beyond narrow policing functions and, as with federal economic regulation, this evolution has progressed from policing terms to broad planning and political ones. As noted in an earlier study of the OSC, for example, the commission has shifted from being a largely quasi-adjudicative agency concerned with policing, to being more markedly a planning and rule-making administrative body.[8] Moreover, economic development objectives on the part of provincial governments, particularly in Quebec, have resulted in the creation and implementation of significant policies aimed at the restructuring of the capital markets and the financial services industry under provincial jurisdiction. As a consequence, efforts to evolve uniform statutes and regulations governing the capital markets have been interrupted. Today, greater challenges than ever before face interprovincial regulators: Quebec has forged ahead with plans to alter, where jurisdictionally possible, the financial services industry. Under the banner of improved competition, the Quebec government has moved unilaterally to de-regulate the financial services sector.

The changes in regulatory environments, approved and contemplated, appear to be a complex interaction of competitive pressures and a technological imperative. The competitive pressures just mentioned are themselves a complicated mixture of provincial political objectives and evolving economic forces within the financial services industry. As for the technological imperative, it is the building "knowledge revolution" evidenced particularly by the growing importance of computers in the securities markets. The result of these forces interacting, however, is a jockeying for advantage by the two major regulatory environments, Ontario and Quebec. Friction between these two regulatory regimes has been limited to date, yet the complicated interaction of political objectives, capital market dominance by Ontario, and impending technological change portend a potentially highly fractious interprovincial regulatory environment.

This examination reveals, also, that the interprovincially regulated capital markets and a mixed-jurisdiction national financial system may be inadequate in the context of these significant changes. The current examination, by various groups, of financial services, and the unilateral changes by Quebec to its financial institutions, have been done at the expense of any thorough discussion of the broader national institutional context. Equally, discussion over the abandonment of traditional barriers among the four pillars (banking, trusts, insurance and securities industries) have been carried on with little attention paid to their ultimate impact on directing national industrial adjustment. It appears that these financial service changes are being considered with little critical assessment of their impact on the vitality of capital markets and their ability or inability to serve Canadian industrial capital needs. It may be that the real failure of interprovincial regulation over capital markets and mixed regulation over the national financial system is that such questions as those just noted are difficult if not impossible to deal with, both jurisdictionally and politically.

Canada's National Financial System

Industrial Strategies and the National Financial System

Like other industrialized countries in North America, Europe and Asia since the Second World War, Canada has become deeply involved in economic management. Though policy mixes have differed substantially, all governments have set economic policies to expand employment and productivity and to ease the swings in their economic cycles.[9] As a result the Canadian government, like so many others, finds itself with a vastly expanded universe of social and economic programs.[10] The tools employed to implement programs have proven to be correspondingly numerous. They range from traditional tax, monetary and tariff tools to the ownership of companies in the infrastructure industries, such as transportation and energy. In addition, there is a range of new tools including unemployment insurance, procurement policies, loan guarantee strategies and export loans. As has been pointed out earlier, regulation, especially economic regulation, is also a prominent instrument guiding governmental policy. Through both independent regulatory agencies and departmental bureaus, regulators have fashioned the development of numerous sectors of the Canadian economy.

The expansion of the governmental role in Canada, it should not be forgotten, has occurred at both federal and provincial levels. In the 1960s and 1970s, as the concept of province building took hold, provincial governments joined in economic management with almost as wide a range of tools as the federal government.[11] As an example, in these decades, provincial and federal governments both became involved in industrial development — industrial assistance — as these broad developmental policies have been tagged by Allan Tupper.[12] The maturing of the global international trade and monetary systems fashioned at Bretton Woods and in subsequent trade negotiations, largely at the insistence of the United States, strengthened interdependence.[13] As a result, however, international competition became a domestic concern as goods from abroad began to strain less competitive industries, creating pressures throughout the industrialized world, including Canada and the United States. Textiles, shoes and consumer electronics for example, and even North America's seemingly untouchable industries like automobiles and steel found themselves increasingly threatened by European, Japanese and other Asian products. Both levels of government, cooperatively or alone, became involved in responding to these economic sector pressures.

In North America, the increasing success of external competitors focussed attention on the role the relevant governments had played in engineering these economic miracles.[14] The Europeans, especially the French, and the Japanese were examined in great detail in order to understand and to replicate, where possible, the directive role that government had played. By the mid-1970s even the Americans, who were the most opposed to the directive and intrusive role of government, were advocating reindustrialization.[15] In Canada, a wide range of industrial assistance policies had been put in place, in no small measure, argues Tupper, because tariff policy had become less efficacious in the new international economic system. Moreover, Keynesian measures had proven inadequate when governmental goals included "balanced regional economic development, the maintenance of employment, in particular firms and industries, the Canadian control in important economic sectors and the necessity for government to extend protection to domestic firms comparable to that offered by other states."[16]

Industrial strategies, therefore, have become significant concerns of almost all governments. Nevertheless, as argued recently by John Zysman, the institutional key to industrial policy is the national financial system.[17] As Zysman contends:

> The central argument of this book is that discretion in the provision of industrial finance — in the selective allocation of credit — necessary for the state to enter continuously into the industrial life of private companies

> and to influence their strategies in the way that a rival or partner would. Even with public companies, the financial instruments for selectively allocating credit provide government a refined set of tools to supplement the appointment of management on the imposition of broadly defined government policy directives. Selective credit allocation is the single discretion necessary to all state-led industrial strategies.[18]

Moreover, says Zysman, the way in which the financial institutions are constructed influences the viability of national or subnational industrial policies:

> We have argued that structural differences in national financial systems contribute to the differing capacities of governments to intervene in the industrial economy. The arrangement of the markets for finance helps shape the choices a government confronts, thus influencing the policies it adopts and the political process by which industrial change occurs.[19]

However, as was pointed out by analysts like Peter Katzenstein, Anglo-American states were not necessarily equipped for such governmental policy making. Katzenstein has argued that institutions are important intervening variables[20] but, as he noted, the range of policy tools and their selective qualities are important in fashioning governmental intervention. Katzenstein concluded, at least with respect to the relationship of government to his chief concern of analysis — sign economic policy — that Anglo-American states tended to have fewer policy tools and far more general ones while those like Japan, especially, had a great number with the capacity to affect, very selectively, industrial sectors or even firms.[21]

Thus, it appears to be very important to analyze the structure of the national financial system and to assess the compatability between it and a government directed industrial assistance policy if one wishes to understand the capacity of a state to respond to international economic pressures. As Zysman notes, industrial adjustment can be either government directed, company-led or negotiated among key economic actors — labour, government and industry.[22] Industrial adjustment is a complex process, and the parameters of industrial change are set by three variables, according to Zysman: the national financial system, state structure and economic situation.[23] Difficulties, in particular, emerge in any national setting when the model of adjustment predicted for each parameter differs. While it is not possible to examine in depth all these parameters, we shall examine in the following sections, if all too briefly, the institutional configuration of the Canadian national financial system.

Models of National Financial Systems

For this analysis of the Canadian national financial system, we have adopted the models identified by John Zysman in examining national financial systems in general. Zysman has articulated three models, a credit-based system administered by governments, a credit-based system dominated by financial institutions and a capital-market-based system where resources, especially capital, are allocated by prices. Each system, in a particular manner, allocates capital to industrial actors. The key objective for financial systems with respect to industrial adjustment (of whatever character) is to provide long-term industrial funds to the domestic economic actors. How this is accomplished sets the limit on how effective government will be in accomplishing its industrial objectives.

The financial systems named above are differentiated according to a number of major dimensions. First, the systems are characterized by the means by which savings are converted into investment. Next, the systems are compared according to the assessment basis adopted by financial institutions in lending to industrial borrowers. Another key dimension differentiating models of national financial systems is the way in which prices are set in the capital markets. Finally, financial systems vary in the way that governments operate the financial markets.[24] In other words, how does the government, through its central bank or equivalent, influence financial markets, directly or indirectly? More broadly, how does government manage the financial system; through market forces or administrative controls?

The market-based financial system, as the name implies, is market dominated in allocating resources; it operates through the price mechanism. In a market-based system, bonds and stocks are key instruments in providing long-term investment funds. More generally, as Zysman notes, "in each distinct financial market, capital, loan or money prices are set in plausibly competitive conditions, a situation that implies a wide variety of capital and money-market instruments and a large number of specialized financial institutions."[25] The availability of market financial instruments, particularly long-term funds, means that firms are not dependent on banks or other financial intermediaries to provide long-term credit.

The relatively independent relationship of financial intermediaries and firms means that banks, for instance, focus their attention primarily on short-term lending. Thus, financial intermediaries, such as banks and near-banks, assess their willingness to lend on the basis of historic performance; bank policy, generally, is to obtain the maximum protection through securable assets and, in the case of default, are as likely to sell company assets as to participate in long-range restructuring of management and company performance.

As described above, prices are set not by administrative decision, but rather, by competitive prices. Neither banks nor governments are directly responsible for setting prices in the major financial markets. They cannot significantly allocate capital resources by differentiating price levels. Market competition remains robust enough that companies can find alternative lenders and markets where particular needs are not met.

The central bank in a capital-market-based system plays a vital, though largely marginal, stabilizing role. In such a national financial system, central banks manage monetary aggregates, interest rates and/or money supply by indirect or arm's-length techniques. Reserve levels of banks can be manipulated: when the central bank intervenes in a capital-market-based system, it does so by buying and selling to bring about changes. Central banks do not prefer one type of financial intermediary over another by administratively determining volume of lending, though it does not preclude general regulatory policies regarding specialization. Government is a substantial borrower and lender in many markets. Government securities become important instruments for funding national debt. Government intervention, when it comes, is market oriented rather than achieved through administrative decision making. Thus, a market-based system "puts banks, firms and governments in distinct spheres from which they venture forth to meet as autonomous bargaining powers."[26] The market-based system is one in which government finds it difficult to influence particular outcomes. The result, as Zysman suggests, is a system where:

> Government intervention in corporate affairs will require specific legislative authorization and will operate outside routine market operations. Consequently, individual interventions by government may be broadly opposed by the financial community, not only because of the objective of any specific intervention but also because of the threat that interventionist policies pose to the integrity of market arrangements.[27]

The two credit-based systems can be described together, in some measure, because they are similar along many of the dimensions previously noted. While the central dominant actor varies (government on the one hand and banks on the other), it is evident from the description provided that, even where financial institutions dominate the credit-based system, these institutions are themselves dependent on state assistance.[28] Moreover, banks serve as policy allies for government, on terms negotiated between the government and finance, though government does not have the direct means to dictate allocative choices to the financial institutions.[29]

In both credit-based systems, markets are too weak to serve the financing needs of corporations. "Credit is at the core of systems of corporate finance."[30] In both cases, corporations are dependent on lending from financial institutions. The two credit systems differ, however, in that finance-dominated systems structure lending through markets where prices are bank-determined, whereas, in government administered credit-based systems government allocative decisions determine prices even where banks serve as lending institutions. Prices are no longer dependent on market competition but are, rather, dependent on administered prices whether they are bank- or government-determined.

With the close relationship between industry and the financial lenders, the lenders' calculations are significantly altered from capital-market-based systems. With lenders now actively allocating resources and determining prices, lending calculations are long-term and firm focussed. Banks or government actors focus more on the future prospects of the company and projected cash flow. Their direction of financial resources to borrowers reveals a commitment to the long-term health of the firm and less attention is paid to securing lending with assets. Moreover, where default threatens, lenders focus on reorganizing and managing the corporation rather than protecting their risk capital.

In both credit-based systems the central bank focusses on the direct means of creating money, establishing quantitative limits on what each bank can lend.[31] In addition, the central banks allow extensive access to their own funds to stabilize the financial system. The focus of both systems is based on quantitative objectives rather than market manipulation. However, in the finance-dominated system, the government is left to pursue aggregate objectives through market manipulation, while in the government-dominated system, the government directly seeks quantitatively administered objectives. In effect, banks are the administrative actors in the former system while government allocates resources in the latter. In both systems, the state funds its debt through government or public agencies collecting savings. The government is, thus, a lender of funds rather than a borrower of funds. Finally, the government and/or central bank further directs the allocation of credit by facilitating the rediscounting of financial instruments, thus aiding the transformation of short-term financial instruments into long-term ones. Both credit systems emphasize administrative direction and resource allocation. Credit systems directly link firms and their lenders. Zysman describes the implications for the government-dominated credit-based system this way:

> The political implication is that the state's entanglement with industry becomes part and parcel of the financial system. The borderline between public and private blurs, not simply because of political arrangements, but because of the very structure of the financial markets.[32]

In Zysman's explication, the national financial system is linked to particular models of industrial adjustment.[33] The unique structural elements of each financial system provide a particular capacity for state actors to direct industrial change and to determine how costs will be distributed across societal groups in the process of industrial adjustment. The importance of the government-finance linkages in the credit-based price-administered system lead to the prediction that a state-led industrial adjustment is the role available to state actors. In a credit-based institution-dominated system, state actors are unable to direct industrial adjustment through the national financial institutions.

Instead, the financial institutions, who dominate the financial structure but are linked to the firm and government, dominate in formulating a tripartite, negotiated industrial adjustment strategy. Finally, in the capital-market-based financial system, government carries on a limited role apart from the financial intermediaries and the firms requiring capital. The dominance of markets means that the financial system is, as Zysman says, "the vehicle that allocates resources among competing uses."[34] As a result, industrial adjustment, it is predicted, will be led by company-led industrial change. Choices are made by individual firms interacting through markets.

The predicted relationship between industrial change and the national financial system is not a fixed one. First, it is apparent that any national financial system is not completely one system or another. Almost all states endeavour to direct the allocation of investment funds whether or not the primary financial institution is a government-administered system or a market system. Secondly, it is not a determinative relationship. The institutional system may be strongly market and yet, political objectives may or may not lead to active state intervention. An institutional configuration inimical to government directed industrial change need not preclude a political determination to direct industrial change by state actions. Indeed, Great Britain, possessing a market-based national financial system has, nevertheless, attempted industrial adaptation primarily through state direction. Great Britain's failure to conform to the predictive model highlights a theme running through Zysman's analysis: the need for conformity between institutional forms. What the British examination reveals, as the only non-conforming institutional case, is that the incompatibility between the state's capacity to direct industrial adjustment and the structure of the national financial system may produce little industrial change and exacerbate political tensions between main economic actors.[35] Zysman's conclusions are important in a number of ways. They alert us to the need to examine the state's role in industrial change in relation to the particular institutional framework of the nation's financial system. Next, his conclusions avoid the debate over which state role is preferred. Instead, Zysman encourages us to focus on the fit between state roles and objectives and national institutions. What his examination suggests is that the state-led industrial role is not necessarily better or worse than the company-led one. Instead, what is to be preferred is a state role appropriate to the national institutional system; what is to be avoided is a state role mismatched to the institutional tools provided. We shall focus on these conclusions shortly, when we come to examine Canada.

Canada in Comparative Context

The three analytic models articulated by John Zysman find real world counterparts in several advanced industrial states. Both Great Britain and the United States represent capital-market-based systems. Both have highly developed capital markets. In both states, the major components of the system — banks, industry and government — stand relatively isolated from each other. Banks and other private financial intermediaries focus on short-term lending. Reinforcing the arm's-length relationship between lender and borrower, financial institutions are restricted in the equity positions they may secure in any firm. Markets, not government or banks, determine the prices in loan, capital or money markets, and the governments, while not uninterested in directing funds and pressing industrial change, find their ability to do so limited institutionally and politically.

The financial systems in both France and Japan, on the other hand, are structured in a manner similar to those suggested by Zysman's model of a credit-based government-administered system. Here the markets, particularly bond and stock markets, are weak and incapable of channelling sufficient investment to the industrial sectors to achieve recapitalization. Credit represents the chief source of investment funds. In both countries, price and credit allocation are government controlled and directed to meet bureaucratic objectives established for industrial adjustment. The government and not the market is the leading partner in industrial adjustment.

Finally, Germany appears to be the only case of a credit-based financially administered price system. The distinct quality of the German national financial system is the ubiquitous role played by the large German banks. This role is made possible by the relaxation of laws against equity holdings by banks and their roles in managing corporate direction. As Zysman points out:

> The power of the German banks in industrial affairs rests on 2 pillars: their market power over the sources of finance for industry, and their legal right to own substantial stocks in corporations and to exercise proxy votes for other shareholders. . . . In essence, all routes to corporate external finance — loans, bonds and equity — lead back to the banks.[36]

While banks no longer dominate in quite the way they did early in the post war world, they remain capable of coordinating the activities of industry and government both regionally and in any particular industrial sector.[37]

Before examining some elements of the institutional makeup of the Canadian national financial system, it will be helpful to draw some broad comparisons between Canada and the countries already analyzed by Zysman. Of the three potential financial models — market-dominated, financial-institution-dominated or government-dominated — which best describes the Canadian national financial system?

The primary test is to identify the strength of the capital markets, notably the bond and stock markets. Table 4-1 provides a crude measure of the strength of the capital markets in the various countries. The figures represent the value of each nation's bonds and equity as a percentage of gross domestic product (GDP). Though far from a perfect measure, the table reveals the marked contrast between a capital-market-based system, such as in the United States, and a credit-market-based system, as shown by the German or, especially, the French examples.

TABLE 4-1 Credit Based and Capital-Market-Based Financial Systems, end of 1977

	Securities as percentage of Gross Domestic Product	
Country	**Bonds**	**Equity**
Canada	63	35
United States	59	53
France	16	7
Germany	35	7
United Kingdom	45	37

Source: Value of Outstanding Securities;
OECD, *Financial Statistics, Vol. 12* (Paris: OECD, 1978).

When Canada is contrasted with these other examples, it is apparent that the Canadian figures are far closer to those examples which are market based rather than those which are credit based. The value of its equities as a percentage of GDP are substantially larger than either credit-based system. Canada's figures contrast favourably even with the principal example of a market-based financial system, the United States, though the value of equities is not as large as that of the United States. Additionally, it is somewhat surprising to discover that the value of our bonds as a percentage of GDP exceeds that in the United States (see Appendix, Table A-1). Though the categories are not fully comparable, they do show the enormous governmental bond sector in Canada. In addition, they point out a rather underdeveloped corporate bond sector in Canada, as opposed to the United States, particularly if the financial institutional sector is removed from the Canadian private figure.

A second test employed in Zysman's study compares the investing institutions and the long-term credit institutions. These figures are replicated in Table 4-2. What they point out is a notable long-term loan component in the French case, as revealed by the claims figure under long-term credit institutions. This figure emphasizes the credit component, and, since the institutions which fund long-term credit are public or quasi-public, it highlights the role that government plays in creating industrial change. Significantly, the American figure is substantially smaller in the long-term credit arena. Instead, the investing institutions which deal in market securities represent a more significant portion of lending in the American figures. What these percentages reflect is the arm's-length nature of the relationship between long-term borrower and lender in the U.S. context which is exactly as expected by the market-based U.S. system.

TABLE 4-2 Share (in Claims and Liabilities) with Non-Financial Sector

Country	Investing Institutions		Long-Term Credit Institutions	
	Liabilities	Claims	Liabilities	Claims
		(percent)		
France	11.3	9.3	8.2	32.9
United States	32.3	31.2	5.5	7.9

Source: J. Zysman, *Governments, Markets and Growth* (Ithaca: Cornell University Press, 1983), p. 66.

When comparisons are made with Canadian figures, totals appear to fall in line with the U.S. figures, though a "hard" comparison is not available. The different bases of reporting Canadian figures and the lack of provincial data make a comparison unavailable, other than in rough, quantitative terms.[38] Nevertheless, the Canadian federal figures appear to be as low or lower than the U.S. figures for long-term credit institutions. The Canadian figures for investing institutions appear roughly to resemble the American 30 percent figures. Using rough comparisons, then, the Canadian figures appear to reinforce the view that Canada's national financial system is a market-based as opposed to a credit-based structure. In order to confirm our analysis, it is necessary to look more closely, if only briefly, at the components of the national financial system.

Financial Intermediaries

Institutional Overview

Given our earlier findings, it is not surprising that there is some resemblance between the structure of American and Canadian financial intermediaries (see Appendix, Tables A-2 and A-3). The basic institutions of a market-based system are present in both countries, and they perform relatively similar functions.

Nonetheless, differences are apparent and should not be underestimated. Our general finding, from Table 4-1, revealed that while Canada is, like the United States, a market-based system, nevertheless, even at the aggregate level there is a significant contrast between the United States and Canada, at least with respect to the "equity category." In the following individual institutional overview, other differences will be made apparent. Regulatory environments and policy decisions, of private and public actors especially, will help to differentiate individual institutional functions in the overall national financial systems. The result is that Canada's national financial system, while clearly market-based, is less strongly so than that of the United States.

BANKS

As in the United States, banks and near-banks in Canada are the preeminent financial intermediaries. The distinctions between these two types of intermediaries have, generally, dissolved. In fact, the near-banks are essentially domestic, personal savings banks as opposed to demand deposit institutions. In contrast to the U.S. free banking structure, Canada has a natural centralization and highly concentrated banking system (see Appendix, Table A-5). The banking world in Canada is dominated by the big five: the Royal Bank of Canada, the Bank of Montreal, the Bank of Nova Scotia, the Canadian Imperial Bank of Commerce and The Toronto-Dominion Bank.[39] The banking structure looks, if anything, more like that of Germany than that of the United States though, importantly, the regulatory restrictions on Canadian banks prevent them from acting like universal banks of the German variety.

The Canadian banking sector, beginning in 1967, has undergone a series of significant legislative changes.[40] The most notable alteration is the recent opening of the Canadian banking sector to foreign banks. As of 1983, 58 so-called Schedule B or foreign banks had been approved. Though foreign banks represent a new competitive element in the banking sector, their potential impact has been restricted by the extensive limitations built into the *Bank Act*.[41] Until recently, each foreign subsidiary was restricted to two offices. Also, Schedule B banks may not have domestic assets in excess of 20 times their authorized capital, which is a level approved by the minister of finance (see s. 174(2)(e) of the Act). In addition, the collective assets of these foreign banks cannot exceed 8 percent of the domestic markets (see s. 302(7) of the Act). While pressures from these banks have encouraged the government to introduce legislative revisions which would double the 8 percent ceiling, such legislation has not been approved.[42] The limitations imposed on these banks, as well as the entrenched position of Canadian banks, has meant that the area of most serious competition between domestic and foreign subsidiaries has been restricted to the corporate lending sector.

The most serious additional regulatory restrictions in the entire banking sector are those related to corporate holdings. Current banking legislation limits the voting rights that a bank may hold of a Canadian company to 10 percent of the total number of votes.[43] It is not surprising, therefore, that on a consolidated balance sheet of banks for 1982 calculated by Shearer, Chant and Bond, the mortgages and other loans totalled $160,136 million while securities totalled $10,345 million.[44] Banks have been circumscribed in their financial roles by regulatory authorities. Until recently, banks were excluded from holding mortgages and, in the securities field, from playing a role in underwriting. Finally, until very recently, banks played no role of consequence in the secondary market transactions either.

Thus, while much criticism has been raised in the past over the highly concentrated nature of the banking sector, less attention has been paid to the circumscribed role afforded these large financial firms. Particularly in respect of the national financial system, the banks have assumed a short-term credit role. This enormous financial resource has played only a limited institutional role in the capital markets, and they have not played any sustained role in directing industrial adaptation.

NEAR-BANKS

One of the anomalies of the regulatory environment, as it now exists, has been the failure of federal banking legislation to define "banking." As a result, a bank in Canada is an entity which has been issued a charter under the terms of the *Bank Act* or the *Quebec Savings Bank Act*.[45] This legal, as opposed to functional, definition has provided the opening for the substantial expansion of institutions which, though not banks, act and look very much like banks. This category of near-banks is notable for its contrasting regulatory authority. The great majority of near-banks in Canada are provincially regulated (see Appendix, Tables A-6 and A-6a). With the expansion of services provided by trust companies, credit unions and caisses populaires, Canada has in fact created two banking systems, one regulated federally, and one provincially. One of the main differences has been the less demanding restrictions imposed generally by provincial authorities on trust companies, especially with respect to reserve requirements.[46] Still, cooperation has not been impossible. Indeed, all provinces except Quebec joined the federally established Canada Deposit Insurance Corporation, thereby extending protection for deposits to provincially regulated trust and loan companies. Even though Quebec established its own insurance scheme, steps have been taken to coordinate companies operating in both jurisdictions and to facilitate loans from the CDIC to the QDIC if such measures are required.[47]

An examination of the asset basis of such institutions (see Appendix, Table A-4) shows that these institutions place a relatively heavy emphasis on mortgage claims with only a secondary interest in equities. These percentages contrast with the investing institutions, in which greater attention has been paid to equities in their investment strategies.

OTHERS

Of the other institutions, insurance companies represent a significant institutional actor in the investing institutional category. Insurance companies, domestic and foreign, have played an important investing role since the late nineteenth century. At the beginning of this decade there were 402 insurance companies registered with the federal government, of which 160 were incorporated in Canada.[48] Both life insurance and general insurance companies have substantial equity holdings in their assets (see Appendix, Table A-4). Even the figures provided in the Appendix somewhat underestimate the importance of insurance companies to the capital markets. For example, if a comparison of life insurance and general insurance holdings of non-government bonds, preferred shares and common shares is made, you find that these holdings represent 35 percent and 46 percent, respectively, of their total assets, making insurance companies major institutional actors in the capital markets.

One last investment entity, the venture capital firms, not identified in this roll call of investment institutions, is worthy of mention. Though not viewed as a traditional financial intermediary, venture capital firms, private and public, have gained some prominence for their capacity to target industrial firms more precisely, particularly promising, high technology ones. The concept has been vital enough for the Ontario government to have encouraged the creation of venture capital firms through tax grants under the small business development corporations program (SBDC). Even more directly, the Ontario government has created its own venture capital Crown agency, the Innovation Development for Employment Advancement Corporation (IDEA Corporation). Alberta and Quebec also have established major venture capital incentive programs.

Most agreements to lend result in the venture capital firms' taking equity positions in companies that otherwise would likely be unable to obtain equity financing. This widening of equity financing is, of course, a positive result of venture capital activity, but a number of drawbacks appear evident in Canada. First, the amount of money invested remains relatively small. The entire amount invested by the Association of Canadian Venture Capital Companies (ACVCC) from 1974 to 1981 amounted to only $400 to $500 million.[49] Next, the kind of choices being made by venture capital firms are somewhat unclear. The demand for a high early return on capital may lead to promising ventures being ignored in the rush to fund the possible "high flyer." Finally, the trend has been to focus on the high technology segment of the market, leaving less glamorous but equally vital sectors without the same possibilities for new capital.

The Pattern of Borrowing

The institutional pattern just completed shows both similarities and some noticeable contrasts with the market-based U.S. national financial system. The same thing also shows up when we examine the pattern of borrowing. Even more than with the institutional overview, the pattern of borrowing reveals the prominent role of government.

As we pointed out in our comparison of bonds and equities, (Table 4-1) cross-nationally Canada, as of 1978, maintained the highest figures for bonds as a percentage of gross domestic product. A further examination of sources of those bonds (see Appendix, Table A-1) reveals that a substantial portion were issued by federal and provincial governments and their enterprises, notably utilities. Examining the pattern of net new issues of securities reinforces this view of goverment dominance in the securities markets (Appendix, Table A-7). It is apparent that recent corporate borrowing in new securities represents a small, even a nominally diminished role, despite the generally healthy market activity, particularly in 1982 and 1983. It is also evident from the figures that corporate bonds have suffered a significant decline and now represent the minor portion of total corporate securities. Finally, the figures reveal that the federal government has become the dominant securities issuer, outrunning even the provinces. It is also apparent that the pattern of bond holding federally has shifted as the volatility of interest rates has increased. Now, shorter-term treasury notes fund a significantly greater portion of the federal government's debt.

Though it is important to record the diminished corporate position in new securities, it is even more revealing to examine the sources of corporate funds (see Appendix, Table A-8). If one examines the sources of external funding by all Canadian non-financial private corporations, one notes the relative increase in loans in the early 1980s (even given the rather volatile figures for the year 1982). This pattern fits with general claims that Canadian companies, particularly energy companies, took on significantly greater debt as the 1970s ended. Though it is an uncertain pattern, still, the increase in debt by Canadian companies accords with the figures on new net issues of securities. A trend to greater debt and away from equity and fixed securities by companies would signal an unhealthy turn by Canadian corporations, particularly in a period of high and/or volatile interest rates.

Conclusion

The pattern that emerges from this brief examination of borrowing and the analysis of financial intermediaries in no way upsets the view that Canada maintains a financial environment in which corporations are dependent for recapitalization on financial markets as opposed to banks or the state. Still, there are worrying features in the national financial system. While government remains a borrower and not a lender (which corresponds to a market-based system), the borrowing role is large and there is apparently some inhibiting effect on corporate borrowing. Behind these deficiencies, and only partly revealed by the analysis, is the significant role played by governmental actors not only as regulators but also as players in the marketplace.

All this suggests, in some measure, a degree of weakness in our capital markets which may inhibit a company-led industrial adaptation policy. Though such a conclusion can be only tentatively reached, given the evidence as presented, it suggests minimally that closer attention be given to the needs of corporations and capital markets as long as the national financial system remains structurally a market-led system. This is especially required if the industrial adaptation model most compatible with Canada's national financial system is hypothesized to be a company-led and not a state-led model.

Examining the Industrial Adaptation Model

Government Industrial Assistance

Earlier, we argued that government involvement in credit and investing, while apparent in Canada as in most countries, did not in any significant way alter the proposition that Canada's national financial system was market-based and not credit-based. All the features of Canada's system appeared to correspond to the characteristics of a market-based financial system. Besides the conclusion that prices are set by markets and that banks, the largest financial institutions, focussed on short-term credit, there was the obvious fact that the Bank of Canada was a classic marginal stabilizer with its "eyes" trained on the managing of aggregates. Moreover, the government was, as noted, a vast borrower of money to fund its debt rather than a lender. Finally, the federal government's regulatory rules (such as those pointed to for the banks) were designed not so much to determine resource allocation as they were to create the conditions of competition.[50]

Nonetheless, a brief examination of government policies, particularly with respect to credit and investment, should not be ignored. First, there are governmental expenditures; beyond the expenditures there remains the rhetoric of industrial strategies, and beyond even the rhetoric, real programs at both levels of government. This suggests that industrial change is thought of as being led by the state and not by the private sector. If, however, the picture of the national financial system as presented here is correct, i.e., if, for all its deficiencies, it is a market-based system and still this government attitude exists, i.e., one which encourages, in part, state-led change as opposed to company-led change, then it may well produce a mismatch between the industrial adaptation model and the national financial system. As we have already suggested, such a conflict may significantly undermine industrial change and produce political conflict.

Indeed, Canada appears to be in the even more unenviable position of having the three critical parameters of industrial change identified in Zysman's analysis: the institutional nature of the financial system, the autonomy of state structures and the economic circumstances facing the country — pointing to different models of industrial change.[51] The first parameter, the national financial system, predicts a company-led model of industrial adjustment as we have discussed. The second and third parameters would suggest a state-led or negotiated model. Historically, government has played a significant role in economic development. It no doubt explains, in some measure, the current attitude and behaviour of both levels of government in Canada in the drive to adapt Canadian industry to international economic pressures. However, while the spending and programs are explicable in historical and political terms, government direction may, according to this analysis, be relatively inefficient, given a continuing market-based national financial system.

Government programs, both federal and provincial, are far too numerous and complicated to examine extensively in this chapter. Only a few salient features can be touched on. As noted by Allan Tupper in his recent analysis of industrial assistance programs, government policies at both levels have encompassed broad objectives — from regional policy to Canadianization. In a further reference he argued, "there is, moreover, no indication that Canadian governments will curtail their economy-building efforts in the foreseeable future. Indeed, disorder and uncertainty in the domestic and international political economy have recently evoked consistently interventionist responses."[52]

If we look at the government lending institutions as a means of identifying the federal government's efforts to allocate resources, we can identify a wide range of governmental credit schemes (see Appendix, Table A-9). The table, reproduced from a study by Allan Maslove, reveals that the federal government has sought to direct credit to firms and individuals to improve their international competitiveness, e.g., the Enterprise Development Program; to provide long-term credit for hard-pressed farmers, e.g., the Farm Credit Corporation; to aid small businesses, e.g., the Federal Business Development Bank. Still, one thing that is readily apparent is that the total funds provided pale in comparison to the funds provided by the private financial intermediaries previously discussed. What is less apparent is the non-directive and secondary role of many of these programs which further detract from a state capacity to lead industrial adaptation. For example, for both the Farm Credit Corporation and the Federal Business Development Bank, credit is provided only after the borrower has found it impossible to obtain funds from private financial institutions. Under the Enterprise Development Program, now called the Industrial and Regional Development Program (IRBD) directed by the Department of Regional and Industrial Expansion (DRIE), specific applicants were not sought; rather, as Tupper points out, the program was designed merely to respond to private sector applications and "involves no explicit judgments about which industrial sectors merit state support."[53]

These programs and Crown corporations do not nearly encompass the wide range of interventionist efforts that could be broadly termed industrial assistance. There are numerous individual assistance programs, not to mention the regional efforts under DREE and now DRIE. An examination of the figures provided in the federal budget of April 1983 suggests spending out of the economic and regional development envelope at $8.5 billion.[54] This figure in no way reflects federal tax incentive efforts to encourage various forms of assistance. Even these figures may not fully comprehend federal efforts. Recently the federal government established the Canadian Development Investment Corporation (CDIC) which now controls Crown corporations in manufacturing like de Havilland and Canadair, Eldorado Nuclear and Teleglobe Canada.[55] Further, the government has found itself extending support to a number of companies mainly through loan guarantee agreements; these include Massey-Ferguson, Maislin Trucking and Chrysler Canada. As Tupper argued:

> A survey of these programs does little to explain why certain industries are supported, while others are ignored. But such a disparate collection of programs indicates that Ottawa has achieved a strategy of promoting "leading sectors" or of exploiting Canada's comparative advantages.[56]

In summary, several types of conclusions are apparent. First, it is not always clear, but it is frequently the case that, in those broad areas of continuing credit assistance, the government's efforts are secondary and frequently reactive. More generally, where the government is more directive, there are extensive programs but they appear uncoordinated, and the initiatives frequently seem dictated by political imperatives. Thus, the federal government appears to be ideologically and politically handicapped in its approach to industrial adaptation. Moreover, even while the sums calculated for federal loans and assistance to the private sector are substantial, one estimate as of 1980 putting the figure at $14 billion, they are certainly less significant than one might have anticipated from the level of discourse over industrial strategies.[57] What one is left with federally is the rhetoric of state-led industrial adaptation and the reality of a market-based, though somewhat weakened, national financial system.

Up to this point, we have not taken into account the extent of provincial government programs. Rough estimates suggest that provincial programs of loans and assistance to the private sector totalled some $5 billion as of 1980.[58] Michael Jenkin, in a recent analysis of provincial industrial policies, points to a broad array of assistance programs provided by the provincial governments in Canada.[59] Of all the provincial programs,the most interesting effort appears to be that of the Quebec government. This is true, in part, because of this government's conscious efforts to direct industrial change for the benefit of Quebec.

In Quebec's efforts to channel industrial change, there are three important financial corporations: the Société générale de financement du Québec, an investment and holding corporation; the Société de développement industriel du Québec, a vehicle for the delivery of industrial development loans and grants; and the Caisse de dépôt et placement du Québec, an investment agency for the assets of the Quebec Pension Plan.[60] The last, in particular, highlights the Quebec government's more directive approach. The Caisse's investment strategies contrast rather sharply with those taken by the federal government with respect to the CPP (see Appendix, Table A-10). While the Canadian government invests virtually all its funds in provincial governments' non-negotiable securities, and while the Caisse has held to a relatively conservative strategy to avoid risky investments, nevertheless, recent conflict with the federal government over investments by the Caisse in Canadian Pacific point to the Quebec government's capacity to influence the course of the province's economy.[61] Furthermore, as Jenkin argues, 60 percent of the Caisse's industrial assets as of the late 1970s were invested in Quebec-based companies like Provigo, Bombardier and Marine Industries Ltd.[62] The present government's directive efforts have gone even further than mere financing. The government has developed plans for specific electronic specializations. It has also established the Société de développement des industries de la culture et des communications to promote the application of new electronics technologies in communications.[63] In biotechnology, the Société générale de financement and several Crown corporations are prepared to make major investments along with private sector partners.[64]

Quebec is not alone. The commitment of all provincial governments to industrial change has grown in recent years. Besides the government assistance to venture capital noted in Ontario, there are numerous Ontario policies, many of them directed today through the Board of Industrial Leadership and Development (BILD). The board, it now appears, directs all the government's development spending on industrial, resource, transportation and regional development, human resources and community infrastructure.[65] In addition, the government has created a number of technology development centres to expand resources for Ontario companies in areas such as microelectronics, auto parts, resource machinery and robotics, to name only a few.[66]

Even more recently, the Alberta government has announced tentative plans to become more directly involved in industrial adaptation. The plans announced include proposals to invest substantially more public funds in the resource and transportation sectors. As the government made clear, the province would be more than willing to use the billions-rich Heritage Trust Fund to achieve its development objectives.[67]

Conclusion

Adding the provincial picture alters but does not fundamentally change the picture of a company-led model of industrial adaptation influenced by numerous, if uncoordinated, governmental industrial policies at both levels of government. It is simply impossible to describe here the wide variety of programs established by provincial and federal governments to influence economic development. However, even this limited picture (including the split in programs between less intensive incentives and precise industrial projects) adds to the sense of confusion characteristic of Canadian industrial adaptation, particularly when the programs of both levels of government are taken together.

Possibly, this confusion in Canada as to how to deal with industrial change (to accommodate the ideological and institutional limitations that we've already discussed) can best be illustrated with a brief glance at what must be considered Canada's most bold economic stroke -- the National Energy Policy. This program was touted, after the Liberal election victory of 1980, as a bold federal government strategy to make Canada energy self-sufficient, to expand exploration under federal control and to Canadianize the energy sector itself.[68] The program was seen as confirmation of the federal government's determination to plan industrial development. However, a closer look at the policy and its progress reveals many of the limitations to which such a plan was subject in the Canadian political and economic environments. For all the government's commitment, the great bulk of financing was to be accomplished by the private sector, particularly the banks. The banks believed the government to be so deeply committed to the sector that little risk would attend large loans to energy companies, especially to favoured companies like Dome Petroleum. None of the actors, neither the government nor the banks, had the type of control over the direction of the sector, particularly companies like Dome, that might have provided the needed restraint required in the situation. As Peter Foster noted in his examination of the relationship between Dome, the banks and the government:[69]

> Between the banks and the government, meanwhile, the underlying wrangle continued about just who was bailing out whom. Were the banks bailing out Ottawa's chosen instruments or was Ottawa bailing out a company that had been massively overindulged by the banks?[70]

The near-bankruptcy of Dome and subsequent bailout efforts are important because they highlight the difficulties of either governmental or institutional control in a context devoid of the institutional means needed for such precise administrative direction. The dangers of the mismatch between the industrial adaptation model and the national financial system are only too apparent in this one, but important, instance of government-encouraged, though not controlled, industrial policy. It points to a dilemma not seriously addressed by most governments in Canada: how to increase their involvement in planning industrial change without developing the institutional means to accomplish the task.

The alternatives are painfully obvious. If the federal and provincial governments insist on directing further industrial change, then far greater attention must be paid to altering the financial system in this country to enable state direction to proceed with some chance of success. On the other hand, if the institutional system is to be left in market hands, as it still is, then much more thought must be given to improving the quality of all the markets in order to sustain a company-led industrial policy. Policies must be put in place designed to encourage funds into the securities markets and to reduce the competition between government debt funding and corporate funding.

The Canadian picture, as briefly as we have sketched it, seems particularly confused. Our national financial system is clearly market based yet more strongly influenced by government than might otherwise be anticipated. Governments at both the provincial and federal levels are deeply involved in industrial change, yet have not really developed the institutional capacity nor provided the real commitment and resources to direct change in most cases. Notwithstanding the above, however, anticipation of governmental direction by numerous private actors and the intrusion of governments in the markets may have inhibited company-led industrial adaptation in any case.

In most liberal democratic states, the clash between market direction and administrative direction is an all too well-known battle. In that respect, Canada is not unique. Canada may be unique, however, in its inability to address the issue and to resolve the choice before it. Without a decision, Canada will never be capable of matching its institutions to its preferences.

Planning Regulation and Capital Markets

Our examination of the national financial system has revealed that both levels of government have taken on an expanded role in economic management. In addition, we have noticed that both federal and provincial governments have employed a wide range of tools and resources to direct industrial adaptation.

Regulation has been one favoured instrument that governments have employed in fashioning the national financial system. Indeed, the national financial system is influenced by a host of statutes, regulators and state-mandated insurance nets, and all financial intermediaries are regulated by federal and/or provincial agencies (see Appendix, Table A-11).

Moreover, we noted earlier some of the restrictions imposed on intermediaries with the intention of limiting the roles of these institutions in the overall financial system. To this end, regulations were written so that banks played a savings and loan role but did not encroach in a major way on the trust function concerning mortgage creation. Regulations also restricted banks from acting as agents for clients seeking to invest in secondary markets, and banks were not encouraged to play a major role in the underwriting of corporate equity issues, though they were invited to be active in the government bond market.

Besides these and other functional roles assigned financial intermediaries, there were significant regulations regarding broader questions of ownership, particularly rules on foreign ownership. Regulations of this sort, particularly, alert us to the exogenous quality of such rules. It is apparent that financial regulation, like other areas of regulation examined in these case studies, points to the use of regulation beyond simply pricing, as is apparent in the *Interest Act*.[71] The regulatory framework extends beyond just promoting the health of the national financial system through a broad variety of entry controls crystallized in such statutes as *The Bank Act* and various trust and loan acts.[72] Foreign ownership restrictions attempt to retain the Canadian character of the financial sector such as banks. These restrictions are, therefore, instances of regulation being employed to achieve other broad governmental purposes beyond the economic objectives of fair prices or efficiency.

A closer examination of securities regulation, as was suggested earlier, reveals a similar pattern of evolution. In the key regulatory environments of Ontario and Quebec, governmental actions by independent regulatory agencies and/or governmental departments have expanded the regulatory objectives. In both jurisdictions, regulators have sought to direct the future development of the capital markets. Regulations have not been restricted to simple policing functions. Regulators have become increasingly unwilling to limit their actions to narrow reactive activities. While the pace of change, particularly technological change, has increased pressures on those responsible for securities regulation to review broad areas of regulation, it is apparent that some of the incentives for planning, particularly in Quebec, reflect a determination to improve a province's competitive position and to achieve broader political objectives. This expanded role for regulation by governments, we believe, explains the "tensions" that surround securities regulation today. Furthermore, the broad regulatory agenda points to a future of potentially significant conflict among the provinces.

In Ontario, securities regulation has been directed, in large measure, by the regulatory agencies created under securities legislation and the self-regulatory organizations, particularly the Toronto Stock Exchange, and the Investment Dealers Association. Securities regulation itself had a somewhat ill-defined beginning in Ontario. James Baillie,[73] a leading securities lawyer and a former chairman of the Ontario Securities Commission (OSC), has suggested that securities regulation in Ontario can be traced back to the *Directors' Liability Act, 1891*.[74] It seems that this legislation was adapted from similar English legislation. More significant securities legislation was adopted in 1928, in Ontario, first in the *Securities Fraud Prevention Act*[75] and then by a series of securities statutes through the 1930s.

In Ontario, no administrative agency was readily identifiable before 1930. However, under the *Security Frauds Prevention Act, 1931*,[76] a government board was set up to regulate the securities industry in Ontario. By 1933, according to Dey and Makuch, this board was referred to as the OSC.[77]

Securities legislation evolved through a series of legislative changes that reflected changes in regulatory objectives in other countries, notably the United States and Great Britain. Early Ontario laws, as their titles indicated, were concerned with conduct, primarily questions of fraud. The legislation required registration of securities and issuers and, in early statutes, regulation extended to secondary trading as well as primary distributions.[78]

The 1930s saw the legislation in Ontario move from merit and misrepresentation to disclosure, principally with respect to new issues of securities. This shift to disclosure from the earlier merit evaluation reflected Ontario 's acceptance of British views on securities regulation. As James Baillie has written, however, this move away from the U.S. view of merit evaluation, commonly referred to as "blue-sky," was never as striking as proponents claimed.[79]

The modern framework of securities regulation in Ontario emerged in the 1945 *Securities Act*.[80] This act was substantially amended in 1947.[81] Modern statutes, while still retaining broad registration requirements, increasingly emphasized disclosure: first, primary market disclosure through the prospectus and more recently, continuous disclosure requirements in secondary markets. *The Securities Act of 1966*,[82] which was largely a product of the report of the Kimber Committee, was particularly noteworthy for the widened scope it brought to securities regulation. In this act, significant improvements in the system of initial distribution of securities were introduced. As well, the act introduced requirements for the annual and semi-annual financial disclosure by issuers; regulatory standards to govern takeover bids; proxy solicitation and the information circulars accompanying the solicitations; and, finally, the reporting by corporate insiders of their trading, together with civil liability provisions for improper use by them of inside information.[83]

The Kimber Report, which was important in bringing expanded regulation to secondary trades, was additionally noteworthy for recognizing that securities regulation was addressing a broadened set of objectives. As Gray Taylor points out:

> The Kimber Committee recommended that responsibility be transferred to another Minister because the purpose of regulation was drifting from the prevention of fraud to the enhancement of the securities industry in the economic life of the province.[84]

The most recent revisions in securities regulation, the *Securities Act 1978*,[85] have reinforced these broadened regulatory trends. For the first time, the closed system of trades was introduced in Ontario. In addition, continuous disclosure provisions were written specifically into the legislation.[86]

The extended regulatory environment can be assessed by other means than those identified above. One of the signs of a strong interventionist regulatory environment is the way in which the agencies responsible for administering the act perceive their role. H.N. Janisch has suggested that administrator agencies are capable of a number or roles:[87] these can vary from a more or less narrow policy adjudicative role to a broad policy-making role. As Janisch argues:

> The difference, of course, is only one of degree, but it is of the greatest significance. In an adjudicative role, an agency concentrates on deciding matters on a case by case basis, seeking to apply known principles to the facts of each case. In an extreme form, this leaves little room for policy making, because it is assured that the policy contained in the empowering legislation and the agency simply has to apply it in the particular case. At the other end of the spectrum is the role of the conscious policy maker, wherein a regulatory agency embarks on an essentially legislative role and seeks to set out in advance the factors that it will take into account in deciding individual cases.[88]

Administrative agencies relying on a policing regulatory environment are likely to act in a more adjudicative manner. Whereas, in environments where regulation has become promotional or planning, we are likely to find that the administrative agency takes more of a policy-making stance. Though the evidence is limited, there is indeed some indication that the OSC has shifted to more of a rule-making stance.[89] As the accompanying table shows (Table 4-3), there has been a significant expansion in the number of regulations and policy statements that accompany the various Ontario securities acts. Of the two, the policy statements are even more significant, since the statements reflect the commission's own policy-making efforts as opposed to those regulations passed by the lieutenant-governor in council.

TABLE 4-3 The Growth of Policy Statements and Regulations in Ontario

Edition	Policy Statement	Regulations
The Securities Act and Regulations 1972, Richard de Boo (1966 Act)	23 pages/ 23 policy statements	40 pages/ 84 Regulations
The Ontario Securities Act and Regulations 1978, 8th edition (1966 Act)	78 pages/ 38 policy statements	53 pages/ 89 Regulations
The Ontario Securities Act and Regulations 1979, 9th edition (1966 Act)	84 pages/ 40 policy statements	77 pages/ 176 Regulations
Ontario Securities Act and Regulations 1982, 11th edition (1978 Act)	112 pages/ 48 policy statements	77 pages/ 175 Regulations
Ontario Securities Act and Regulations 1983, 12th edition	115 pages/ 43 policy statements	81 pages/ 175 Regulations

Source: A. Alexandroff, "Policemen or Architects: Ontario Securities Commissioners' Self Perceptions of Acting in the Public Interest" (unpublished manuscript) (Montreal: McGill University, 1984), p. 47.

A further indication of the growth of rule making is the significant number of hearings that have occurred or are planned by the commission. These apply to such matters as discount brokerage, the role of financial institutions, the prompt offering prospectus, the uncommon common share and the discussion of the report relating to takeover bids and issuer bids. Hearings of this nature undermine the creation of policy through the adjudicative case-by-case approach. They give substance to a view expressed by former commissioners (interviewed elsewhere by this author) suggesting that adjudication has become a less significant aspect of commissioner responsibility.[90] All of these administrative actions and procedures suggest that the OSC has altered its practices to conform to a broader policy-making approach. It suggests, furthermore, that securities regulation is no longer confined simply to policing regulation and that the administrative agency has become more deeply involved in planning regulation.

Quebec's securities laws have recently undergone extensive revision. With the passage of what was formerly Bill 85,[91] Quebec joined Ontario and a number of other provinces in modernizing its securities regulation.

As pointed out in a recent examination,[92] this new legislation is "probably the most innovative" of the recent legislative enactments across Canada[93] and furthermore,

> It [the new securities act] also shows the greatest diversity of influences. Its drafting owes most to the *Ontario Act*, but it has also been much influenced by the federal proposals for a Securities Market for Canada, more than any other provincial act to date. It also appears to have been influenced by present and proposed securities law in the United States. And of course it has been drafted against the background of Quebec's Civil Code, although the Code's direct influence is the least of all the sources mentioned.[94].

Quebec's legislation has followed the general path already indicated in the case of Ontario. Thus, there has been an evolution of the disclosure requirements, while maintaining a continuing merit aspect.

Significant disclosure regulations were introduced first in Quebec in 1924.[95] The most notable requirement was the filing of a financial information statement as a requirement for a corporation's issuing bonds, shares or other securities. As in Ontario and some other provinces, Quebec moved to pass its own version of the *Security Frauds Prevention Act* in 1930;[96] this was further supplemented by a *Companies Information Act* in 1933.[97] The modern disclosure rules did not appear in Quebec until passage of the *Securities Act* in 1955.[98] It was by this act that the Commission des valeurs mobilières du Québec (CVMQ) was created. Though revisions were passed allowing Quebec to broaden its disclosure requirements, it was not until the current passage of Bill 85 that Quebec substantially modernized its securities legislation. As pointed out by La Rochelle, Pépin and Simmonds, the new securities legislation equals and, in some instances, even surpasses Ontario's legislation.[99] For example, the act has described the discretionary powers of the commission, including the legislative authority to draw up policy statements. Also, the act has gone further in allowing the commission to grant authority to the self-regulating organizations to assist in regulating securities markets. Finally, the current act now provides for the closed system in Quebec and new, rather important, disclosure procedures, including the prompt-offering qualification system and the permanent information record.[100]

Though the act has brought Quebec securities regulation into closer balance with other Canadian jurisdictions, small but nagging problems continue to exist. For instance, periodic disclosures under the "timely disclosure" requirements call for quarterly filings every 45 days, while in Ontario the time limit is 60 days. More serious problems are raised by the French language requirements, a product of the Charter of the French Language and its interpretation by the CVMQ in the securities regulation field.[101] There are also minor differences in the content of a Quebec prospectus. With the exception of language requirements, which impose serious obligations on certain reporting issuers, the other differences are more irritating than burdensome.

There are still continuing technical differences, though there have been repeated calls for integration to facilitate national markets. Moreover, these persistent differences belie more serious problems that further diminish the prospect of national financial markets. Before examining the problems of the search for regulatory uniformity, it should be mentioned that the revision of Quebec's securities laws are just part of a broad set of regulatory revisions by the Quebec government. These revisions point to a government committed to regulation as a means of controlling Quebec's provincial economy. As active as the CMVQ has been and, particularly under Paul Guy, it has been quite active, the focus of regulatory activity in Quebec remains with the government.

Search for Uniformity

With ten provincial jurisdictions and no direct federal presence, there have been periodic efforts to integrate the various statutory regimes to facilitate national market activity in securities. The difficulties of achieving a national securities market regime can be exaggerated somewhat by drawing attention to the multifarious provincial jurisdictions. In reality, Ontario is the dominant securities environment with the most active market, the Toronto Stock Exchange. Ontario legislation has provided the example for smaller jurisdictions in the evolution of securities regulation in Canada. However, steps toward integration of the various provincial acts through copying Ontario's legislation have always been followed up by individual provincial amendments that have reversed the trend toward unification.

The earliest and, perhaps, the most successful attempt to integrate securities laws across Canada came in the 1930s. After the passage of the 1928 *Ontario Security Frauds Prevention Act*, the provinces met and eight of them adopted acts quite similar in form to the Ontario legislation.[102] However, as Williamson pointed out, by the time the one remaining province, New Brunswick, adopted a similar act, the other provinces had substantially amended their statutes, and the uniformity achieved to that point slowly dissipated.[103] Changes in the Ontario act periodically brought on renewed efforts by the provinces to achieve uniformity among the provincial jurisdictions, but none have proven to be entirely successful.

Efforts to provide uniformity have not ended with the effort to draft identical legislation, however. In addition, provincial administrators have met yearly to discuss policies and problems of securities regulation. These meetings by provincial administrators led, in part, to the creation of a rather formal organization, the Provincial Securities Administrators.[104] This organization was also a response to growing interest by the federal government in establishing a presence in the securities regulation field in the 1960s. Together, the securities administrators have produced a set of uniform policy statements.

The uniform policy statements have been the most serious effort to integrate provincial regimes. These policy statements are organized into three classes: the National Policy Statements that apply in all provinces except Newfoundland and Nova Scotia; the Uniform Act Policies that apply in Ontario and the Western provinces, and finally the Provincial Policies that apply in only the one province.[105] While these efforts to harmonize policy statements should not be ignored, their spillover effect has not been significant. In some ways, the multiple sets of statements only highlight the difficulties in moving to uniformity in such a complex regulatory environment, and, finally, harmonized policy statements are no substitute for a uniform statutory environment.

Considering the limited success at complete harmonization that we have examined, it might well be asked how harmful these legally diverse regulatory environments really are. As already suggested, a degree of harmony has resulted from the dominant position maintained by Ontario. This market dominance has encouraged other jurisdictions to remain sensitive to Ontario's rules. Moreover, the differences, while troublesome, may not seriously impede national market activity, certainly not to the extent of seriously impairing market efficiency. In addition, it may well be that the diversity of jurisdictions provides for new ideas and greater vitality in the regulatory environment.[106] Indeed, as the authors of the assessment of Quebec's new securities legislation suggest:

> It may be that, in the present federal context, the differences between the legislation in force from province to province will simply mirror the greater vitality of the regulatory authorities in each jurisdiction as they assert and express through legislation their own specific views of certain issues.[107]

Nonetheless, the potential for serious conflict between jurisdictions is always present, and the more that regulation takes on a planning aspect, the greater the potential for political conflict damaging this critical national resource. An episode of the 1970s reveals the potential for serious jurisdictional conflict as opposed to healthy competition. By Policy No. 4 issued by the Quebec Securities Commission, Quebec brokers were advised to execute a securities trade in Quebec, where possible, even if the broker could obtain better execution for his client on a market outside Quebec.[108] Though this policy position was later withdrawn, the policy statement reveals the serious political interference possible through the administrative process. Indeed, in both jurisdictions there had been recommendations in various reports to keep certain transactions of registered brokers within the separate jurisdictions.[109] Though these recommendations were never followed, they revealed the potentially harmful balkanization possible where regulation was fragmented and exogenous political factors were not excluded from regulation.

Contending Futures

The securities regulatory environments in Ontario and Quebec illustrate the contending economic and political pressures now affecting Canada. As pointed out in the Introduction, these pressures are complex and lead to divergent results. For instance, there are technological changes, particularly in the area of computer-assisted market transactions, which push toward a national market system. This outcome illustrates the role that technology has in outpacing and overwhelming any political or regulatory barriers.

Technology is a major influence when linked to market forces, but political forces are capable of deflecting, limiting or delaying technological changes. Political forces are quite capable of distorting the efficiencies inherent in market forces. Political pressures, as we shall show, have apparently encouraged competition between the capital markets of the two jurisdictions. What is less clear is whether the increase in competition between the exchanges, for instance, is likely to improve the overall health of securities markets or is intended to gain advantages for one market at the expense of the other. Additionally, it is unclear whether these pressures, for example Quebec's unilateral decision to "de-regulate" the financial services sector, are ultimately a move which improves the efficiency of financial services nation-wide or one intended as a means to other political ends which may well fragment the financial markets.

In looking at these technological and policy-making changes, one begins with the present structural reality that the Toronto Stock Exchange (TSE) far exceeds the volume traded by the Montreal Exchange.[110] The Montreal Exchange remains a junior actor compared to the much larger TSE. This market relationship has a bearing on the consequences of the technological and political forces that now influence the development of capital markets.

The TSE began to examine the potential of a computer-controlled execution system in the late 1960s. Its program, CATS, or the Computer-Assisted Trading System, was intended to enable this computer system to execute trades via terminals in members' offices.[111] As Clelland pointed out, this project was designed to replace traders meeting face-to-face and, even if it were still not possible to replace all face-to-face trades, then it would at least be capable of making more efficient trades by electronic communication.[112]

CATS has made major progress since the first-stage system began in 1975. By 1978, CATS executed the trades of some 80 relatively inactive stocks.[113] This number has increased since, and today CATS handles something like 20 percent of the trades of the TSE. Though there are still concerns that the CATS may not be able to handle both active and volatile stocks, there is no question that computer-assisted trading shows a growing presence in securities markets. Indeed, at the Tokyo Exchange, which operates a system like the TSE's CATS, the system handles far in excess of the present Toronto volumes.[114]

While there are concerns expressed by TSE floor traders and members as to the adequacy of the computer-assisted system, this technology has made a significant impact on the way the market operates and could, in the future, completely revolutionize trading. What is apparent, however, is that such a system as CATS cannot be introduced without affecting the position of the current markets and their regulators. Indeed, the decision by the TSE to begin automated transactions encouraged the Montreal Exchange to suggest an even broader program. A successful computer-based trading system designed by the TSE threatened certain Quebec interests. As Williamson pointed out, "This (CATS) would probably be of little concern to the Montreal members who also trade on the Toronto Exchange but would be a serious blow to a few firms that are members only of the Montreal Exchange, and it might be painful, too, for the government of Quebec."[115]

A committee was formed consisting of representatives of the Toronto, Montreal and Vancouver exchanges plus representatives of the national Investment Dealers Association and later the Alberta Exchange. By 1975, the committee had submitted a plan that was, in effect, a proposal for a new securities market, in other words a Canada-wide securities market. In the plan, it appeared that this new entity would be proposed as an Ontario corporation and would then likely come under the regulatory umbrella of the Ontario Securities Commission (OSC), though a new regulatory agency was possible.[116] Whatever the possibilities, it appears that this Canada-wide system, separate from though linked to the evolution of CATS, has not progressed. Instead, it appears that the expansion of computer-assisted trading will be dominated by the TSE. Such a result poses the uncomfortable possibility of an Ontario-imposed framework.

This possibility can hardly fit the plans of the Montreal Exchange or the Quebec government. Indeed the Montreal Exchange under the guidance of Pierre Lortie has done much to improve its competitiveness. In recent figures, the Montreal Exchange shows a significant increase in trading volume. In the first five months of 1984, for instance, Montreal's value of trading was 23.4 percent of the TSE's value, up from 14.5 percent in the comparable 1983 period.[117]

This improvement in the position of the Montreal Exchange is itself a result of significant changes in exchange policy as well as governmental support in Quebec. The Montreal Exchange has shifted to a modified

U.S. system of specialists in which one trader is responsible for making a market in a stock.[118] The Montreal Exchange has capped the maximum price that can be charged by a brokerage firm for any one transaction.[119] Beyond the aggressiveness of the exchange itself, the Quebec government has aided in its revitalization. It has provided a wide range of tax incentives. One plan encourages investment by offering a write-off of 166 percent on Quebec taxes for companies exploring for natural resources.[120] Another plan provides a tax-free grant to a maximum of $10,000 for developing companies that go public. Finally, the Quebec government has drawn up plans recently to give special tax benefits to professional market makers on the trading floor. The hope is to attract more capital to the exchange and make Montreal more competitive.[121]

Pointing out the increased competitiveness of the Montreal Exchange is not done to criticize these greater efforts but only to indicate the possibilities of severe conflict between Ontario and Quebec as computer-assisted market transactions dominated by the TSE become a growing possibility. Certainly, the current objectives of the Quebec government are not to build a more competitive national system but to improve the capital position of Quebec. A Toronto-dominated computer-assisted marketplace is hardly likely to be the end sought by Quebec's present government. At a minimum, technological changes and political objectives seem to be on a collision course. The more determined the Quebec government is to plan the province's economic development, the more likelihood there is of serious interprovincial conflict which could impede the securities markets and ultimately impose national economic costs.

The Quebec government's interventionist stance in revising Quebec's provincial financial services sector appears to hasten the pace of full-service financial institutions, at least as far as provincial jurisdiction allows. These changes appear to advance competitiveness by allowing a greater range of actors to enter fields that have, hitherto, been closed to many of them. Thus, former Quebec Finance Minister Parizeau's regulatory revisions appear to increase competitive forces. Once again, such actions may lead to interprovincial as well as federal-provincial conflict, particularly if such actions are, in fact, aimed at strengthening Quebec's capital markets and its institutions, even at the expense of others. It is not at all clear that the de-regulation of financial services will, in the long run, improve the health of securities markets, primary or secondary.

There have been increasing pressures from various financial intermediaries to expand the range of services that each may perform. Notable examples include the request by The Toronto-Dominion Bank to actively offer discount stock services — the so-called Green-line Service.[122] There was a request by Daly Gordon to the TSE to allow it to be linked to a large Belgian holding company. The request posed difficult questions regarding foreign ownership restrictions:[123] ownership by any single non-resident owner is restricted to a maximum of 10 percent.[124] Finally Midland Doherty, duplicating the cash management accounts pioneered by the U.S. stockbroker, Merrill Lynch Pierce Fenner & Smith Inc., is prepared to create similar accounts which amount to a form of chequing service.[125] These requests are the latest actions by various companies to diversify their financial services. In response, the Ontario government, or at least the regulatory agency most involved, the OSC, has undertaken a number of hearings to deal not only with the specific requests, but also to understand the broader consequences of the regulatory framework. The Ontario and the federal governments, as well, have decided to examine the broader questions posed by these de-regulatory pressures.

As noted earlier, Quebec has struck out on its own and plans to complete its de-regulatory steps by the end of 1985. Although Finance Minister Parizeau indicated, before his resignation, a willingness to consult with both the Ontario and the federal governments, he made it clear that Quebec would not slow its legislative timetable.[126]

What Quebec has done, through a series of legislative changes, is to ease the ownership rules and to permit the extensive diversity of functions in the financial markets. In 1983, the Quebec *Securities Act* was amended to remove ownership restrictions on provincially regulated securities dealers. The powers of mutual insurance and stock ownership insurance companies have been, or are about to be, broadened, as will the powers of the credit unions and trust companies.[127] The result in Quebec is evident. The Laurentienne Group of general life insurance companies has bought stock in the Quebec brokerage firm of Geoffrion Leclerc Inc. Standard Life Assurance Company acquired an interest in Trust général du Canada. Trust général has now acquired a limited brokerage licence. Montreal Trust Company has applied for a limited brokerage licence, and there are other changes completed or contemplated.[128]

Finance Minister Parizeau, while still holding that portfolio, was a strong advocate of de-regulation. Parizeau argued that his actions were absolutely necessary, since he believed that the specializations in the financial services sector could not be maintained against the need to diversify by the four pillars: banks, trusts, stock brokerage and insurance companies.[129] Quebec's actions may, in fact, be more and less than what they seem to be. First, the use of the term de-regulation is a misnomer. Quebec's policy is more appropriately called re-regulation with the integration of financial services functions added. One of the keys to the Parizeau plan was an expanded regulatory environment established under the Inspector General of Financial Institutions. This regulatory agency now oversees the trust companies, caisses populaires and insurance companies in Quebec. Thus, the policy provides for new functional regulation by one powerful regulatory agency which provides better surveillance and control.

The ends of "de-regulation," moreover, may be more than simple integration. Robert MacIntosh, president of the Canadian Bankers' Association, recently argued, "Obviously the whole strategy is to bolster Quebec based institutions."[130] And Parizeau himself, while still finance minister, argued, "It is clear that this approach could change nonbanking financial institutions into direct competitors with the banks. This is not in itself a bad thing."[131] In fact, it appears that behind the structure of de-regulation lies the Quebec government's objective, i.e., strengthening Quebec's financial sector by concentrating capital resources. Behind the discussion of de-regulation lies the desire to encourage a Quebec financial sector capable of sustaining itself against other Canadian companies. Quebec's actions are backed by new rules and new regulations. How willing Quebec would ultimately be to opening the sector to other Canadian companies is not clear. One need only remember the Quebec government's unwillingness to allow Credit Foncier to be sold to non-Quebec interests.

De-regulation appears to be a Quebec move to rewrite the regulatory environment: to control the sector while arguing for a more open competitive environment. At a minimum, Quebec's unilateral actions force the pace of change — particularly in Ontario. While the issues posed by integration of financial services must be faced, preparing for integration in Ontario and Quebec in isolation, and possibly in haste, may prove to be detrimental to Canada's capital markets. One result may well be that regulatory environments of Ontario and Quebec will not match. Such a result may, in fact, lead to a further balkanization of financial services across Canada. If Ontario's regulators impose stricter limitations, then, in order to do business in Quebec, firms will find it necessary to establish separate Quebec entities if they wish to continue operations in both environments.

In addition, as noted earlier, the rapid entry into integrated or diversified financial services is being undertaken with only limited attention being paid to the consequences of such an institutional arrangement for the financial markets. Concerns have been raised as to the effects of integration for the concentration of capital within the sector, the influence of large institutions, such as the banks, on the brokerage industry, and the possibilities of conflict of interest through integration but little has been said concerning the consequences of de-regulation for the health of the securities markets. In part, this is not surprising, since the debate really concerns the structure of the financial services industry, but the structural pattern will likely influence the health of the markets. It is certainly not apparent that an integrated financial services sector will be more attentive to the securities markets. Indeed, full service financial institutions may well be a real detriment to the capital markets as specialized services are ended and, as we have argued, Canada has a need for strong financial markets. However, the political and regulatory environments appear to inhibit serious discussion of the health of financial markets.

Securities regulation in Canada has been dominantly provincial. Like other cases we have examined, provincial securities regulation has served as a major tool for policing a vital segment of the financial markets. Like other policy areas, regulation has emerged as a planning tool for provincial governments and their agents. Policy planning, particularly in the major provincial jurisdictions, has imported wider political objectives. Harmonization of policies has become a more remote possibility. This, in and of itself, as we noticed, is not highly damaging. What it does is to reflect the divergences that exist. Because technological and political pressures have created a highly uncertain environment, the potential for serious differences has increased. Moreover, the differing provincial agencies have made it more difficult to discuss changes. Thus, while the need for change has become more pressing, the capacity for uniform action has declined. Even in the face of broad economic and technological changes, financial markets are faced with the real possibility of damaging policy actions. Such competitive political action is not likely to enhance Canadian capital markets or improve financial market capacity. Once again, Canada is left poised between underdeveloped market forces and inefficient political forces. In an increasingly competitive international economy, such a situation cannot be contemplated with indifference.

Chapter 5

Conclusions: *Issues and Options*

The Royal Commission on the Economic Union and Development Prospects for Canada has a comprehensive and ambitious mandate. One of its central concerns is Canada's capacity to adapt to the changing nature of the world economy, and a significant aspect of that mandate is the concern for the impact of the federal system on that capacity. More specifically, there is a concern about the need to harmonize government activities related to the economy so as to manage intergovernmental conflicts effectively and to achieve efficiency and effectiveness in such activities. The purpose of this research project has been to focus on one important aspect of the intergovernmental dimension of economic management, namely the intergovernmental politics of economic regulation. Such a focus is derived from the fact that, as noted by the Commission in its report *Challenges and Choices*, there has been a transformation in the manner in which governments involve themselves in the lives of Canadians.[1] One of the more important aspects of this transformation has been the use of economic regulation as a major policy instrument. Although it is difficult to establish precise measurements to support our claim, we would contend that, in certain sectors of the economy, some of which are central to our economic prospects, economic regulation has emerged as a rival to spending and taxing as an instrument for shaping and influencing the nature of economic activities. Such a development, it is our contention, has had significant consequences for intergovernmental relations in Canada, consequences that go to the heart of the Commission's mandate, and the wider general concerns about a conflict-laden intergovernmental system. This project has sought, through a series of case studies, to identify the causes of those conflicts involving economic regulation and the impact they have had on economic policy making.

In this concluding chapter it is not our intention to summarize the findings and the conclusions of the three individual case studies. The case studies were undertaken, as indicated in Chapter 1, not with the presumption that they could prove the central hypothesis that has guided this project, but with the belief that they could effectively illustrate that hypothesis and lend support for the general arguments of the study. In this chapter, we propose, instead, to review the general issues that arise from the employment of economic regulation as a primary policy instrument as they relate to the Commission's central concerns about the intergovernmental politics of economic policy making and the impact of such politics on Canada's capacity to adapt. The second section of the chapter will review some of the major possible responses for ameliorating the problems that have developed. We must emphasize that, in the latter section, we will not attempt to propose possible policies for any of the individual sectors that have provided the basis for our case studies. Nor will we attempt to recommend specific courses of action either for the Commission or for a more general audience. We will confine ourselves to an overview of the major options that, in our opinion, merit consideration.

Economic Regulation and the Federal System: The Issues

In Chapter 1, we provided what was described as a "working definition" of economic regulation. For our purposes, such regulation involves the employment of the coercive power of the state to influence and/or control the economic behaviour or choices of firms and individuals. With respect to economic behaviour, we confined regulation to three specific areas: entry into an activity, price-setting and standard-setting with the last being distinctly tertiary. In much of the literature there is an assumption, sometimes explicit, usually implicit, that economic regulation as an instrument of governance has served but one function, namely to police specific economic activities so as to prevent what society, via the political process, has defined as unacceptable corporate behaviour.

Our contention, and it is central to our analysis, is that to confine regulation a priori to the strait-jacket of a single function is unacceptable. To the extent that regulation is defined as a problem area, the single-function assumption may not only misdirect any analysis of the problem, it will also misdirect the search for solutions. Economic regulation, as it has been employed in Canada, has been multi-functional. It has been employed as an instrument for government influence or control over economic activities to serve positive, prescriptive functions over and above the negative, proscriptive function of policing. We have used the terms promoting and planning to describe the positive functions of regulation.

In itself, there is little that is particularly novel about our attempt to delineate the multi-functional use of regulation. James Landis, in a pioneering American study, recognized this as early as 1936.[2] Similarly, J.A. Corry, after describing the regulatory activities of the Canadian government in 1941, concluded that "in each, the aim goes beyond the negative one of trying to discourage individuals from embarking on particular kinds of action. It transcends the criminal law type of social control, in that it seeks positive objectives, some modification of the economic and social environment."[3] In this respect, our contribution, if worthwhile, has been to provide a framework to permit a more systematic analysis of the nature of the different functions and how they differ from one another.

For purposes of distinguishing them, we feel that there are two major perspectives from which one can view the three, admittedly "ideal," types of regulatory functions — policing, promoting and planning. The first is from the viewpoint of the decisional processes employed by the regulator, and the second is from the viewpoint of the scope of regulatory decision making. We have suggested that there is a cluster of characteristics that typify the decisional processes of policing regulation. Such processes are usually reactive, remedial and issue specific. If one conceptualizes the three functions as constituting a continuum with planning and policing the polar types, planning incorporates a far more "proactive" or initiating role as well as a generalized, problem-solving, policy-oriented approach to decision making.

The second dimension useful for distinguishing the individual regulatory functions pertains to the scope of regulatory decision making. Using the three concepts of structure, conduct and goals or objectives as indicators of regulatory scope, we suggested that there were major differences associated with the individual functions. The argument was that policing regulation, as a polar type, was less likely to be concerned with structural questions and more likely to regulate a limited range of corporate activities. Planning regulation, on the other hand, played a role in structural matters and subjected a much more comprehensive set of business activities to regulation. Promoting regulation, on these measures, would fall somewhere in between the two poles, depending on the purpose of promotion. By far the most significant point of differentiation involves the objectives or goals. Policing regulation, we maintain, is employed to pursue a fairly narrow, circumscribed set of public objectives that are primarily internal or endogenous to the industry regulated. By this latter point, we mean that regulatory policy objectives in a policing regime are usually confined to those involving the most immediate participants, the firms and their customers. Planning regulation, however, is employed to attain a much broader, more comprehensive set of goals, including, and possibly primarily, exogenous objectives. Such objectives involve the use of the sector or the firm for goals external to the main participants. An example would be regulation of railroads to promote regional development; another would involve regulating telecommunications for national unity objectives.

Building on the preceding, we suggested a further distinction which is that policing regulation focusses primarily on rules, whereas planning emphasizes outcomes. In other words, the former concentrates on patrolling the boundaries within which corporate behaviour must operate, while the latter seeks to direct economic activity toward the attainment of publicly determined objectives. The conceptual analysis, while perhaps somewhat abstract, is crucial to understanding the central analytical concern that provides the focus for an investigation of the politics of regulation. That concern is the degree of autonomy permitted corporate decision makers to make essential economic decisions. We argued that policing regulation endows corporate executives with the greatest degree of autonomy to make the central decisions affecting their firms. In planning regulation, however, corporate autonomy is diminished significantly with government emerging as the primary goal setter not only for the firm, but also for the industry or sector of economic activity. We suggested that a useful shorthand method for further distinguishing the principal types of regulation is to characterize policing regulation as *firm-led* or *firm-dominant* economic decision making, and planning regulation as *state-led* or *state-dominant* economic decision making.

A central concern for the Royal Commission is with the politics of economic policy making and, specifically, how the politics and structures of economic policy making affect the development and attainment of national goals and policies. The preceding is directly relevant to this concern. The central argument advanced in this study is that the individual regulatory functions are characterized by distinctive patterns of politics, that is, patterns of political relationships and conflicts and, further, that the nature of the pattern has an impact on the attainment of public goals. We contend that changing the regulatory function changes, significantly, the politics of regulation. No doubt other aspects could be usefully included; however, we have chosen to concentrate on two in particular because they provide the bridge to understanding why and how the politics of regulation can affect the satisfactory pursuit of economic policy objectives. These two facets are first, the patterns of interest representation and participation in the regulatory process and second, the pattern of relationships between regulatory issues, institutions and processes and other political issues, institutions and processes.

In this study we have not attempted a comprehensive test of our basic argument that changes in the degree of corporate autonomy cause changes in the patterns of political processes and relationships. We have limited the study to an analysis of the significance of the intergovernmental politics of economic regulation for the politics of economic policy making. More specifically, we advanced the hypothesis that that there is a causal connection between intergovernmental conflict and changes in the function of regulation. The conflict increases as economic regulation performs less of a policing function and more of a planning function. Why should conflict increase? If we put to one side considerations of partisanship, personalities, status and simple territorial imperatives, all of which in varying degrees play some role, we come to the basic reason. Public policies are not neutral in their impact. They can confer or create advantages for some individuals over others, for some firms over others, for some industries over others. Changing the function of regulation so as to enhance the role of the state at the expense of corporate decision makers gives those who occupy state decision-making positions another set of tools and policies for conferring or creating advantages.

In Canada, we have eleven sets of state decision makers. When the function of regulation is changed so as to enhance the role of one set of those decision makers, it is inevitable that all or some of the others will be affected. We have suggested that a useful approach for understanding those effects is to analyze their impact on the tripartite roles of governments as interest representatives, as owners of regulated firms and as policy makers. If some governments perceive that their vital interests, as defined by these roles -- and there could be others -- are adversely affected, potentially or actually, they will not automatically defer to the goal setting of others. This is true, we suggest, both across and between levels of government. The result is increased intergovernmental conflict, although we would suggest that the intensity of the conflict may vary with the specific governmental role affected. Governments are more likely to do battle with other governments when they perceive their policy role to be influenced or constrained by other governments than if they see their representative or ownership roles being challenged.

Of course, the problem is not intergovernmental conflict per se. Conflict can be healthy if it leads to offering alternative definitions of public issues and policy options. Conflict in this sense is normal in a democratic society and not only to be expected, but also encouraged. Consequently, to ask the question, "What has been the impact of changing the function of economic regulation on intergovernmental relations?" and to get the answer that it leads to increased conflict is nothing new. The far more important question is, "What is the significance of intergovernmental conflict, so caused, for economic policy making?" More specifically, what are the policy consequences of such conflict, and if they are negative, how are they to be ameliorated? These, then, are the important questions and issues to which this study gives rise and that need to be addressed. In the remainder of this chapter, we shall first sketch out some of our reasons for believing that the consequences are indeed serious and then, secondly, delineate some of the possible responses.

In its first round of public hearings, the Commission "found federal-provincial conflict discussed most often in terms of problems not solved, interests not served, priorities not set and opportunities lost for want of a common purpose."[4] Elsewhere, it quotes a senior Canadian corporate executive who decried the all too common impact on the economic union of "government against government."[5] These two observations accurately and concisely sum up what we believe to be the consequences of intergovernmental conflict caused by changes in the function of regulation. Our case studies of airlines and telecommunications illustrate some of these consequences most graphically. In particular, they illustrate how the conflicts can immobilize governments and prevent them from accomplishing their objectives.

The most serious consequence of such conflicts is that they can create barriers to adaptation and effective public response in areas of economic policy where change is perceived to be necessary. A related facet of this is that governments may choose to use their often significant resources to undermine the goals of other governments, and this may lead to socially unjustifiable and wasteful intergovernmental competition. A further unfortunate consequence of intergovernmental conflict and one that is all too common regardless of the policy instruments involved, is that distinctly second-order questions of who or which level of government will decide can effectively pre-empt first-order questions about the appropriate public policy goals and objectives. This is not to deny that the former may be surrogates for the latter but simply to suggest that intergovernmental disputes can easily degenerate into battles over turf to the detriment of substance.

When focussing on policy consequences, it is imperative that we do not adopt an unduly government-centred perspective. The costs of such conflicts are not only those of public "immobilisme" and wasted resources; there are also significant costs borne by the firms and industries that are embroiled in intergovernmental disputes and borne also by their customers, suppliers and competitors. There are two primary categories of corporate costs.

The first costs arise from the need to expend greater resources monitoring and, where necessary and possible, participating in the policy development process. A move from policing to planning regulation increases these costs in two respects. First, there is the additional cost imposed because government in general is a much more significant actor in corporate decision making, so that sound strategic planning requires greater attention to be paid to government activities. Second, there is the cost of the intergovernmental process itself. If such a process emerges as an important forum with a significant impact on corporate decision making, then resources must be spent monitoring and, where possible, influencing the decision making in that forum. It should be acknowledged that dealing with governments is an unavoidable reality in an era of the active state and therefore, any increase in costs associated with changing the nature of regulation are, at worst, incremental. Moreover, it should not be forgotten that some of the costs of dealing with governments are the result of corporate demands on government for benefits and not simply responses to government influence on business.

It is the second major category of costs, which are both financial and psychological and which are incurred as a result of increased intergovernmental conflict, that are the more troublesome. Under a policing regulatory regime, corporate decision makers have considerable discretion in their response to technological and economic changes. When corporate executives are responsible for planning their destinies, the corporate capacity to adapt is, all other things being equal, primarily a function of corporate abilities and processes. Planning regulation and, more importantly for us, intergovernmental conflict over such planning, profoundly alter this relationship. Whatever the merits of government planning exercises (merits we do not choose to assess), when governments in relative isolation attempt to plan, firms must take government initiatives into consideration and, indeed, these intiatives become primary. However, when one government proposes to plan, but other governments object, the result is not status quo ante with the regulated firm maintaining its decision-making autonomy as the result of the intergovernmental stand-off. The most likely outcome is the creation of a planning vacuum. Corporate decision makers must wait for state decision makers to resolve their conflicts.

This may not be a major source of concern in a relatively stable, insulated environment. However, in a dynamic environment, characterized by considerable technological change and one not protected from external forces such as international developments, putting planning on hold may severely impair corporate adaptability. Equipment may not be purchased or updated; investments may not be made in research and development. This is a situation in which corporate decision makers must respond to uncertain but unavoidable economic forces as well as to government decision makers, but they are unable to respond effectively to either because the latter cannot decide. A further impediment to corporate adaptability is that the emphasis corporate executives would place on such objectives as efficiency is not likely to bear the same weight in the intergovernmental disputes over plans for industrial activities. As a result the context for corporate adaptability is heavily influenced by governments, both in the conflicts themselves and in the priorities for their resolution.

On the other hand, all the costs of intergovernmental conflicts must not be placed on the backs of governments. Although they may have more autonomy to shape both their policy agenda and their decisions than is commonly assumed, governments do not, in a democratic society such as ours, exist and operate in a vacuum. They reflect and respond to demands and pressures from within their individual constituencies. Those pressures emanate, generally, from electorates but more specifically and directly from interested parties, most notably businesses. Governments do not confer advantages and disadvantages in a vacuum; they are persuaded to act. The regulatory process, or the "regulation game" as it has been astutely described, is a major arena where private actors pursue, through the instruments of government, the attainment of advantage over competitors.[6] Any discussion of the costs of government would be remiss in ignoring this important aspect of the reality of policy making.

There is a final set of costs that result from intergovernmental conflict over regulatory planning. These costs, however, are imposed only when such planning is assigned to an independent regulatory agency. To the extent that regulatory planning is attempted by a government department, the following considerations do not arise. The costs that we believe intergovernmental conflict may cause, as a result of a shift from a policing to a planning functon for a regulatory agency, involve the legitimacy and the capacity of such an agency.

Our contention is that by assigning a planning role to an independent regulatory agency, the resulting degree of politicization (especially to the extent that the agency becomes embroiled in the wider political conflicts) may undermine the legitimacy of the agency as a public decision maker. It will be recalled from Chapter 1 that regulatory agencies, by and large, were created not so much to take issues "out of politics" as to change the political arena and, consequently, the relationship between regulatory political issues and elected authorities. There was a presumed need for impartial, specialized decision makers who would be relatively removed and insulated from wider political conflicts. In order to reinforce the legitimacy of their role, members of agencies developed an organizational ethos that complemented their legislative mandates. They did this by concentrating on specific, narrowly-defined issues and by emphasizing the importance of precedent in their decision making. One major measure of their success was that, prior to the late 1960s, there was no significant questioning of their accountability. The issue did not arise because their legitimacy was established.

One of the major consequences of a shift to planning regulation is to remove the insulation, the buffer, that protects the regulatory agency. Although the architects of planning by agency may take it for granted, there is no inherent reason why other affected parties should defer to the competence of the agency as a planner. In other words, the specialized competence granted to legitimized agency decision making in a policing function is denied that agency in a planning role. For the agency, the cost of such a development is that there is no automatic reason for their decisions being respected or obeyed. This is particularly troublesome when planning is not the sole or major function of the agency because the loss of legitimacy extends to other roles, and the continuing effectiveness of the agency may, ultimately, be called into question.

A related aspect of this is the debate concerning the accountability of regulatory agencies. In the last decade, and it is no coincidence, there has been widespread criticism of the independent decision-making capacity of these agencies, especially at the federal level. Such criticism has come, not surprisingly, from provincial governments, but it has come, as well, from federal ministers to whom such agencies report. This has led to the development of proposals for increased political control which, in turn, raises concern about potential political interference in areas where regulatory independence is deemed to be necessary.[7]

Although a decline in legitimacy can by itself undermine the effectiveness of regulatory agencies, equal attention needs to be paid to the impact on the decision-making capacity of such agencies as a result of a shift from policing to planning with its attendant politicization. There is good reason for asking whether or not regulatory agencies might lose their "comparative institutional advantage" in the process. Politicians have considerable flexibility in determining their agenda; regulatory agencies do not. Of particular importance is the fact that once a matter is before them, regulatory agencies unlike politicians have, as indicated earlier, "a duty to decide." In addition, political processes are more appropriate for the negotiating, adjusting and accommodating of diverse interests than the typical adversarial regulatory process. Further, the regulatory decision-making instruments are fairly restricted compared to those of more traditional political decision makers. In particular, regulatory agencies, while they have the means to confer advantages on participants, are even more confined than political decision makers in placating those who lose as a result of their decisions. Finally, there is the more general consideration as to whether or not the tools designed for "command and control" regulation are functional for the open-ended goal-setting process that is necessary in areas of dynamic technological and economic change, especially where efficiency, productivity and technological development need to be fostered.[8] Although concerns about the capacity of regulatory agencies as agents for planning need to be addressed on their own, the intergovernmental conflicts caused by a shift to planning both bring them to the fore and reinforce them.

Economic Regulation and the Federal System: The Options

We believe that there are substantial costs imposed on both the public and corporate sectors in Canada by intergovernmental conflicts arising from changes in the function of economic regulation. If the regulated sectors are to contribute to the efficiency and adaptability of the Canadian economy and, given their vital infrastructural role, it is essential that they do, then these costs must be lowered. In this concluding section, we describe four major options that address these costs: maintaining the status quo; joint regulatory mechanisms; "political regulation"; and de-regulation. Before turning to these options, we must comment briefly on two other options which, at first glance, one might reasonably think should be discussed: interdelegation of powers and parliamentary approval or ratification of federal regulatory appointments. While we believe that there is considerable merit in principle in both these solutions for addressing some of the intergovernmental problems associated with the workings of regulatory systems, it is our opinion that neither addresses the core problem analyzed in this study.[9] To reiterate, our concern has been with changes in the function of economic regulation as a cause of intergovernmental conflict.

Maintaining the Status Quo

Inclusion of maintenance of the status quo as an option is not pro forma. There are those who would contend that this is the most attractive of all options. The reasons for this position are twofold. In the first place, it can be argued that changes in the function of economic regulation do not play the causal role that we have assigned to them. Consequently, if the problem has been misdiagnosed or overemphasized, then significant changes in the existing system of roles and relationships will be misguided. The second argument for the status quo is straightforward. Whatever the defects of the existing system, any alternative may be worse. This approach was suggested in a recent conference on Canadian–U.S. regulatory issues in the communications sector by Ian P. Sharp. He argued that the only thing worse than the existing situation, in which public policy was ten years behind technology, was the prospect that some day it might catch up. As he explained it:

> We will be okay as long as this time gap remains, as long as the legislators never get to the stage where they say, "We have to solve this problem because it is today's problem, and therefore, we have to solve it today." If that time ever comes, that is when we are all going to get into terrible trouble.[10]

We believe that the arguments in favour of the status quo are defective in two respects. Obviously, we reject the argument that we may have misdiagnosed the problem, although it should be emphasized again that we have not argued that changes in the regulatory function are the sole cause of the conflicts analyzed in the three case studies. We are persuaded by the evidence, however, and additional studies (for example, in the broadcasting and energy sectors) could only reinforce our contention that the intergovernmental conflicts have in very large part been caused by such changes. In drawing this conclusion, however, we remind the reader that it pertains to only one aspect of the politics of regulation. We have not attempted a broader analysis that would identify the causes of the changes in the regulatory function and the subsequent intergovernmental conflicts.

The second argument in defence of the status quo is less easily refuted. If government "immobilisme" was the primary consequence of the type of intergovernmental conflict we have studied, then perhaps the problems are not so serious as to warrant substantial policy changes. The underlying premise of such a position, of course, is that in the absence of authoritative public policy, it is business as usual for corporate decision makers. However, this premise may be highly suspect. There may be a serious problem, in the first place, if, as a result of intergovernmental conflict, the legitimacy and capacity of regulatory agencies are eroded and this erosion adversely affects the conduct of business in regulated sectors. More important, however, is the potential impact of intergovernmental conflict on corporate planning. If such conflict causes a planning vacuum, which we have suggested to be a real possibility and, therefore, a significant cost, then the status quo is clearly not defensible. Furthermore, the status quo is even less acceptable if two jurisdictions, either across or within levels of government, employ their regulatory powers to create barriers to the free flow of goods, capital or services. In other words, the status quo may be acceptable if it can be established that its impact on corporate decision making or on the operations of the economic union is minimal. Absent such a defence, the status quo is not easily defensible.

Joint Regulatory Mechanisms

The second major option is some variant of joint regulation across jurisdictional lines, either federal-provincial or interprovincial, depending on the source of the regulatory conflict. There are several major variants of this option. One would have existing regulatory agencies, federal or provincial, meet together to engage in joint hearings at least and at most, joint decision making on common problems. Various proposals along these lines have been made to deal with regulatory conflicts in securities, telecommunications and aspects of the transportation sector.[11] A second major variant would entail the power of appointment by one level of government of members of a regulatory agency established by another level.[12] Although it is possible that the flow of such appointments would be federal to provincial agencies, the most common proposal is for provincial appointments to federal agencies.

Although there are substantial differences among the various proposals that call for joint regulation, there is little utility, for our purposes, in discussing all of them. What is significant is that all accept the principle that there should be some form of shared decision making because different governments have legitimate interests in a particular area. In effect, all such proposals rest, in varying degrees, on the acceptance of de facto concurrency in the exercise of regulatory power. It is this principle that needs to be addressed in an assessment of this option.

The advantages of joint regulation premised on concurrency are obvious and immediate. Such a regulatory system would provide the participating governments with substantial policy influence to ensure that their interests, however determined, are respected. The argument has been emphasized by Lesser who noted that " . . . concurrency should imply a form of partnership. Even if the partners are not exactly equal in status, each should have an effective role to play in the decision-making process."[13] If this is the result, the consequence for governments is that the price of intergovernmental conflicts would be reduced significantly, if not eliminated entirely. For companies that are regulated, a joint regulatory system has an equal potential for reducing their costs. Such a system would provide a single forum for regulatory decision making — "one stop regulation" — which should provide for the elimination of overlaps and conflicts. Even more importantly, joint regulation should reduce the costs of dealing with several regulators and permit both the regulated and the regulators to avoid the problems of either two-tier regulation, i.e., federal-provincial, or dual regulation, i.e., provincial-provincial. Most significantly, perhaps, the vacuum in planning should be eliminated by terminating the intergovernmental conflicts inasmuch as the rules and objectives of regulation would be agreed upon. Finally, joint regulation if accepted by the governments should attenuate the loss of legitimacy for the regulatory agencies involved. Indeed, by providing an intergovernmental foundation for regulation, the legitimacy of the regulator could be enhanced.

Attainment of these advantages would be dependent, however, in surmounting some significant hurdles. The first major hurdle would be the development of a system for regulatory appointments to the joint agency. In particular, the allocation of members to each government would be a serious problem. In the telecommunications industry, for example, the following are only five of many proposals that have been made for the membership of a joint regulatory body:

- six federal appointees, five provincial appointees;
- six provincial, three federal;
- ten provincial, three federal;
- ten provincial, one federal; or
- federal government has one less than provincial appointees.[14]

The central point at issue is that no government wants to be assigned permanently to a minority position and so become a potential perpetual "loser" in the regulatory system. This problem, which would be less of a concern for policing regulation, is obviously a central issue for those governments which believe that regulation can and should be employed as a more positive instrument of governing. In this situation, the regulatory stakes are clearly greater and the issue of membership is even more crucial.

Even if the allocation of appointments could be agreed upon, a joint regulatory system would need to confront the difficult problem of the nature of regulatory representation. Simply put, are members of a joint regulatory agency representatives, i.e., delegates, of their respective appointing governments or are they, once appointed, independent members of a quasi-judicial agency? Under the existing systems, federal and provincial, regulators, once appointed, are not assumed to represent their appointers any more than members of the judiciary. As adjudicators, they are presumed to be independent of those who made their appointment, and such a presumption is a necessary condition for agency or judicial legitimacy. The problem with independent regulators is closely linked with the function of regulation. If regulation is confined to a policing function, the issue is not that pressing, if indeed it is a problem at all. However, if planning regulation is attempted, then governments will want to ensure that their objectives are achieved. If the members of a joint agency are not independent but are delegates, the result can only be that the Intergovernmental conflicts will continue. They are simply transferred to another political arena, the regulatory agency. Such a development would not only undermine the legitimacy of the agency as far as affected interests are concerned but, undoubtedly, result in the same stalemates and impasses typical of the wider intergovernmental system. If this is the result, the costs for governments and regulators are not reduced.

If governments accept the principle that regulators, once appointed, are independent agents and not delegates, they will have to confront the problem that has been central to the debates over the Canadian Radio-television and Telecommunications Commission (CRTC) at the federal level. How does a government ensure that policy making remains the responsibility, primarily at least, of elected authorities and is not unduly delegated to an independent agency? Again, this was not normally deemed to be a problem with policing regulation. If regulation is to play a planning role with elected authorities given responsibility to determine the policies that regulators are to implement, we are left with the problem of resolving the intergovernmental policy disputes. In other words, a joint regulatory system may be a structure without an agreed upon set of purposes or objectives. For governments, this may be acceptable, inasmuch as they will no longer face the threat of an independent agency as "loose cannon," but for corporate decision makers, the situation would be little different from the planning vacuum that existed as a result of intergovernmental conflicts prior to the creation of the joint agency.

Political Regulation

The third option would entail radical, although not novel, changes in the nature of the regulatory process. Under this option, the search for a solution to the intergovernmental problems would focus on the independence of regulatory agencies. More specifically, this option involves a fully politicized model of regulation without recourse to independent regulatory authorities. Under this option, there could be several choices, such as cabinet or an individual minister exercising regulatory responsibilities or integrating the regulatory body within a department of government and assigning it advisory powers only.

Variations on this politicized model of regulation are not new. It will be recalled that, prior to the creation of independent agencies, regulatory powers were vested in cabinets, cabinet committees, ministers and Parliament itself. Recently, moreover, there has been recourse to such as models. Among the available current examples are the Foreign Investment Review Agency, the Prairie Rail Action Committee, the Northern Pipeline Agency, the Grains Commissioners, the Petroleum Monitoring Agency and the Canada Oil and Gas Lands Administration (COGLA). The recent licensing process and decision by the minister of communications for cellular radio telephone systems under the *Radio Act* is an example of individual ministerial regulatory decision making.[15]

There are a number of potential advantages in this option. In terms of intergovernmental relations, it provides an opportunity, if the governments are agreeable, to recognize the "special status" of governments and to incorporate that status into the regulatory process. The FIRA mandating legislation, for example, requires that any determination of the acceptability of reviewable investments take into consideration the views of affected provincial governments.[16] Regulation under COGLA goes even further, as Doern and Toner note:

> COGLA also works with provincial governments to ensure that their needs and responsibilities are addressed. It is the Government of Canada's intention that COGLA's mandate be integrated with that of other levels of government. In March 1982, the federal and Nova Scotia governments signed an agreement creating the Canada–Nova Scotia Offshore Oil and Gas Board. Through the Board, which is chaired by the COGLA Administrator, representatives of the federal and Nova Scotia governments jointly manage resource development off the Nova Scotia coast. Under the agreement, the Nova Scotia representatives can if necessary delay decisions for up to one year in order to ensure full consideration of provincial concerns.[17]

In terms of the regulatory process, there are two possible advantages. The first is that the process can be speeded up considerably because politicized regulation does not require the use of the trial-type adversarial proceedings typical of independent agencies. Secondly, with the integration of the regulatory function into wider political processes, the problem of political control over independent regulatory agency decision making does not arise.

The disadvantages of the politicized regulatory model are not insignificant. In the first place, to the extent that political, rather than bureaucratic, authorities are responsible for making regulatory decisions, the demands on their time, especially for making individual decisions rather than establishing the policy to be implemented, can be considerable. This was, for example, regarded as a major defect of the FIRA process.[18] Secondly, this model of regulation undermines one of the fundamental rationales for the creation of separate independent agencies, namely to transfer a subset of politically contentious decisions from the partisan political arena to another, less overtly political, forum. Consequently political regulators may be required to assume political responsibility for their decisions, although the example of FIRA suggests that under certain circumstances such responsibility may be deflected. A third disadvantage arises from the fact that providing a decision-making system more conducive to intergovernmental accommodation does not ensure that such accommodation will occur. Unlike regulatory agencies, politicians do not have a "duty to decide" and consequently, having to confront one's adversaries face-to-face, as it were, without the advantage of shifting responsibility may easily result, not in more effective, efficient or even faster decision making, but in no decision making at all.

There are also significant disadvantages for affected parties in the regulatory process, including not just the regulated companies but broader interests. Politicized regulation will require that impartial decision making be foregone as there will be neither any requirement nor any method of imposing such a demand on decision makers. Moreover, given that political decision makers are not bound to give reasons for their decisions, the regulatory process would lose its predictability for regulated parties. Closely related to this would be the loss of what is, perhaps, one of the major characteristics of the process of regulation by independent agency, namely its openness to broader public participation and scrutiny than that possible through political regulation. A recent Federal Court decision on the issue of disclosure of information in cabinet appeals highlights the three preceding problems. In that decision Justice LeDain stated:

> It would not in my opinion be reasonable to ascribe to Parliament an intention that the duty to act fairly should impose on the Governor in Council . . . any particular manner of considering a petition or appeal, any

particular limits to the right to consult, or any particular duty of disclosure with respect to intragovernmental submissions. These are all matters which go to the very heart of the Cabinet's need to be master of its procedure and to receive from governmental sources the advice it requires concerning policy under the protection of the secrecy which all members of the Council have sworn to observe.[19]

A final disadvantage is the danger that, while political regulation would mean political control over decision making, it would not lead to enhanced political accountability. Paradoxically, political control may result in diminished accountability, if the FIRA example is any guide.[20]

De-regulation

The fourth and final option that we consider is de-regulation. We do so with some trepidation because it is often difficult to have a reasoned discussion about its merits and weaknesses. For some, it carries with it the spectre of selfish, unbridled market forces; for others, of course, that spectre is the ideal. In addition, in the current geopolitical environment, to introduce de-regulation as an option worthy of serious consideration is to risk being dismissed as "un-Canadian." So powerful are the currents of emotion surrounding the concept, that the former government refused to label its new policy on airline regulation as de-regulation, preferring instead the more innocuous term "liberalization." This is unfortunate. If this study has accomplished anything, it will have established that regulation is not one dimensional. If this is the case, then de-regulation must be treated as equally multi-faceted.

If regulation is a policing function, de-regulation can, indeed, constitute a substitution of market for political control. On the other hand, if regulation is employed for planning purposes, then de-regulation would not constitute, necessarily or even probably, a transfer of control to the market but rather a move away from planning back to promoting or policing regulation. For this situation, some would perhaps prefer the term "re-regulation." We believe this to be unnecessary obfuscation. For us, de-regulation is a legitimate, neutral, generic term to indicate not necessarily a total removal, but a lessening of public control over corporate decision making. In analyzing the merits of de-regulation, we will confine the discussion to de-regulation which involves a move away from regulatory planning. The justification for this is derived from the central concern of this study, which is how to lessen intergovernmental conflicts caused by a shift from policing to planning regulation.

De-regulation as we envisage it, namely, as the termination of planning regulation, would have the immediate advantage of removing the most proximate cause of intergovernmental conflict. To be more accurate, it would remove the cause of conflict only from the regulatory arena because, undoubtedly, the conflicts would be transferred to other political arenas. This would be, however, a small success. To the extent that the regulatory agency or process was restricted to a policing role, this would lead to a significant depoliticization of the function of regulation. In the present environment, this would enhance the legitimacy of the regulatory agencies as well as remove the major threats to their decision-making capacity.

For corporate decision makers, the termination of regulatory planning would enhance their decision-making autonomy vis-à-vis regulatory authorities. This would result from the fact that corporate planning would be no longer tied to public planning via regulatory licensing and price setting. This, of course, would not mean that corporate planners could act in complete isolation. It would simply mean that "command and control" public tools would not be employed to impose positive goals. Corporate decision makers could still be influenced by a broad range of government instruments such as tax and subsidy policies as well as by a new competition policy if this could be enacted. In short, governments would not be totally bereft of influence over corporate decision makers. They would, however, have to place a greater emphasis on incentives rather than coercion.

The only major disadvantage that we can identify with the de-regulation option is that the governments choosing this option will be surrendering their use of what has emerged as a major policy tool for directing corporate decision makers. Over the past two or three decades, regulation has become attractive as a governing instrument for a number of reasons. It has an immediate impact; its full costs are dispersed and do not show up as a significant component of public spending. In addition, the regulatory instrument appears to be flexible and, not insignificantly, given the tradition of specialized, impartial agencies, provides an opportunity (to paraphrase Schultze) for the "public use of the corporate interest" that gives regulation the appearance of being far less political than it might otherwise be.

Given the arguments contained in the preceding paragraph, it will be difficult to persuade governments to relinquish voluntarily what appears to be a very attractive instrument of government. We believe, however, that the basic argument of this study and the individual cases used to illustrate this argument should convince governments, at both levels, to reassess the purpose and value of regulation. We face the prospect that intergovernmental conflicts over government regulation may not only waste public and corporate resources but may rob regulation of any utility. Charles Schultze has argued that:

> Precisely because the legitimate occasions for social intervention will continue to multiply as society becomes more complex, congested and technologically sophisticated, the collective-coercion component of intervention should be treated as a scarce resource.[21]

We would conclude by urging that, at a time when Canadian decision makers, public and corporate, are faced with tremendous challenges, we cannot afford to squander the resource of regulation. Our study has sought to demonstrate that this is a very real possibility.

Appendix: Selected Tables

TABLE A-1 Bond Issuers

Country	End of 1977	Amount	Percentage of Total
Canada in Cdn$ millions	General government and its enterprises	100,885	75
	Private non-financial enterprises and financial institutions	33,554	25
	Total	134,439	
United States in US$ millions	Central government	284,454	26
	Central government lending agencies	166,042	15
	State and local governments	271,343	24
	Domestic, private and foreign	390,686	35
	Total	1,112,525	
France in F Fr billions	Central government (nominal value)	22.47	7
	Public sectors	192.71	64
	Private sector	85.17	28
	Total	300.35	
U.K. in £ millions	Central government	39,419	77
	Local government	2,934	6
	Public non-financial enterprises	1,900	4
	Private non-financial enterprises	5,742	11
	Financial institutions	1,260	2
	Total	51,255	
Germany in DM millions	General government	83,811	18
	Public non-financial enterprises	22,897	5
	Private non-financial enterprises	7,969	2
	Banks	303,243	65
	Total	417,920	

Source: OECD, *Financial Statistics*, Vol.12 (Paris: OECD, 1978).

TABLE A-2 Total Assets of Canadian Financial Institutions in Millions of Canadian Dollars

	1975	1980	1981	1982
Chartered Canadian banks	100,380	248,418	311,923	348,000[c]
Schedule B	—	—	5,668	18,990
Quebec savings banks[a]	8,971	1,774	4,243	4,588
Trust companies (including guaranteed funds)	14,604	38,968	43,641	47,360
Assets in trust (ETA)	32,332	64,629	75,165	88,808
Mortgage loan companies	8,077	16,075	21,017	28,681
Local credit unions and caisses populaires	12,791	30,546	32,061	33,527
Central credit unions	2,602	6,464	7,313	8,880
Sales finance and consumer loan companies	10,336	14,054	14,493	12,516
Finance/leasing companies	806	2,181	2,381	2,167
Life insurance companies (assets in Canada)	28,834	32,191	35,784	39,034
Other insurance companies (property and casualty)	5,556	11,187	12,244	13,630
Investment dealers	3,673	6,673	7,534	8,448
Mortgage investment trust corporations (real estate investment)	1,052	2,008	1,323	811
Mutual funds (investment funds)	2,769	4,459	4,962	5,233
Closed-end funds	921	1,183	1,023	1,116
Trusteed pension funds[b] (private pension plans)	20,962	51,685	61,514	71,925
Total	241,606	532,495	642,279	733,714

Source: Statistics Canada, *Financial Institutions*, cat. no. 61–006.

a. *Bank of Canada Review*.

b. Statistics Canada, *Trusteed Pension Plans; Financial Statistics*.

c. As of Feb. 23, 1983, Supplement to the *Canada Gazette*, Chartered Banks.

TABLE A-3 Comparison of the Structures of the Financial Systems of Canada and the United States: Total Assets of Major Financial Intermediaries, December 31, 1980

	United States		Canada	
	$ Billions	Percent	$ Billions	Percent
Commercial Banks	1,887	43	171	44
Near-Banks	873	20	91	23
Savings and loan companies	630	14	—	—
Mutual savings banks	172	4	—	—
Credit unions	72	2	32	8[a]
Trust and loan companies	—	—	55	14
Quebec savings banks	—	—	2	—
Government depositories	—	—	2	1
Other Intermediaries	1,626	37	127	33
Life insurance companies	476	11	38	10
Other insurance companies	187	4	20	5
Pension funds	729	17	50	13
Mutual funds	58	1	5	1
Finance companies	175	4	14	4
Total	4,385		389	

Source: Reproduced in R.A.Shearer, J.F.Chant, D.E.Bond, *The Economics of the Canadian Financial System: Theory, Policy and Institutions* (Scarborough: Prentice-Hall, 1984), Table 15-4.

a. Includes caisses populaires.

TABLE A-4 Partial Categorization of Assets of Canadian Financial Institutions

	Assets in $ Millions			
	Assets as of 1983	Percent of Total Assets[a]		
		Loans	Mortgages	Stocks
1. Deposit-taking Institutions				
Chartered banks	366,990[a]	53	130	4
Quebec savings bonds	4,588	4	62	?
Trust companies	47,360	7	60	4
Mortgage loan companies	28,681	2	83	1
Local credit unions and caisses populaires	33,527	24	48	14?
Central credit unions	8,880	na	na	na
2. Long-Term Credit Institutions				
Federally sponsored credit agencies (CMHC, FBDB, FCC, ED) and mortgage pools	19,309.0	—	—	—
Federal government	121.8	—	—	—
RRSP	7,000	—	59	15
3. Investing Institutions				
Life insurance companies	39,034	—	38	7
Other insurance companies	13,630	—	7	12
Mortgage investment trust corporations (real estate investment)	811	—	na	na
Closed-end funds	1,116	—	—	9
Trusteed pension funds	71,925	—	11	17
ETA accounts	88,808	—	13	30
Mutual funds	5,233	—	23	6
Quebec Pension Plan (end of 1976)	4,000	—	5	15
Public Employer Plans[a]	35,700	—	6	5
Private Employer Plans[a]	18,900	—	25	27
4. Other Financial Institutions				
Sales finance and consumer loans companies	12,516	83	7	—
Financial/leasing companies	2,167	na	na	na
Investment dealers	8,448	na	na	na

Source: Assets – Supplement to the *Canada Gazette*, Chartered Banks. Categorization reproduced in R.A. Shearer, J.F. Chant, D.E. Bond, *The Economics of the Canadian Financial System: Theory Policy and Institutions* (Scarborough: Prentice-Hall, 1984), Tables 10-1, 11-2, 11-3, 11-4, 11-5, 11-6, 12-1, 12-2, 12-3, 12-4, 12-5.

a. As of June 30, 1982.

? The category as described was identified as investments.

TABLE A-5 List of Schedule "A" and Schedule "B" Banks and Summary of Assets as at 28 February 1983

Name of Bank	Total Assets
	(Cdn$)
The Bank of British Columbia	3,098,025
Bank of Montreal	63,757,892
The Bank of Nova Scotia	53,450,465
Canadian Commercial Bank	1,962,642
Canadian Imperial Bank of Commerce	68,334,369
Continental Bank of Canada	4,347,307
The Mercantile Bank of Canada	4,049,325
National Bank of Canada	16,846,443
Northland Bank	649,756
The Royal Bank of Canada	87,372,047
The Toronto-Dominion Bank	44,130,393
Western & Pacific Bank of Canada	2,100
Total Schedule A Banks	348,000,764
ABN Bank Canada	288,314
BT Bank of Canada	323,778
Banca Commerciale Italiana of Canada	63,258
Banca Nazionale del Lavoro of Canada	67,145
Banco Central of Canada	23,571
Bank of America Canada	1,111,812
Bank of Boston Canada	82,732
Bank of Credit and Commerce Canada	94,331
Bank Hapoalim (Canada)	84,324
Bank Leumi le-Israel (Canada)	84,527
The Bank of Tokyo Canada	554,696
Banque Nationale de Paris (Canada)	1,090,936
Barclays Bank of Canada	1,248,068
The Chase Manhattan Bank of Canada	469,075
Chemical Bank of Canada	1,251,640
Citibank Canada	2,767,084
Commerica Bank Canada	96,495
Continental Illinois Bank (Canada)	716,232
Crédit Commercial de France (Canada)	112,274
Crédit-Lyonnais Canada	757,923
Crédit Suisse Canada	364,236
Dai-Ichi Kangyo Bank (Canada)	160,647
Deutsche Bank (Canada)	117,587
Dresdner Bank Canada	258,942
First Interstate Bank of Canada	59,100
The First National Bank of Chicago (Canada)	307,639
Fuji Bank Canada	186,735
Grindlays Bank of Canada	87,292
Hanil Bank Canada	45,491
Hongkong Bank of Canada	300,224

TABLE A-5 (CONT'D)

Name of Bank	Total Assets
	(Cdn$)
The Industrial Bank of Japan (Canada)	146,162
International Commercial Bank of Cathay (Canada)	23,270
Irving Bank Canada	142,523
Israel Discount Bank of Canada	60,292
Korea Exchange Bank of Canada	47,282
Lloyds Bank International Canada	398,604
Manufacturers Hanover Bank of Canada	399,136
Midland Bank Canada	388,748
Mitsubishi Bank of Canada	145,021
The Mitsui Bank of Canada	180,072
Morgan Bank of Canada	653,421
Morguard Bank of Canada	197,654
National Bank of Detroit, Canada	248,766
National Bank of Greece (Canada)	64,879
National Westminster Bank of Canada	694,438
Overseas Bank (Canada)	8,964
Overseas Union Bank of Singapore (Canada)	5,412
Paribas Bank of Canada	96,647
Rabobank Canada	—
Republic National Bank of New York (Canada)	12,715
Seattle-First Bank Canada	57,536
Security Pacific Bank Canada	166,322
Société Générale (Canada)	599,980
Standard Chartered Bank of Canada	234,481
State Bank of India (Canada)	6,469
Swiss Bank Corporation (Canada)	551,489
Union Bank of Switzerland (Canada)	210,261
Wells Fargo Bank Canada	73,621
Total Schedule B Banks	18,990,273

Source: Statistics Canada, *Financial Institutions*, cat. no. 61–006 (1983).

TABLE A-6 Assets of Trust Companies

		Number of Canadian Trust Companies	
		1982	1981
		77	75
Aggregate Figures		$000	$000
Total company funds		2,328,771	2,293,384
Total guaranteed funds (funds derived from deposits)		37,333,243	35,767,989
Estates, trusts and agencies		88,808,272	75,165,621
	Total	128,470,286	113,226,994

	Assets (at book value)		
	Federal	Provincial	Total (1982)
	$000	$000	$000
Company funds	1,297,423	992,675	2,290,098
Guaranteed trust funds (funds derived from deposits)	22,121,013	14,416,434	36,537,447

Provincial Figures	1981	
Ontario (=113,141,447,000[a])	37,212,056,000	
Quebec[a]	6,088,446,656	
British Columbia (as at 31 March 1982, unavailable for 1981)	6,700,000,000	(Rounded)
Alberta[b] (as at 31 March 1981)	33,909,260,000	

Sources: For Aggregate Figures: Trust Companies Association of Canada, *General Information Bulletin*, No. 67 (August 1983).
For Assets (at book value): Canada, Department of Insurance, *The Superintendent's Report*, November 1,1983.
For Provincial Figures: Ontario, Registrar of Business of 1981; Quebec, l'inspecteur des compagnies de fidéicommis 1981; British Columbia, Ministry of Consumer and Corporate Affairs, *Annual Report, 1982*; and Alberta, Department of Consumer and Corporate Affairs, *Annual Report for the Fiscal Year ended 31 March 1981.*

a. Figures include estates, trusts and agencies.
b. Total assets (may include estates, trusts and agencies).

TABLE A-6a Trust Companies

Federal Trust Companies (31 December 1982)

Atlantic Trust Company of Canada (N-S 1964/Fed 1981)
Bayshore Trust Company (1977)
Canada Permanent Trust Company (1874)
The Canada Trust Company (1894)
Central Trust Company (1981)
Citizens Trust Company (1979)
Colonial Trust Company (1978)
Commercial Trust Company Limited (1904)
Continental Trust Company (1973)
Co-operative Trust Company of Canada (1967)
Discovery Trust Company of Canada (1974)
Eaton Bay Trust (1974)
Equitable Trust Company (1970)
Evangeline Trust Company (1980)
The Fidelity Trust Company (Man 1909/Fed 1972)
Guaranty Trust Company of Canada (1925)
Income Trust Company (1972)
The Interior Trust Company (Man 1909/Fed 1972)
The International Trust Company (1977)
Marcil Trust Company (1978)
The Merchant Trust Company (1978)
Montreal Trust (1978)
Morgan Trust (1979)
Morguard Trust Company (1972)
Norfolk Trust Company (Sask 1916/Fed 1982)
The North Canadian Trust Company (Man 1913/Fed 1980)
Nova Scotia Savings and Trust Company (1980)
Peace Hills Trust Company (1980)
Pioneer Trust Company (1974)
The Premier Trust Company (1973)
The Regional Trust Company (1976)
Standard Trust Company (1963)
Sterling Trust Corporation (1911)
Western Capital Trust Company (1979)

Federal Trust Companies (31 December 1975)

Canada Permanent Trust Company (1872)
The Canada Trust Company (1894)
The Central and Nova Scotia Trust Company
Commercial Trust Company Limited (1904)
Continental Trust Company (1973)
Co-operative Trust Company of Canada (1967)
Eaton Bay Trust (1974)
Equitable Trust Company (1970)
The Fidelity Trust Company (Man 1909/Fed 1972)
Guaranty Trust Company of Canada (1925)
Income Trust Company (1972)
Morguard Trust Company (1972)
Nelcon Trust Company (Que 1971)
Pioneer Trust Company (1974)
The Premier Trust Company (1913)
Standard Trust Company (1963)
Sterling Trust Corporation (1911)

TABLE A-6a (CONT'D)

Provincial Trust Companies (1982)
Subject to Federal Inspection
The Acadia Trust Company (N-S 1920)
British Swiss Trust Company (PEI)
Cavendish Trust Company Inc. (PEI)
Charlottetown Trust Company (PEI 1934)
Custodian Trust Company Ltd. (PEI 1939)
Earnscliffe Trust Limited (PEI)
Elgistan Trust (PEI 1963)
Gulf Trust Corporation (PEI 1940)
Inland Trust & Savings Corporation Ltd. (Man 1965)
Interprovincial Trust Company (PEI)
Investors Group Trust Co. Ltd. (Man 1968)
Pan-American Trust Company (PEI 1940)
Provincial Trust Company (PEI)
The Regent Trust Company (Man 1954)

Provincial Trust Companies (1975)
Subject to Federal Inspection
The Acadia Trust Company (N-S 1920)
Atlantic Trust Company of Canada (N-S 1964/Fed 1981)
Fort Garry Trust Company (Man 1964)
Inland Trust & Savings Corporation Ltd. (Man 1965)
Interior Trust Company (Man)
Investors Group Trust Co. Ltd. (Man 1968)
North Canadian Trust Company (Man 1913/Fed 1980)
The Regent Trust Company (Man 1954)

Provincial Trust Companies (1982)
Except for those Subject to Federal Inspection
Cabot Trust Company (Ont 1978)
Columbia Trust Company
Community Trust Company, Limited (Ont 1975)
Compagnie de Fiducie Citicorp/Citicorp Trust Company (Que 1960)
Compagnie de Fiducie Guardian/Guardian Trust Company (Que 1929)
Compagnie de Fiducie Imperiale
Compagnie Sherbrooke Trust/Sherbrooke Trust Company (Subsidiary, Trust General)
Counsel Trust Company (Ont 1977)
Credit Foncier/Credit Foncier Trust (Que 1974)
Crown Trust Company (Ont 1895)
District Trust Company (Ont 1964)
The Effort Trust Company (Ont 1978)
Executive Trust Company (Ont 1981)
Family Trust Corporation (Ont 1976)
Fiduciaires de l'Alcan Limitée/Alcan Fiduciaries Ltd.
Fiduciaires de la Cité et du District de Montréal Limitée/Montreal City and District Trustees Limited
Fiducie Canadienne Italienne/Canadian Italian Trust Co.
Fiducie du Québec/Quebec Trust Company (Que 1962)
Fiducie Populaire
Fiducie Prêt et Revenu/Savings & Investment Trust (Que 1960)
Financial Trust Company (Ont 1977)
First City Trust Company (Alta 1962)

TABLE A-6a (CONT'D)

Greymac Trust Company (Ont 1977)
HFC Trust Limited
Highfield Savings and Trust Company
Huronia Trust Company (Ont 1977)
Mennonite Trust Ltd.
Monarch Trust Company (Ont 1977)
The Municipal Trust Company (Ont 1978)
National Trust Company Limited (Ont 1898)
North American Trust Company (Que 1962)
North West Trust Company
Pacific & Western Trust Corporation
Peoples Trust Company
Principal Savings and Trust Company
Saskatchewan Trust Company
Seaway Trust Company (Ont 1978)
Security Trust Company (Ont 1977)
Settlers Savings and Mortgage Corp.
Société de Fiducie Banker's Trust (La)/The Bankers' Trust Co. (Que 1905)
– (Subsidiary of Royal Trust)
Société de Fiducie Lombard Odier/Lombard Odier Trust Company
Trust Général du Canada/General Trust of Canada
Trust General Inc.
Trust Hellénique Canadien/Hellenic Canadian Trust
Vanguard Trust of Canada Limited (Ont 1974)
Victoria and Grey Mortgage Corporation (Ont 1897)
Yorkshire Trust Company

Sources: For Provincial Trust Companies (1982) Canada, Department of Insurance, "Report of the Superintendent of Insurance for Canada," for the year ended 31 December 1982: Trust and Loan Companies. For the Superintendent's Report, the figures for those provincial companies subject to inspection by the federal Department of Insurance are included with those of the federal companies. For Provincial Trust Companies (1975): same, for the year ended 31 December 1975. For Provincial Trust Companies (1982) except for those subject to federal inspection: *Canadian Almanac and Directory 1984* (Toronto, Copp Clark Pitman, 1984); Trust Companies Association of Canada, *Directory of Members and Certain Non-Members of the Trust Companies Association of Canada* (Toronto: Trust Companies Association of Canada, Revised 1984); Ontario, Ministry of Consumer and Commercial Relations, *Report of the Registrar of Business in 1981; Loan and Trust Corporations (85th Report)*; Quebec, Ministère des Institutions financières et coopératives, *Rapport annuel de l'inspecteur des compagnies de fidéicommis 1981*; Alberta, Department of Consumer and Corporate Affairs, *Annual Report for the Fiscal Year Ended 31 March 1981*. Dates of incorporation available from the Ontario Registrar of Business.

TABLE A-7 Net New Issue of Securities in Millions of Dollars

	Government of Canada				Provincial		Municipal		Non-Financial Corporations				
Year	Bonds	%	Bills	%	Bonds	%	Bonds	%	Bonds	%	Common and preferred stock	%	Total
1972	1,269		330		2,990		445		941		445		
1973	−677		530		2,614		399		712		442		
1974	3,272		940		3,785		553		1,210		466		
1975	3,397	22	570	4	6,752	45	1,119	7.5	2,149	14	871	6	14,858
1976	2,588		1,645		8,980		1,240		2,258		1,050		
1980	5,913	22	5,475	20	8,639	32	650	2.0	2,317	9	4,060	15	27,054
1981	12,784		−35		12,524		521		4,083		5,204		35,116
1982	13,975	33	5,025	12	14,882	35	446	1.0	3,727	9	4,081	10	42,136
1983	13,083	28	13,300	28	11,901	25	384	1.0	2,539	5	5,492	12	46,699
			56		25		1				17		

Source: For 1972–76: *Bank of Canada Review*, July 1977, Tables 28, 31, 32 and 34.
For 1980–83: *Bank of Canada Review*, February 1984, Tables 28, 31, 32 and 34.

TABLE A-8 Sources of Funds of Canadian Non-Financial Private Corporations in Millions of Dollars

External Sources	1975	%	1980	%	1981	%	1982	%
Bank loans	1,307	23	6,474	37	17,571	50	20	0.2
Other loans	905	16	1,616	9	3,150	9	2,241	21
Short-term paper	90	2	11	0.1	964	3	503	5
Mortgages	332	6	1,788	10	1,599	5	1,337	13
Bonds	2,112	37	2,141	12	5,381	15	2,838	26
Stocks	960	17	5,565	31	6,643	19	3,805	35
	5,706		17,595		35,308		10,744	

Source: Statistics Canada, *Financial Flow Accounts*, various issues.

TABLE A-9 Government Lending Institutions and Programs in Millions of Dollars

	Loans		Loan Guarantees	
	Outstanding Total 31-03-82	**Extended During FY 1981–82**	**Outstanding Total 31-03-82**	**Extended During FY 1981–82**
Federal Government	121.8	7.4	1,426.4	91.2
Extended under Enterprise Development Program	7.9	−0.4	101.1	50.7
Canada Mortage & Housing Corporation	8,996.4	416.3	26,800.0	−100.3
Federal Business Development Banks	2,112.5	476.0	19.4	n.a.
Farm Credit Corporation	3,627.7	499.8	—	—
Export Development	4,564.5	1,508.2	2,455.6	2,772.8

Source: A. Maslove, "Loans and Loan Guarantees: Business as Usual versus the Politics of Risk," in *How Ottawa Spends: The Liberals, the Opposition and Federal Priorities, 1983*, edited by G. Bruce Doern (Toronto: James Lorimer, 1983), pp. 121, 126.

TABLE A-10 Public and Private Pension Plans Assets as of the end of 1976

Canada Pension Plan	$10.9 billion
Quebec Pension Plan	4.0 billion
Public Employer Plans	35.7 billion
Private Employee Plans	18.9 billion
RRSPs	7.5 billion
Total	77.1 billion

	Investments (%)				
	Claims on Government	**Corp. Bonds**	**Corp. Equities**	**Mortgages**	**Others**
Canada Pension Plan	100	—	—	—	—
Quebec Pension Plan	62	10	15	5	8
Public Employer Plans	81	5	5	6	4
Private Employer Plans	15	21	27	25	13
RRSPs	10	10	15	59	6
Total	59	9	11	15	6

Source: Arthur Donner, *Financing the Future: Canada's Capital Markets in the Eighties* (Toronto: James Lorimer, 1982), p. 119.

TABLE A-11 Functions and Responsibilities of the Regulators of Deposition Institutions, 1975

	Federally Incorporated		Provincially Incorporated		
	Chartered Banks	**Trust & Mortgage Loan Companies**	**Trust & Mortgage Loan Companies**	**Credit Unions**	**Caisses Populaires**
Federal					
Bank of Canada	Lender of last resort; regulator of liquidity				
Inspector General of Banks	Inspector; administrator of Bank Act				
Canada Deposit Insurance Corp. (CDIC)	Insurer of deposits; lender of last resort	Insurer of deposits; lender of last resort	Insurer of deposits (outside Quebec); lender of last resort	Lender of last resort	
Superintendent of Insurance		Inspector, administrator of Trust & Loan, Act, administrator of Small Loans Act	Administrator of Small Loans Act	Administrator of Small Loans Act	Administrator of Small Loans Act
Minister of Consumer and Corporate Affairs	Administrator of Interest Act	Administrator of Interest Act	Administrator of Interest Act	Administrator of Interest Act	Administrator of Interest Act

Provincial					
Quebec Deposit Insurance Board (QDIB)			Insurer of deposits (in Quebec); lender of last resort		Insurer of deposits; lender of last resort
Registrar of Trust and Loan companies		Licenser of business in provinces	Inspector; administrator of Trust & Loans Act; licenser of business in province		
Ministry of Financial Institutions (Quebec)	Changes made in 1983				(Delegated Inspector to centrals); administrator of Caisses Populaires Act
Supervisor of Credit Unions				Inspector; administrator of Credit Union Act	
Credit Union Reserve Board (some provinces only)				Insurer of deposits; lender of last resort	

Source: Economic Council of Canada, "Efficiency and Regulation." Reproduced from R.A. Shearer, J.F. Chant and D.E. Bond, *The Economics of the Canadian Financial System: Theory, Policy and Institutions* (Scarborough: Prentice-Hall, 1984) pp. 280–81.

Notes

CHAPTER 1

1. Canada, Royal Commission on the Economic Union and Development Prospects for Canada, *Research for the Commission on Canada's Future* (Ottawa: Minister of Supply and Services Canada, 1984), p. 2.
2. C. Lloyd Brown-John, *Canadian Regulatory Agencies* (Toronto: Butterworth, 1981), p. 7.
3. Margot Priest, W.T. Stanbury and Fred Thompson, "On the Definition of Economic Regulation," in *Government Regulation: Scope, Growth, Process*, edited by W.T. Stanbury (Montreal: Institute for Research on Public Policy, 1980), p. 5.
4. U.S. Senate Committee on Government Operations, *Study on Federal Regulation*, vol. 1 (Washington, D.C.: Government Printing Office, 1977), p. 5.
5. Douglas G. Hartle, *Public Policy Decision Making and Regulation* (Montreal: Institute for Research on Public Policy, 1979), p. 1.
6. Economic Council of Canada, *Regulation Reference: A Preliminary Report* (Ottawa: Minister of Supply and Services Canada, 1978), p. 15.
7. Barry M. Mitnick, *The Political Economy of Regulation* (New York: Columbia University Press, 1980), p. 7.
8. Ibid., p. 9.
9. Michael J. Trebilcock, Leonard Waverman, and J. Robert S. Prichard, "Markets for Regulation," in *Ontario Economic Council, Government Regulation* (Toronto: Ontario Economic Council, 1978), p. 11.
10. Theodore J. Lowi, *The End of Liberalism: The Second Republic of the United States*, 2d ed. (New York: W.W. Norton, 1979), p. 273.
11. Douglas Needham, *The Economics and Politics of Regulation: A Behavioral Approach* (Boston: Little, Brown, 1983), p. 1.
12. Robert E. Litan and William D. Nordhaus, *Reforming Federal Regulation* (New Haven: Yale University Press, 1983), pp. 5–6.
13. Richard J. Schultz, *Federalism and the Regulatory Process* (Montreal: Institute for Research on Public Policy, 1979), p. 8.
14. Mel Dubnick and Alan R. Gitelson, "Regulatory Policy Analysis: Working in a Quagmire," *Policy Studies Review* 1 (3) (1982), p. 424.
15. Stephen Breyer, *Regulation and Its Reform* (Cambridge, Mass.: Harvard University Press, 1982), p. 7, and William T. Gormley, Jr., *The Politics of Public Utility Regulation* (Pittsburgh: University of Pittsburgh Press, 1983).
16. Fred Thompson and L.R. Jones, *Regulatory Policy and Practices: Regulating Better and Regulating Less* (New York: Praeger, 1982), p. 11.
17. Richard B. Stewart, "Regulation, Innovation and Administrative Law: A Conceptual Framework," *California Law Review* 69 (1981): 1263–1377, and Richard J. Schultz, "Regulation as Maginot Line: Confronting the Technological Revolution in Telecommunications," *Canadian Public Administration* 26 (1983): 203–18.
18. Board of Railway Commissioners for Canada, *Judgements, Orders, Regulations and Rulings* (Henceforth *J.O.R.R.*) (1919), p. 63.
19. Ibid., 1966, p. 718.
20. F.M. Scherer, *Industrial Market Structure and Economic Performance*, 2d ed. (Chicago: Rand McNally, 1980); Christopher Green, *Canadian Industrial Organization and Policy* (Toronto: McGraw-Hill Ryerson, 1980); and Richard Caves, *American Industry: Structure, Conduct, Performance*, 4th ed. (Englewood Cliffs, N.J.: Prentice-Hall, 1964).
21. Scherer, *Industrial Market Structure*, p. 4.
22. Caves, *American Industry*, p. 14.
23. Railway Act, R.S.C. 1970, c. R-2, s. 265.

24. National Transportation Act, R.S.C. 1970, c. N-17, s. 3 and s. 23(2) respectively.
25. Canada, *An Act to Amend the National Transportation Act* (Bill C-33). First Reading, January 27, 1977, found in W.T. Stanbury, ed., *Studies on Regulation in Canada* (Montreal: Institute for Research on Public Policy, 1978), Appendix 2.
26. *Pipe Lines Act*, S.C., 1949, c-20, s.12(3).
27. *National Energy Board Act*, R.S.C., 1970, c. N-6, s. 44.
28. *Canadian Broadcasting Act*, R.S.C., 1952, c. 32, s. 21(1).
29. *Broadcasting Act*, R.S.C., 1970, c. B-11, s. 3.
30. Canada, *Telecommunications Act* (Bill C-43). First Reading, March 22, 1977.
31. K.W. Studnicki-Gizbert, "Regulatory Policy Options in Transport," *Transportation Research Forum Proceedings*, 12 (1971), pp. 1–30. See also Marc Porat, "Communication Policy in an Information Society," in *Communications for Tomorrow: Policy Perspectives for the 1980's*, edited by G.O. Robinson (New York: Praeger, 1978), p. 12.
32. Such an analysis is attempted for the transportation, energy and communications sectors in Richard J. Schultz, "Governments in Miniature: Critical Events in the Politics of Federal Regulation" (in progress).
33. Theodore J. Lowi, "Four Systems of Policy, Politics and Choice," *Public Administration Review* 32 (1972), p. 229.
34. This method of characterization is inspired by John Zysman's "Three Models of Adjustment," in his *Governments, Markets and Growth* (Ithaca: Cornell University Press, 1983).
35. Howard Darling, *The Politics of Freight Rates: The Railway Freight Rate Issue in Canada* (Toronto: McClelland and Stewart, 1980), and Carmen Baggaley, "Belling the Cat: The Art of the Possible and the Introduction of Federal Telephone Regulation in Canada, 1880–1910," unpublished paper prepared for Institute for Research on Public Policy, 1981.
36. See W.T. Stanbury, "The Consumer Interest and the Regulated Industries," in *Transportation Policy: Regulation, Competition and the Public Interest*, edited by K. Ruppenthal and W.T. Stanbury (Vancouver: Centre for Transportation Studies, 1976), p. 139. The most comprehensive discussion of this issue is found in Richard B. Stewart, "The Reformation of American Administrative Law," *Harvard Law Review*, (1975): 1667–1813.
37. CRTC, Telecom Rules and Procedures, SOR/79–554, July 27, 1979.
38. Theodore Lowi, "American Business, Public Policy, Case Studies and Political Theory," *World Politics* 16 (1963–64), p. 691.
39. Lester C. Thurow, *The Zero-Sum Society: Distribution and the Possibilities for Economic Change* (New York: Basic Books, 1980), and Charles L. Schultze, *The Public Use of Private Interest* (Washington, D.C.: Brookings Institution, 1977).
40. A.W. Currie, "The Board of Transport Commissioners as an Administrative Body," in *Canadian Public Administration*, edited by J.E. Hodgetts and D.C. Corbett (Toronto: Macmillan, 1960), p. 224.
41. Ibid., pp. 231–32.
42. Ibid., p. 236.
43. Ibid., pp. 236–37.
44. Howard Darling, *The Politics of Freight Rates* (Toronto: McClelland and Stewart, 1980), pp. 116–21.
45. Canada, Parliament, *Sessional Papers, 1902*, Vol.36, No.20A, "Reports upon Railway Commissions, Railway Rate Grievances and Regulative Legislation by Prof. S.J. McLean."
46. Currie, "The Board of Transport Commissioners," p. 229.
47. As quoted in ibid., p. 229.
48. Arthur R. Wright, "An Examination of the Role of the Board of Transport Commissioners for Canada as a Regulatory Tribunal," *Canadian Public Administration* 6 (1963), p. 285.

49. Caroline Andrew and Rejean Pelletier, "The Regulators," in *The Regulatory Process in Canada*, edited by G. Bruce Doern (Toronto: Macmillan, 1978), pp. 147–64.
50. Richard J. Schultz, "Regulatory Agencies and the Dilemmas of Delegation," in *The Administrative State in Canada*, edited by O.P. Dwivedi (Toronto: University of Toronto Press, 1982), pp. 89–106.
51. Richard J. Schultz, "Boards and Bureaucracies: An Overview," paper presented to McGill University Management Institute Conference on Regulation in Transition, Calgary, November 11–13, 1981.
52. Anthony Downs, *Inside Bureaucracy* (Boston: Little, Brown, 1967), especially chap. 17.
53. Cited in Robert J. Buchan and C. Christopher Johnston, "Telecommunications Regulation and the Constitution: A Lawyer's Perspective," in *Telecommunications, Regulation and the Constitution*, edited by Robert J. Buchan et al. (Montreal: Institute for Research on Public Policy, 1982), p. 117.
54. J. Evanson and R. Simeon, "The Roots of Discontent," in Economic Council of Canada, *The Political Economy of Confederation* (Ottawa: Minister of Supply and Services Canada, 1978), p. 176.
55. H.V. Nelles, *The Politics of Development* (Toronto: Macmillan, 1974), and Christopher Armstrong, *The Politics of Federalism* (Toronto: University of Toronto Press, 1981).
56. See Michael Jenkin, *The Challenge of Diversity* (Ottawa: Minister of Supply and Services Canada, 1983); H.G. Thorburn, *Planning and the Economy* (Ottawa: Canadian Institute for Economic Policy, 1984); and Alan Tupper, *Public Money in the Private Sector* (Kingston: Queen's University, Institute of Intergovernmental Relations, 1982).
57. Darling, *Politics of Freight Rates*.
58. Schultz, "Regulatory Agencies."
59. H.N. Janisch, "Policy-making in Regulation . . . ," *Osgoode Hall Law Journal* 17 (1979): 46–106.
60. Schultz, "Regulation as Maginot Line."
61. Janisch, "Policy-making in Regulation."
62. Stewart, "Reformation of American Administrative Law," p. 1683.

CHAPTER 2

1. For background on the years prior to 1937, see G.P. de T. Glazebrook, *A History of Transportation in Canada*, vol. 2 (Toronto: McClelland and Stewart, 1964), pp. 256–64, and David Corbett, *Politics and the Airlines* (Toronto: University of Toronto Press, 1965).
2. Corbett, *Politics and the Airlines*, p. 106.
3. Ibid., p. 108.
4. Ibid., pp. 108–14 and John W. Langford, "Air Canada," in *Public Corporations and Public Policy in Canada*, edited by Allen Tupper and G. Bruce Doern (Montreal: Institute for Research on Public Policy, 1981), pp. 252–55.
5. *Trans-Canada Air Lines Act*, S.C. 1937, c. 43, s. 14.
6. Canada, *House of Commons Debates*, March 22, 1937, p. 2042.
7. *Transport Act*, S.C. 1938, c. 53, s. 13(5).
8. Ibid., s. 5(1).
9. *Act to amend the Aeronautics Act*, S.C. 1944–45, c. 28, s. 12(6).
10. Canada, *House of Commons Debates*, April 2, 1943, p. 1776.
11. Ibid.
12. Canada, *House of Commons Debates*, Feb. 2, 1944, p. 125.
13. *Act to amend the Aeronautics Act*, S.C. 1944–45, c. 28, s. 12.

14. For information on S-31, *The Corporate Shareholding Limitation Act*, see Allan Tupper, "Bill S-31 and the Federalism of State Capitalism," Discussion Paper 18 (Kingston: Queen's University, Institute of Intergovernmental Relations).

15. Canada, *House of Commons Debates*, March 17, 1944, p. 1573.

16. See Corbett, *Politics and the Airlines*, pp. 165–67, and G.B. Hunnings, "Canadian Government Aviation Policy Involving CP Air," in *Perspectives on Canadian Airline Regulation*, edited by G.B. Reschenthaler and B. Roberts (Montreal: Institute for Research on Public Policy, 1979), pp. 165–70.

17. See John R. Baldwin, *The Regulatory Agency and the Public Corporation* (Cambridge, Mass.: Ballinger Publishing, 1975), esp. chap. 6.

18. The Hon. George Hees to Stephen F. Wheatcroft, February 4, 1958, as cited in S.F. Wheatcroft, *Airline Competition in Canada* (Ottawa: Department of Transport, 1958), Foreword.

19. For details see Corbett, *Politics and the Airlines*, pp. 177–80, and Baldwin, *The Regulatory Agency and the Public Corporation*, chap. 4. It might be noted, in terms of Baldwin's theory and model, that he neglects to mention the first decision and, even more importantly, stresses that the regulatory agency rather than the government made the decisions.

20. See Corbett, *Politics and the Airlines*, pp. 179–80.

21. The government's planning approach also involved rationalizing international services, but we will not include a detailed analysis of this aspect which, in any event, only reinforces our claim that the government was seeking to employ regulation as an instrument to plan the airline industry.

22. Statement by minister of transport, April 24, 1964. Canada, *House of Commons Debates*, May 1, 1964, Appendix B, p. 2855. (Henceforth *1964 Statement*.)

23. Canada, *House of Commons Debates*, June 1, 1965 pp. 1814–15 (Henceforth *1965 Statement*.)

24. *1964 Statement*.

25. Minister of Transport, Hon. J.W. Pickersgill, Press Release, March 27, 1967, pp. 1–2 (Henceforth *1967 Statement*.)

26. *1964 Statement*, Principle 3.

27. *1965 Statement*.

28. Minister of Transport, Hon. J.W. Pickersgill, Press Release, October 20, 1966. (Henceforth *1966 Statement*.)

29. Minister of Transport, Hon. Don Jamieson, Press Release, August 15, 1969, p. 2.

30. *1966 Statement*.

31. Ibid.

32. Ibid.

33. Ibid.

34. Ibid.

35. Statement of purpose quoted in Canadian Transport Commission, Air Transport Committee Decision No. 3735, October 24, 1973, p. 3.

36. Cited in "Judgments of the Minister in the Matter of the Aeronautics Act and in the Matter of Decision No. 3735 of the Air Transport Committee dated October 24, 1973," p. 6.

37. CTC, Air Transport Committee Decision 3735, p. 9.

38. Ibid., pp. 10–11.

39. Canadian Transport Commission, Air Transport Committee Decision No.3832, March 25, 1974, p. 1.

40. See the Dissent included in CTC, Air Transport Committee Decision 3735, p. 2.

41. See the exchange in the Ontario Legislature on November 2, 1973.

42. See, for example, Richard J. Schultz, *Federalism, Bureaucracy and Public Policy* (Montreal: McGill-Queen's University Press, 1980), and Richard J. Schultz, *Fed-*

eralism and the Regulatory Process (Montreal: Institute for Research on Public Policy, 1979) for more general discussion of these issues.

43. Much of the information on this subject is drawn from Allan Tupper, "Pacific Western Airlines," in *Public Corporations and Public Policy in Canada*, edited by Allan Tupper and G. Bruce Doern (Montreal: Institute for Research on Public Policy, 1981), as well as interviews with federal and provincial officials conducted in 1976–77 by Schultz as part of the research for his *Federalism and the Regulatory Process*.
44. Tupper, "Pacific Western Airlines," pp. 288 and 289.
45. "PWA Ruling *has* Alberta Spitting Fire," *Financial Post*, August 14, 1976.
46. Canadian Transport Commission Research Branch, "Transportation and the Capital Markets" (76-28E) and "Transportation Capital Expenditure Forecasts" (76-29E) (Ottawa).
47. *Act to amend the Aeronautics Act and the National Transportation Act*, S.C. 1976–77, c. 26, s. 1 and 3.
48. Quoted in Tupper, "Pacific Western Airlines," p. 297.
49. *Ottawa Citizen*, August 7, 1976.
50. Canadian Transport Commission, Air Transport Committee Decision No. 4886, July 5, 1976, pp. 1 and 3.
51. *Ottawa Citizen*, August 7, 1976.
52. Most of the following information on Transair is drawn from Tupper, "Pacific Western Airlines."
53. Canadian Transport Commission, Air Transport Committee Decision No. 4060, February 27, 1975.
54. Canadian Transport Commission, Air Transport Committe Decision No. 3729, October 1, 1973.
55. The information on the development of this conflict is based on a publicly released Telex from the Manitoba Minister of Industry and Commerce, Leonard Evans, to the prime minister, dated November 21, 1975 and confirmed in interviews with federal officials.
56. "Row Over Airline Sweeps the Prairies," *The Globe and Mail*, January 3, 1976.
57. See, for example, Western Premiers' Task Force on Constitutional Trends, *Third Report*, March 1979, p. 26.
58. Ibid., p. 52.
59. Canadian Transport Commission, Air Transport Committee Decision No. 5539, July 1978.
60. This information is drawn from Canadian Transport Commission, *An Analysis of Air Transport Committee Decisions, 1973–1978* (Ottawa: Research Branch, 1979), p. 85.
61. Ibid.
62. Ken Romain, "Quebecair, Great Lakes Bid for Nordair Involves Two New Liners," *The Globe and Mail*, March 17, 1979, B14.
63. Ibid.
64. Wendie Kerr, "Quebecair Seeks Talks with Nordair," *The Globe and Mail*, December 2, 1981, B7.
65. "Quebec Stock Purchase in Airline under Study," *The Globe and Mail*, July 28, 1981, B7.
66. Wendie Kerr, *The Globe and Mail*, March 3, 1983, B3.
67. Ibid., July 7, 1983.
68. Canadian Transport Commission, Air Transport Committee Decision No. 6099, April 9, 1980, p. 6.
69. Ibid.
70. Ibid., p. 7.
71. *Air Canada Act*, S.C. 1977–78, s. 26, c. 5.
72. Ibid., s. 7(2).

73. Langford, "Air Canada," p. 257.

74. *Air Canada Act*, S.C. 1977–78, c. 5, s. 8 and 9.

75. Wendie Kerr, "Officials Hope for Early Public Release of Proposals on Regional Air Policy," *The Globe and Mail*, September 30, 1980, B11.

76. Canada, House of Commons, "Minutes of Proceedings and Evidence of Standing Committee on Transport," Issue No. 41, February 3, 1982, p. 5.

77. For full details of participants, see ibid., Issue No.55, Appendices A and B.

78. See Michael Valpy, "MPs at Their Best: The System Does Work," *The Globe and Mail*, April 8, 1982, A7.

79. "Minutes of Standing Committee on Transport," Issue No. 55, p. 21.

80. Ibid., Issue No. 88, March 15, 1983.

81. Hon. Lloyd Axworthy, Minister of Transport, *A New Canadian Air Policy*, May 10, 1984.

82. Ibid., p. 2.

83. Ibid., p. 7.

84. Ibid., p. 8.

CHAPTER 3

1. H.N. Janisch, "Telecommunications Ownership and Regulation in Canada: Compatibility or Confusion," paper prepared for the 12th Annual Telecommunications Policy Research Conference, Airlie, Virginia, April 23, 1984, p. 13.

2. "*An Act to Amend Chapter 156 of the Acts of 1910: An Act to Incorporate the Maritime Telegraph and Telephone Company Act,*" S.N.S. 1967, c. 5, s. 1(3). It is worth noting that the concern was fairly specific, namely, that Maritime Tel & Tel would, to the detriment of local suppliers, shift its equipment purchases to Northern Telecom. There was no wider concern, for example, about the need to control telephone systems for regional economic development purposes.

3. CRTC, *Facts Digest*, January 1984, p. 15.

4. For information on the nature of these companies, see Ontario Telephone Service Commission, *Annual Report — 1983* and Québec, Régie des services publics du Québec, *Rapport annuel 1983*.

5. The CRTC's inquiry officer in the cost inquiry concluded that Bell Canada's methodology, while having a number of positive features, was not suitable because it did not meet the criterion of auditability. CRTC, *Report of the Inquiry Officer with respect to the Inquiry into Telecommunications Carriers' Costing and Accounting Procedures: Phase III — Cost of Existing Services*, 30 April 1984, p. 135.

6. Bell Canada, *Memorandum of Evidence, CRTC Telecom, Public Notice 1984–86, Interexchange Competition and Related Issues*, April 1984, p. 6.

7. W.K. McCourt, "Local Service Pricing: Current Environment and Future Trends," in *Local Telephone Pricing: Is There a Better Way*, edited by Richard J. Schultz and Peter Barnes (Montreal: McGill University, Centre for the Study of Regulated Industries, 1984), p. 12.

8. Richard J. Schultz, "Partners in a Game Without Masters: Reconstructing the Telecommunications Regulatory System," in *Telecommunications Regulation and the Constitution*, edited by Robert J. Buchan et al. (Montreal: Institute for Research on Public Policy, 1982), p. 72.

9. NBTel, *Memorandum of Evidence, in the Matter of a Hearing to Review Issues relating to Interconnection in the Telecommunications Industry in New Brunswick*, Board of Commissioners of Public Utilities of New Brunswick, April 1984, p. 13.

10. Maritime Tel & Tel, NBTel, Newfoundland Telephone and Island Tel, Submission to Department of Communications Policy Review, May 14, 1984, p. 15.

11. B.C.Tel, *Memorandum of Evidence, CRTC Telecom, Public Notice 1984–86, Interexchange Competition and Related Issues*, April 1984, Appendix 2, p. 2.

12. Canada, "Notes for a Statement by the Prime Minister of Canada on Communications," in *Federal-Provincial Conference of First Ministers on the Constitution*, Document: 800–141039 (Ottawa, 1980).
13. The quotation is from s. 92(10)(c) of the *Constitution Act, 1867*.
14. See C.H. McNairn, "Transportation, Communication and the Constitution: The Scope of Federal Jurisdiction," *Canadian Bar Review* 47 (1969): 355–94. C.M. Dalfen, "Constitutional Jurisdiction over Interprovincial Telephone Rates," *Canadian Communications Law Review* 2 (1970); 170–90b; W.R. Lederman, "Telecommunications and the Federal Constitution of Canada," in *Telecommunications for Canada*, edited by H. Edward English (Toronto: Methuen, 1973), pp. 339–87; and Robert J. Buchan and C. Christopher Johnston, "Telecommunications Regulation and the Constitution: A Lawyer's Perspective," in *Telecommunications Regulation and the Constitution*, by Robert J. Buchan et al. (Montreal: Institute for Research on Public Policy, 1982), pp. 115–66.
15. Buchan and Johnston, "Telecommunications Regulation," p. 120.
16. Federal Court of Canada Trial Division, unreported decision by Madame Justice B. Reed, October 26, 1984 (in the matter of the application of CNCP Telecommunications, as applicant, against Alberta Government Telephone, as respondent . . .).
17. *Canadian Communications Network Letter*, November 19, 1984, p. 2.
18. The information for this paragraph is drawn from Lederman, "Telecommunications and the Federal Constitution"; Buchan and Johnston, "Telecommunications Regulation"; and E.B. Ogle, *Long Distance Please: The Story of the TransCanada Telephone System* (Toronto: Collins, 1979).
19. Telecom Canada, *Statistics 1982*.
20. The 1892 amendment is found in *An Act respecting the Bell Telephone Company of Canada*, S.C., 1892, c. 67, s. 3. In 1902, there was a further amendment that made any rate change subject to cabinet approval. (*An Act respecting the Bell Telephone Company of Canada*, S.C. 1902, c. 41, s. 3.) The 1906 legislation is *An Act to amend the Railway Act*, 1903, S.C., 1906, c. 42, ss. 29–35.
21. Canada, Department of Communications, *Instant World* (Ottawa: Information Canada, 1971), p. 214.
22. See Buchan and Johnston, "Telecommunications Regulation," p. 124, and Walter D. Gainer, "The Canadian Telecommunications Industry: Structure and Regulation," in Canada, Department of Communications, *Telecommission Study 2(a)* (Ottawa: Information Canada, 1970).
23. Board of Transport Commissioners for Canada, *Judgments, Orders, Regulations and Rulings* (Henceforth *J.O.R.R.*), 1919, p. 26.
24. Ibid. 1921, p. 15.
25. Ibid. 1966, p. 718.
26. In 1964, the board initiated a public review on "the permissive level of [Bell Canada's] earnings and the basis on which such permissive level may be authorized for telephone rate purposes." See ibid., p. 538.
27. Ibid. 1927, p. 249.
28. Ibid. 1965, p. 718.
29. Canada, Department of Communications, *Telecommission Study 7(a)(b) Regulatory Bodies: Structures and Roles* (Ottawa: Information Canada, 1972), p. 8.
30. Carl Beigie, "An Economic Framework for Policy Action in Canadian Telecommunications," in *Telecommunications for Canada*, edited by H. Edward English (Toronto: Methuen, 1973), p. 150.
31. John C. McManus, "Federal Regulation of Telecommunications in Canada," in *Telecommunications for Canada*, edited by H. Edward English, (Toronto: Methuen, 1973), p. 393.
32. For an early appreciation of the natural monopoly character of telephones, see Canada, *Senate Debates*, May 4, 1982, p. 188 and May 5, 1982, p. 191.
33. *J.O.R.R.*, 1921–22, p. 47.

34. See Canada, *Telecommission Study 7(a)(b)*, p. 4.
35. *An Act respecting The Bell Telephone Company of Canada*, S.C., 1967–68, c. 48, s. 5(5).
36. See Canada, *Telecommission Study 7(a)(b)*, p. 7.
37. This power was acquired in 1929 after concern had been raised about the watering of stock. The amendment is found in *An Act respecting the Bell Telephone Company of Canada*, S.C., 1929, c. 93, s. 1(2).
38. See Canada, *Telecommission Study 7(a)(b)*, p. 3, and *J.O.R.R.*, 1950, p. 246.
39. Canada, *Telecommission Study 7(a)(b)*, p. 3, and McManus, "Federal Regulation of Telecommunications," pp. 396–97.
40. For a useful summary, see McManus, "Federal Regulation of Telecommunications," pp. 397–401.
41. Ibid., pp. 395 and 405–406.
42. See Buchan and Johnston, "Telecommunications Regulation"; Ogle, *Long Distance*; and Gainer "Canadian Telecommunications Industry."
43. See H.N. Janisch and P.B. Huber, *A Critique of Provincial Regulation in the Atlantic Provinces* (Halifax: Dalhousie University, Faculty of Law, 1974), especially pp. 1.23–1.32.
44. On this point see Janisch, "Telecommunications Ownership."
45. Quoted in Ogle, *Long Distance*, p. 232.
46. Figures compiled from Janisch and Huber, *Critique of Provincial Regulation*, Appendix D.1–D.95.
47. McManus, Federal Regulation of Telecommunications.
48. Janisch and Huber, *Critique of Provincial Regulation*, Appendix D.30.
49. McManus, "Federal Regulation of Telecommunications," p.420.
50. Beigie, "Economic Framework," p. 83.
51. On this point, see Edward E. Zajac, *Fairness or Efficiency: An Introduction to Public Utility Pricing* (Cambridge, Mass.: Ballinger Publishing, 1978).
52. See, for example, Richard J. Schultz and Peter Barnes, eds., *Local Telephone Pricing: Is There a Better Way* (Montreal: McGill University, Centre for the Study of Regulated Industries, 1984).
53. Canada, *Telecommission Study 7(a)(b)*, p. 3.
54. Canada, Department of Communications, *Instant World*, p. 211.
55. These, of course, were not the only decisions that were crucial, but in a number of important respects, these two decisions taken back to back, have come to symbolize the dramatic shifts in technology and public policy. For background on these and other U.S. decisions and on their impact see G.O. Robinson, ed., *Communications for Tomorrow: Policy Perspectives for the 1980's* (New York: Praeger, 1978), and J.R. Meyer et al., *The Economics of Competition in the Telecommunications Industry* (Cambridge, Mass.: Oelgeschlager, Gunn & Hain, 1980).
56. See, for example, H.N. Janisch and Y. Kurisaki, "The Reform of Telecommunications Regulation in Japan and Canada: A Comparative Analysis," in *Telecommunications Policy* (forthcoming).
57. The following material is drawn from Schultz, "Partners in a Game Without Masters," pp. 47–50.
58. See *The New York Times*, October 21, 1984, p. 3-1.
59. It is of considerable interest that a Canadian company, Olympia and York, is in the forefront of developing by-pass systems in the United States. See Andrew Pollack, "Landlord to Start a Phone Network," *The New York Times*, November 16, 1983, D.1.
60. For a good discussion of these issues and their relevance to Canada, see H.N. Janisch, "Winners and Losers: The Challenges Facing Telecommunications Regulation," paper prepared for IRPP Conference on Competition and Technological Change: The Impact on Telecommunications Policy and Regulation, Toronto, September 25–26, 1984) and the rich set of sources cited therein.

61. See Daniel Bell, *The Coming of the Post Industrial Society* (New York: Basic Books, 1973), and Simon Nora and Alain Minc, *The Computerization of Society* (Cambridge, Mass.: MIT Press, 1980) as well as the studies cited in S. Serafini and M. Andrieu, *The Information Revolution and Its Implications for Canada* (Ottawa: Minister of Supply and Services Canada, 1981).
62. Serafini and Andrieu, *Information Revolution*, p. 68.
63. An earlier indication came in 1967 when the government released a white paper entitled, "A Domestic Satellite Communication System for Canada," outlining its intentions to create such a system to offer a nationwide television service in English and French as well as to provide telephone service to northern parts of Canada. In preparing this paper, a task force consulted with a wide range of individuals and organizations. The one notable exception is that it did not consult with provincial governments, especially those whose telephone carriers would be asked to share in the burden of creating such a system.
64. *An Act respecting the Department of Communications*, R.S.C. 1970, c. C-24, s. 5.
65. Canada, *House of Commons Debates*, February 27, 1969, p. 6016.
66. Ibid., February 28, 1969, p. 6079.
67. Canada, *Telecommunications Act* (Bill C-43). First Reading, March 22, 1977.
68. Canada, *House of Commons Debates*, February 28, 1969, p. 6080.
69. Canada, Department of Communications, *Instant World* and the extensive Telecommission Studies were the product of this activity.
70. Canada, Minister of Communications, "Proposals for a Communications Policy for Canada: A Position Paper of the Government of Canada" (Ottawa: Information Canada, 1973). Although this paper also dealt with broadcasting matters we shall, for the most part, exclude them from our discussion.
71. Ibid., p. 3. These objectives were further expanded when the government introduced legislation regarding telecommunications in 1977. (The full list was cited earlier in chap. 1, subsection on "Telecommunications.")
72. Ibid., p. 14.
73. Ibid., p. 16.
74. Ibid., p. 7.
75. Ibid.
76. Ibid., p. 8.
77. Canada, Minister of Communications, "Communications: Some Federal Proposals" (Ottawa: Information Canada, 1975).
78. For details and documentation see Schultz, "Partners in a Game Without Masters," pp. 58–62.
79. *Canadian Radio-television and Telecommunications Commission Act*, S.C. 1974–75–76, c. 49.
80. See Schultz, *Federalism and the Regulatory Process*, chap. 2, note 45, pp. 66–67.
81. See Schultz, "Partners in a Game Without Masters," p. 62.
82. For details, see CRTC Telecom Decision CRTC 81–13, July 7 1981, especially pp. 33–37.
83. Canada, *House of Commons Debates*, March 4, 1975, p. 3782.
84. CRTC, "Telecommunications Regulation — Procedures and Practices," Ottawa, July 20, 1976, p. 3.
85. Ibid.
86. Ibid., p. 12.
87. CRTC, Public Announcement, June 6, 1978.
88. These examples are all drawn from CRTC decisions on Bell Canada rate applications in the period from 1977 to 1980.
89. *J.O.R.R.*, 1966, p. 718.
90. *Broadcasting Act*, R.S.C. 1970, c.B-11, s. 3(a).

91. CRTC, *CNCP Telecommunications: Interconnection with Bell Canada*, Telecom Decision 79–11, May 17 1979.
92. CRTC, Telecom Decision 80–13, August 5, 1980, and Telecom Decision 82–14, November 23 1982.
93. CRTC, Telecom, Public Notice 1978–18.
94. For a review of provincial actions following the CRTC decision see NBTel, *Memorandum of Evidence*, Note 9, Evidence of Richard Schultz, especially pp. 38–54.
95. CRTC, Telecom Decision 79–11, May 17, 1979, p. 78.
96. Ibid., p. 74.
97. Ibid., p. 99.
98. Ibid., p. 101.
99. Quoted in *The Globe and Mail*, April 19, 1976.
100. See CRTC, Telecom Decision 79–11, p. 113.

Chapter 4

1. The major exception to national regulation, besides Canada, is Australia. In addition, the United States provides an example of dual regulation where both levels of government regulate the capital markets and the national financial system more generally. Still, in the American regulation of capital markets there is a strong federal/ national component which, in fact, sets the minimum standards, precluding permissive competition between jurisdictions.
2. The national financial system is not an easy institutional environment to describe. However, a good starting point is the figure provided by Hugh Clelland in his piece included in the 1979 Consumer and Corporate Affairs study. The figure includes what Clelland calls the financial sector, that is, pension funds, caisses populaires and credit unions, banks, finance companies, mortgage companies, venture capital companies, investment brokers, life insurance companies, mutual funds and trust companies; secondly, the securities markets, that is the dealer markets, money markets, bond markets and over-the-counter companies and the agency markets, stock exchanges and stockbrokers; finally it includes the real sector, meaning individuals, business and government. See Hugh Clelland, "Application of Automation in the Canadian Securities Industry: Present and Projected," in *Proposals for Securities Market Law for Canada: Background Papers*, vol. 3, edited by P. Anisman, W.M.H. Grover, J.L. Howard and J.P. Williamson (Ottawa: Minister of Supply and Services Canada, 1978) (hereinafter *Proposals, Vol. III*), p. 956.

   Another helpful description is that suggested in the study by Dimitri Vittas. This study focusses on central banks, a country's deposit-taking institutions, long-term credit institutions, investing institutions, other financial institutions, bond and stock markets. See D. Vittas, T. Hindle, P. Frazer,and R. Brown, *Banking Systems Abroad: The Role of Large Deposit Banks in the Financial Systems of Germany, France, Italy, the Netherlands, Switzerland, Sweden, Japan, and the United States* (London: Inter-Bank Research Organization, 1978).

   Both descriptions tend to under-emphasize the governmental financial system connections. Thus the national financial system, as described here, also includes direct and indirect governmental instruments from government-owned institutions, to government credit and investment programs, to government regulatory agencies.
3. The OSC has moved to alter the function of the financial services sectors. A decision by the commission following an intensive study and hearing by the OSC staff resulted in the approval, in late 1983, of the Toronto-Dominion Bank's Green Line Investor Service. This service allows registered financial institutions to actively market stock services through discount brokerage houses.

   The fall 1984 hearings of the OSC to inquire into foreign ownership and financial industry ownership in the securities industry was a broad policy review sparked by the Daly Gordon Securities plan to create a larger investment company involving a link with a Belgian holding company, Lambert Bruxelles Group. More broadly, the

OSC, in examining the restrictions placed on ownership of the securities industry — 10 percent for any individual firm and 25 percent total foreign ownership — again inquires into the advisability of excluding financial institutions from securities industry ownership.

4. The Ontario task force, under the direction of J. Stefan Dupré, was provided with a two-year mandate to inquire into the possible detriment or benefit to be derived from more integrated financial services, particularly the consequences for capital markets.
5. The federal committee was an advisory committee headed by Roy MacLaren. "The report was expected to address six key topics: solvency, conflict of interest, concentration and efficiency, foreign ownership, regulation by institution compared with function and federal-provincial jurisdictions." See, "OSC Plans to Hold Hearing on Impact of Growing Change on Canadian Securities Firms," *The Globe and Mail*, July 4, 1984, B11. It is unclear as to whether the new (1984) federal government plans to continue the examination of these issues at this time.
6. J. Zysman, *Government, Markets and Growth: Financial Systems and the Politics of Industrial Change* (Ithaca: Cornell University Press, 1983).
7. Ibid., p. 286.
8. A. Alexandroff, "Policemen or Architects: Ontario Securities Commissioners' Self Perceptions of Acting in the Public Interest"(unpublished manuscript) (Montreal: McGill University, 1984), pp. 45–48.
9. For a detailed analysis of U.S. postwar economic power, see C. Maier, "The Politics of Productivity: Foundations of American International Economic Policy after World War II," in *Between Power and Plenty: Foreign Economic Policies of Advanced Industrial States*, edited by P. Katzenstein (Madison: University of Wisconsin Press, 1978), pp. 23–49.
10. The best general examination of the expansion of the role of government in Canada is G. Bruce Doern and R.W. Phidd, *Canadian Public Policy: Ideas, Structure, Process* (Toronto: Methuen, 1983). For an insightful analysis of social policy, see K. Banting, *The Welfare State and Canadian Federalism* (Kingston: Queen's University, Institute of Intergovernmental Relations, 1982). For an excellent recent analysis of regional policy, see D. Savoie, *Federal-Provincial Collaboration: The Canada – New Brunswick General Development Agreement* (Montreal: McGill-Queen's University Press, 1981). Finally, for an insight into the process of decision making in Ottawa in the 1970s, see R. French, *How Canada Decides* (Ottawa: Canadian Institute for Economic Policy, 1980).
11. For a recent, excellent description of provincial policies see M.Jenkin, *The Challenge of Diversity: Industrial Policy in the Canadian Federation* (Ottawa: Minister of Supply and Services, Canada, 1983).
12. A. Tupper, *Public Money in the Private Sector* (Kingston: Queen's University, Institute of Intergovernmental Relations, 1982).
13. For general background on monetary and trade policies, see J.E. Spero, *The Politics of International Economic Relations* (New York: St.Martin's Press, 1981), and D. Blake and R. Walters, *The Politics of Global Economic Relations* (Englewood Cliffs, N.J.: Prentice-Hall, 1976). For a more detailed analysis of postwar monetary issues, see R. Solomon, *The International Monetary System, 1945–1976* (New York: Harper and Row, 1977). For trade, see A. Shonfield, ed., *International Economic Relations of the Western World, 1959–1971, vol. 1: Politics and Trade* (London: Oxford University Press, 1976).
14. An early analysis of the mixed economic system was provided by A. Shonfield, *Modern Capitalism: The Changing Balance of Public and Private Power* (London: Oxford University Press, 1965). A more recent analysis comes from Harvard's R. Reich, *The Last American Frontier* (New York: Basic Books, 1983).
15. President Carter, before his defeat, had established a board of key industrial, labour and governmental actors to fashion industrial policy in the United States. With the Reagan victory of 1980, this was all tucked away.
16. Tupper, *Public Money*, p. 2.
17. Zysman, *Government, Markets and Growth*.

18. Ibid., p. 76.
19. Ibid., p. 286.
20. P. Katzenstein, ed., *Between Power and Plenty*, pp. 295–336.
21. Ibid., pp. 302–306.
22. Zysman, *Government, Markets and Growth*, p. 286 ff.
23. Ibid., p. 304.
24. Ibid., pp. 63–69.
25. Ibid., p. 70.
26. Ibid.
27. Ibid., p. 71.
28. Ibid., p. 72.
29. Ibid.
30. Ibid.
31. Ibid., p. 68.
32. Ibid., p. 72.
33. Ibid., pp. 80–95.
34. Ibid., p. 92.
35. Ibid., pp. 171–232.
36. Ibid., p. 261.
37. Ibid., p. 265.
38. The comparative figures are constructed in so complex a manner that it was impossible to produce a certain figure. At best, we looked at the gross figures in the subcategories and measured them against the totals.
39. The five banks represent approximately 91 percent of all assets of Canada's domestic banks.
40. See *The Bank Act*, S.C. 1966–67, c. 87, and *The Bank Act*, S.C. 1980, c. 40.
41. *Bank Act*, S.C. 1980, c. 40, ss. 173(2), 174(2)(e), 193(4), 200(a) (the sections on limitations on foreign banks).
42. *The Globe and Mail*, April 12, 1984, B1.
43. *Bank Act*, R.S.C. 1970, c. B-1, s. 76. The act limits the shares of capital stock to 10 percent for companies but allows that share to rise to 50 percent for small companies. In the current legislation, see *Bank Act*, S.C. 1980, c. 40, ss. 193(4), 194.
44. R.A. Shearer, J.F. Chant and D.E. Bond, *The Economics of the Canadian Financial System: Theory, Policy and Institutions* (Scarborough: Prentice-Hall, 1984), p. 200.
45. *Quebec Savings Bank Act*, R.S.C. 1970, c. B-4, as amended.
46. For a description of the differing regulatory environments, see J.F. Chant and J.W. Dean, "An Approach to the Regulation of Banking Institutions in a Federal State," *Osgoode Hall Law Journal 10 (1982)*, pp. 737–44.
47. Shearer, Chant and Bond, *Economics of Canadian Financial System*, p. 363.
48. Ibid., p. 262.
49. "Venture Capital," in *Canadian Business* (June 1983), p. 67.
50. Zysman, *Government, Markets and Growth*, p. 68. Zysman here distinguishes between regulatory rules and directive control.
51. Ibid., p. 304. Zysman identifies the factors which make up the three parameters.
52. Tupper, *Public Money*, p. 4.
53. The institutional structure of the Canadian government, which is concerned with regional and industrial programs, went through extensive changes in the Trudeau period and again under Turner, even during the short period of that government. For a description of some of these changes, see Doern and Phidd, *Canadian Public Policy*, pp. 393–452. The quote is from Tupper, *Public Money*, p. 14.
54. G.Bruce Doern, "The Liberals and the Opposition: Ideas, Priorities and the Imperatives of Governing Canada in the 1980's," in *How Ottawa Spends: The Liberals, the*

Opposition and Federal Priorities, 1983, edited by G.Bruce Doern (Toronto: James Lorimer, 1983), p. 16.

55. Ibid., p. 21.
56. Tupper, *Public Money*, p. 14.
57. This figure is calculated from data provided in the study by the Economic Council of Canada. See Economic Council of Canada, *Intervention and Efficiency: A Study of Government Credit and Credit Guarantees to the Private Sector* (Ottawa: Minister of Supply and Services Canada, 1982).
58. This figure is taken from the Economic Council of Canada's study and reproduced in A. Maslove, "Loans and Loan Guarantees: Business as Usual Versus the Politics of Risk,"in *How Ottawa Spends: The Liberals, the Opposition and Federal Priorities*, edited by G. Bruce Doern, (Toronto: James Lorimer, 1983), p. 125.
59. Jenkin, *Challenge of Diversity*.
60. Ibid., p. 79.
61. A. Donner, *Financing the Future: Canada's Capital Markets in the Eighties* (Toronto: James Lorimer, 1982), p. 126.
62. Jenkin, *Challenge of Diversity*, p. 79.
63. Ibid., p. 81.
64. Ibid.
65. Ibid., p. 73.
66. Ibid.
67. The outline of the plan was announced by Alberta Premier Peter Lougheed. See *The Globe and Mail*, July 12, 1984, p. 9.
68. For a thorough examination of the NEP, see G. Bruce Doern and G. Toner, *The NEP and Canadian Energy Politics* (forthcoming).
69. Peter Foster, *Other People's Money: The Banks, the Government and Dome* (Toronto: Totem Books, 1983).
70. Ibid., p. 221.
71. *Interest Act*, R.S.C. 1970, c. I-18, as amended.
72. The various trust acts include: federally, *Trust Companies Act*, R.S.C. 1970, c. T-16, as amended; in Ontario, *Loan and Trust Corporations Act*, R.S.O. 1980, c. 249, as amended; in Quebec, *Trust Companies Act*, R.S.Q. 1977, c. C-41, as amended; in British Columbia, *Trust Company Act*, R.S.B.C. 1979, c. 412, as amended; in Alberta, *Trust Companies Act*, R.S.A. 1980, c. T-9, as amended; in Saskatchewan, *The Trust and Loan Corporations Act*, S.S. 1980–81, c. T-22.1, as amended; in Manitoba, *The Corporations Act*, S.M. 1976, c. 40, part xxiv, as amended; in New Brunswick, *Trust, Building and Loan Companies Loaning Act*, R.S.N.B. 1973, c. T-13; in Nova Scotia, *Trust Companies Act*, R.S.N.S. 1967, c. 316, as amended; in Prince Edward Island, *Licensing Act*, S.P.E.I. 1976, c. 18, as amended; and in Newfoundland, *The Trust and Loan Companies (Licensing) Act*, R.S.Nfld. 1974, No. 120, as amended.
73. James Baillie, "The Protection of the Investor in Ontario," *Canadian Public Administration* 8 (1965), p. 172.
74. *Directors' Liability Act, 1891*, S.O. 1891, c. 34.
75. *Securities Fraud Prevention Act*, S.O. 1928, c. 34.
76. *Security Frauds Prevention Act*, 1931, S.O. 1931, c. 48.
77. P. Dey and S. Makuch, "Government Supervision of Self-Regulatory Organizations in the Canadian Securities Industry," in *Proposals for Securities Market Law for Canada: Background Papers*, vol. 3, edited by P. Anisman, W.M.W. Grover, J.L. Howard and J.P. Williamson, (Ottawa: Minister of Supply and Services Canada, 1978), p. 1418.
78. For an examination of early securities legislation, see P. Williamson, *Securities Regulation in Canada* (Toronto: University of Toronto Press, 1960).
79. Baillie, "Protection of the Investor," p. 175.

80. *Securities Act, 1945*, S.O. 1945, c. 22 (1st Sess.).

81. *Securities Act, 1947*, S.O. 1947, c. 98.

82. *Securities Act, 1966*, S.O. 1966, c. 142.

83. D.L. Johnson, *Canadian Securities Regulation* (Toronto: Butterworth, 1977), p. 16.

84. Gray Taylor, "Comments on the Mandate and Operation of the Ontario Securities Commission," *University of Toronto Faculty of Law Review* 36 (1978), p. 14.

85. The evolution of the bill is long and complex. Its statutory history includes:
Bill 154, 28th Leg., 4th Sess. (June 1972);
Bill 75, 29th Leg., 4th Sess. (June 1974);
Bill 98, 29th Leg., 5th Sess. (May 1975);
Bill 20, 30th Leg., 4th Sess. (April 1977);
Bill 30, 31st Leg., 1st Sess. (June 1977); and
Bill 7, 31st Leg., 2nd Sess. (February 1978).

86. R. Simmonds, "The Prospectus Closed System in Ontario and Its Context," in *2 Corporate Structure: Finance and Operation. Essays on the Law and Business Practice*, edited by L. Sarna (Toronto: Caldwell, 1982), p. 25.

87. H.N. Janisch, "Policy Making in Regulation: Towards a New Definition of the Status of Independent Agencies in Canada," (1979), *Osgoode Hall Law Journal* 17 (1979), pp. 49–50.

88. Ibid., p. 50.

89. Taylor, "Comments on the Mandate"; Alexandroff, "Policemen or Architects."

90. Alexandroff, "Policement or Architects," pp. 55–56.

91. *Securities Act*, S.Q. 1982, c. 48.

92. L. La Rochelle, F.J. Pepin and R.L. Simmonds, "Bill 85, Quebec's New Securities Act," *McGill Law Review*: 29, (1983) 88–140.

93. Ibid., p. 91.

94. Ibid.

95. *Securities Sale Act*, R.S.Q. 1925, c. 228.

96. *Security Frauds Prevention Act*, S.Q. 1933, c. 85.

97. *Companies Information Act*, R.S.Q. 1935, c. 228.

98. *Securities Act*, S.Q. 1954–55, c. 11.

99. La Rochelle, Pepin and Simmonds, "Bill 85," p. 95.

100. Ibid., pp. 95, 105–107, 113–14.

101. *Charter of the French Language*, R.S.Q. 1977, c. C-11; see also La Rochelle, Pepin and Simmonds, "Bill 85," pp. 133–37.

102. Williamson, *Securities Regulation*, p. 24.

103. Ibid.

104. J.L. Howard, "Securities Regulation: Structure and Process," in *Proposals for Securities Market Law for Canada: Background Papers*, vol. 3, edited by P. Anisman, W.M.H. Grover, J.L. Howard and J.P. Williamson, (Ottawa: Minister of Supply and Services Canada, 1978), p. 1683.

105. Ibid., fn. 168.

106. Indeed, the basis of the market structure is that choice generates healthy competition. Here, however, we are suggesting that political choices do not necessarily generate healthy competition.

107. La Rochelle, Pepin and Simmonds, "Bill 85," p. 137.

108. Howard, "Securities Regulation," p. 1651, fn. 73.

109. Ibid., p. 1651.

110. *The Globe and Mail*, April 23, 1984, B1.

111. Clelland, "Application of Automation," p. 1024.

112. Ibid., p. 1025.

113. Ibid., p. 1031.

114. Discussion with officials at Toronto Stock Exchange, July 1984.
115. J.P. Williamson, "Canadian Capital Markets" in *Proposals for Securities Market Law for Canada: Background Papers*, vol. 3, edited by P. Anisman, W.M.H. Grover, J.L. Howard and J.P. Williamson (Ottawa: Minister of Supply and Services Canada, 1978), p. 126.
116. Ibid., p. 127.
117. *The Globe and Mail*, June 8, 1984, B1.
118. Ibid., April 23, 1984, B1.
119. Ibid., June 8, 1984, B1.
120. Ibid., April 23, 1984, B1.
121. Ibid.
122. Ibid., *The Globe and Mail*, November 22, 1983, B1; *The Globe and Mail*, November 30, 1983, B1.
123. Ibid., April 13, 1984, B1.
124. *Securities Act*, R.S.O. 1980, c. 466, as amended, s. 732.
125. *The Globe and Mail*, June 19, 1984, B1.
126. Ibid., March 10, 1984, B4.
127. Ibid.
128. *The Financial Post*, April 7, 1984, p. 2.
129. Ibid.
130. Ibid.
131. Ibid.

CHAPTER 5

1. Canada, Royal Commission on the Economic Union and Development Prospects for Canada, *Challenges and Choices* (Ottawa: Minister of Supply and Services, 1984), p. 66.
2. James Landis, *The Administrative Process* (New Haven: Yale University Press, 1951), p. 15.
3. J.A. Corry, "The Genesis and Nature of Boards," in *Canadian Boards at Work*, edited by John Willis (Toronto: Macmillan, 1941), p. 27.
4. Canada, Royal Commission, *Challenges and Choices*, p. 22.
5. Ibid., p. 23.
6. B.M. Owen and R. Braeutigam, *The Regulation Game: Strategic Use of the Administrative Process* (Cambridge, Mass.: Ballinger, 1978).
7. See H.N. Janisch, "Policy Making in Regulation . . . ," *Osgoode Hall Law Journal* 17 (1979): 46–106; and Richard Schultz, "Regulatory Agencies and the Dilemmas of Delegation," in *The Administrative State in Canada* edited by O.P.Dwivedi (Toronto: University of Toronto Press, 1982), pp. 89–106.
8. On these points see Richard J.Schultz, "Regulation as Maginot Line: Confronting the Technological Revolution in Telecommunications," *Canadian Public Administration* 26 (1983): 203–18.
9. For a discussion of both these alternatives see Richard J.Schultz, *Federalism and the Regulatory Process* (Montreal: Institute for Research on Public Policy, 1979); and Richard J. Schultz, "Delegation and Cable Distribution Systems: A Negative Assessment," Discussion Paper 11 (Kingston: Queen's University, Institute of Intergovernmental Relations, 1981).
10. Ian P.Sharp, "Responses by the User Community," in *Policy Issues in the Canadian-American Information Sector* (Montreal: McGill University, Centre for the Study of Regulated Industries, 1984), pp. 64–65.
11. See, for example, Robert J.Buchan et al., *Telecommunications Regulation and the Constitution* (Montreal: Institute for Research on Public Policy, 1982); Ontario

Securities Commission *Bulletin* 61 (November 1967); and Richard J. Schultz, "Intergovernmental Cooperation, Regulatory Agencies and Transportation Regulation in Canada," *Canadian Public Administration* 19 (1976): 183–207.

12. See John Howard, "Securities Regulation: Structure and Process," in Consumer and Corporate Affairs Canada, *Proposals for a Securities Market Law for Canada: Background Papers*, vol. 3 edited by P. Anisman, W.M.H. Grover, J.L. Howard and J.P. Williams (Ottawa: Minister of Supply and Services Canada, 1978), and Hon. Jean Chrétien, "Federal Proposal to Ensure Efficient Telecommunication Services Between All Points in Canada," presented to the Continuing Committee of Ministers on the Constitution, August 25, 1980, found in R.J. Buchan et al. *Telecommunications Regulation and the Constitution* (Montreal: Institute for Research on Public Policy, 1982), Appendix C.
13. Barry Lesser, "The Implications of the Federal and Provincial Proposals for Regulating Telecommunications: An Economist's Perspective," in R.J. Buchan et al., *Telecommunications Regulation and the Constitution* (Montreal: Institute for Research on Public Policy, 1982), p. 216.
14. These proposals are all found in the articles in Buchan et al., *Telecommunications Regulation.*
15. See Canada, Department of Communications, News Release, "Fox Announces Award of National Cellular Radio Licence to Cantel . . . ," December 14, 1983.
16. *Foreign Investment Review Act*, S.C. 1973–74, c. 46, s. 2(2)(e).
17. G. Bruce Doern and Glen Toner, *The Politics of Energy: The Development and Implementation of the NEP* (Toronto: Methuen, 1984), p. 241.
18. Richard J. Schultz et al., *The Cabinet as a Regulatory Body: The Case of the Foreign Investment Review Act* (Ottawa: Economic Council of Canada, 1980), especially pp. 113–14.
19. *Inuit Tapirisat of Canada v. Leger* (1979), 95 D.L.R. (3d), p. 675.
20. See Schultz et al., *The Cabinet as a Regulatory Body*, especially pp. 152–59.
21. Charles L. Schultze, *The Public Use of the Private Interest* (Washington, D.C.: Brookings Institution, 1977), p. 6.

THE COLLECTED RESEARCH STUDIES

Royal Commission on the Economic Union and Development Prospects for Canada

ECONOMICS

Income Distribution and Economic Security in Canada (Vol.1), *François Vaillancourt, Research Coordinator*

Vol. 1 Income Distribution and Economic Security in Canada, *F. Vaillancourt* (C)*

Industrial Structure (Vols. 2-8), *Donald G. McFetridge, Research Coordinator*

Vol. 2 Canadian Industry in Transition, *D.G. McFetridge* (C)
Vol. 3 Technological Change in Canadian Industry, *D.G. McFetridge* (C)
Vol. 4 Canadian Industrial Policy in Action, *D.G. McFetridge* (C)
Vol. 5 Economics of Industrial Policy and Strategy, *D.G. McFetridge* (C)
Vol. 6 The Role of Scale in Canada–US Productivity Differences, *J.R. Baldwin and P.K. Gorecki* (M)
Vol. 7 Competition Policy and Vertical Exchange, *F. Mathewson and R. Winter* (M)
Vol. 8 The Political Economy of Economic Adjustment, *M. Trebilcock* (M)

International Trade (Vols. 9-14), *John Whalley, Research Coordinator*

Vol. 9 Canadian Trade Policies and the World Economy, *J. Whalley with C. Hamilton and R. Hill* (M)
Vol. 10 Canada and the Multilateral Trading System, *J. Whalley* (M)
Vol. 11 Canada–United States Free Trade, *J. Whalley* (C)
Vol. 12 Domestic Policies and the International Economic Environment, *J. Whalley* (C)
Vol. 13 Trade, Industrial Policy and International Competition, *R. Harris* (M)
Vol. 14 Canada's Resource Industries and Water Export Policy, *J. Whalley* (C)

Labour Markets and Labour Relations (Vols. 15-18), *Craig Riddell, Research Coordinator*

Vol. 15 Labour-Management Cooperation in Canada, *C. Riddell* (C)
Vol. 16 Canadian Labour Relations, *C. Riddell* (C)
Vol. 17 Work and Pay: The Canadian Labour Market, *C. Riddell* (C)
Vol. 18 Adapting to Change: Labour Market Adjustment in Canada, *C. Riddell* (C)

Macroeconomics (Vols. 19-25), *John Sargent, Research Coordinator*

Vol. 19 Macroeconomic Performance and Policy Issues: Overviews, *J. Sargent* (M)
Vol. 20 Post-War Macroeconomic Developments, *J. Sargent* (C)
Vol. 21 Fiscal and Monetary Policy, *J. Sargent* (C)
Vol. 22 Economic Growth: Prospects and Determinants, *J. Sargent* (C)
Vol. 23 Long-Term Economic Prospects for Canada: A Symposium, *J. Sargent* (C)
Vol. 24 Foreign Macroeconomic Experience: A Symposium, *J. Sargent* (C)
Vol. 25 Dealing with Inflation and Unemployment in Canada, *C. Riddell* (M)

Economic Ideas and Social Issues (Vols. 26 and 27), *David Laidler, Research Coordinator*

Vol. 26 Approaches to Economic Well-Being, *D. Laidler* (C)
Vol. 27 Responses to Economic Change, *D. Laidler* (C)

* (C) denotes a Collection of studies by various authors coordinated by the person named. (M) denotes a Monograph.

Politics and Institutions of Government

Canada and the International Political Economy (Vols. 28-30), *Denis Stairs and Gilbert R. Winham, Research Coordinators*

Vol. 28 Canada and the International Political/Economic Environment, *D. Stairs and G.R. Winham* (C)
Vol. 29 The Politics of Canada's Economic Relationship with the United States, *D. Stairs and G.R. Winham* (C)
Vol. 30 Selected Problems in Formulating Foreign Economic Policy, *D. Stairs and G.R. Winham* (C)

State and Society in the Modern Era (Vols. 31 and 32), *Keith Banting, Research Coordinator*

Vol. 31 State and Society: Canada in Comparative Perspective, *K. Banting* (C)
Vol. 32 The State and Economic Interests, *K. Banting* (C)

Constitutionalism, Citizenship and Society (Vols. 33-35), *Alan Cairns and Cynthia Williams, Research Coordinators*

Vol. 33 Constitutionalism, Citizenship and Society in Canada, *A. Cairns and C. Williams* (C)
Vol. 34 The Politics of Gender, Ethnicity and Language in Canada, *A. Cairns and C. Williams* (C)
Vol. 35 Public Opinion and Public Policy in Canada, *R. Johnston* (M)

Representative Institutions (Vols. 36-39), *Peter Aucoin, Research Coordinator*

Vol. 36 Party Government and Regional Representation in Canada, *P. Aucoin* (C)
Vol. 37 Regional Responsiveness and the National Administrative State, *P. Aucoin* (C)
Vol. 38 Institutional Reforms for Representative Government, *P. Aucoin* (C)
Vol. 39 Intrastate Federalism in Canada, *D.V. Smiley and R.L. Watts* (M)

The Politics of Economic Policy (Vols. 40-43), *G. Bruce Doern, Research Coordinator*

Vol. 40 The Politics of Economic Policy, *G.B. Doern* (C)
Vol. 41 Federal and Provincial Budgeting, *A.M. Maslove, M.J. Prince and G.B. Doern* (M)
Vol. 42 Economic Regulation and the Federal System, *R. Schultz and A. Alexandroff* (M)
Vol. 43 Bureaucracy in Canada: Control and Reform, *S.L. Sutherland and G.B. Doern* (M)

Industrial Policy (Vols. 44 and 45), *André Blais, Research Coordinator*

Vol. 44 Canadian Industrial Policy, *A. Blais* (C)
Vol. 45 The Political Sociology of Industrial Policy, *A. Blais* (M)

Law and Constitutional Issues

Law, Society and the Economy (Vols. 46-51), *Ivan Bernier and Andrée Lajoie, Research Coordinators*

Vol. 46 Law, Society and the Economy, *I. Bernier and A. Lajoie* (C)
Vol. 47 The Supreme Court of Canada as an Instrument of Political Change, *I. Bernier and A. Lajoie* (C)
Vol. 48 Regulations, Crown Corporations and Administrative Tribunals, *I. Bernier and A. Lajoie* (C)
Vol. 49 Family Law and Social Welfare Legislation in Canada, *I. Bernier and A. Lajoie* (C)
Vol. 50 Consumer Protection, Environmental Law and Corporate Power, *I. Bernier and A. Lajoie* (C)
Vol. 51 Labour Law and Urban Law in Canada, *I. Bernier and A. Lajoie* (C)

The International Legal Environment (Vols. 52-54), *John Quinn, Research Coordinator*

Vol. 52 The International Legal Environment, *J. Quinn* (C)
Vol. 53 Canadian Economic Development and the International Trading System, *M.M. Hart* (M)
Vol. 54 Canada and the New International Law of the Sea, *D.M. Johnston* (M)

Harmonization of Laws in Canada (Vols. 55 and 56), *Ronald C.C. Cuming, Research Coordinator*

Vol. 55 Perspectives on the Harmonization of Law in Canada, *R. Cuming* (C)
Vol. 56 Harmonization of Business Law in Canada, *R. Cuming* (C)

Institutional and Constitutional Arrangements (Vols. 57 and 58), *Clare F. Beckton and A. Wayne MacKay, Research Coordinators*

Vol. 57 Recurring Issues in Canadian Federalism, *C.F. Beckton and A.W. MacKay* (C)
Vol. 58 The Courts and The Charter, *C.F. Beckton and A.W. MacKay* (C)

FEDERALISM AND THE ECONOMIC UNION

Federalism and The Economic Union (Vols. 58-72), *Mark Krasnick, Kenneth Norrie and Richard Simeon, Research Coordinators*

Vol. 59 Federalism and Economic Union in Canada, *K. Norrie, R. Simeon and M. Krasnick* (M)
Vol. 60 Perspectives on the Canadian Economic Union, *M. Krasnick* (C)
Vol. 61 Division of Powers and Public Policy, *R. Simeon* (C)
Vol. 62 Case Studies in the Division of Powers, *M. Krasnick* (C)
Vol. 63 Intergovernmental Relations, *R. Simeon* (C)
Vol. 64 Disparities and Interregional Adjustment, *K. Norrie* (C)
Vol. 65 Fiscal Federalism, *M. Krasnick* (C)
Vol. 66 Mobility of Capital in the Canadian Economic Union, *N. Roy* (M)
Vol. 67 Economic Management and the Division of Powers, *T.J. Courchene* (M)
Vol. 68 Regional Aspects of Confederation, *J. Whalley* (M)
Vol. 69 Interest Groups in the Canadian Federal System, *H.G. Thorburn* (M)
Vol. 70 Canada and Quebec, Past and Future: An Essay, *D. Latouche* (M)
Vol. 71 The Political Economy of Canadian Federalism: 1940-1984, *R. Simeon and I. Robinson* (M)

THE NORTH

Vol. 72 The North, *Michael S. Whittington, Coordinator* (C)

Commission Organization

Chairman

Donald S. Macdonald

Commissioners

Clarence L. Barber
Albert Breton
M. Angela Cantwell Peters
E. Gérard Docquier

William M. Hamilton
John R. Messer
Laurent Picard
Michel Robert

Daryl K. Seaman
Thomas K. Shoyama
Jean Casselman-Wadds
Catherine T. Wallace

Senior Officers

Executive Director
J. Gerald Godsoe

Director of Policy
Alan Nymark

Secretary
Michel Rochon

Director of Administration
Sheila-Marie Cook

Senior Advisors
David Ablett
Victor Clarke
Carl Goldenberg
Harry Stewart

Director of Publishing
Ed Matheson

Directors of Research
Ivan Bernier
Alan Cairns
David C. Smith

Co-Directors of Research
Kenneth Norrie
John Sargent

Research Program Organization

Economics

Research Director
David C. Smith

Executive Assistant & Assistant Director (Research Services)
I. Lilla Connidis

Coordinators
David Laidler
Donald G. McFetridge
Kenneth Norrie*
Craig Riddell
John Sargent*
François Vaillancourt
John Whalley

Research Analysts
Caroline Digby
Mireille Ethier
Judith Gold
Douglas S. Green
Colleen Hamilton
Roderick Hill
Joyce Martin

Politics and the Institutions of Government

Research Director
Alan Cairns

Executive Assistant
Karen Jackson

Coordinators
Peter Aucoin
Keith Banting
André Blais
Bruce Doern
Richard Simeon
Denis Stairs
Cynthia Williams
Gilbert R. Winham

Research Analysts
Claude Desranleau
Ian Robinson

Office Administration
Donna Stebbing

Law and Constitutional Issues

Research Director
Ivan Bernier

Executive Assistant & Research Program Administrator
Jacques J.M. Shore

Coordinators
Clare F. Beckton
Ronald C.C. Cuming
Mark Krasnick
Andrée Lajoie
A. Wayne MacKay
John J. Quinn

Administrative and Research Assistant
Nicolas Roy

Research Analyst
Nola Silzer

*Kenneth Norrie and John Sargent co-directed the final phase of Economics Research with David Smith